The French School of Spirituality

An Introduction and Reader

by Raymond Deville
Translated by Agnes Cunningham, sscm

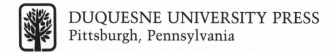
DUQUESNE UNIVERSITY PRESS
Pittsburgh, Pennsylvania

Published in French under the title
L'école française de spiritualité
Copyright 1987 by Desclée, Paris

English Language Copyright © 1994
by Duquesne University Press

Published in the United States of America
by Duquesne University Press
600 Forbes Avenue
Pittsburgh, Pennsylvania 15282

Library of Congress Cataloging-in-Publication Data

Deville, Raymond.
    [Ecole française de spiritualité. English]
    The French School of Spirituality : an introduction and reader /
Raymond Deville : translated by Agnes Cunningham.
        p.   cm.
    Includes bibliographical references and index.
    ISBN 0–8207–0258–7 (pbk.)
    1. Spirituality—France—History—17th century.   2. Catholic
Church—France—History—17th century.   3. France—Religious life
and customs.   4. France—Church history—17th century.   I. Title.
BX1529.D4813   1994
248'.0944'09032—dc20   94-24828

THE FRENCH SCHOOL OF SPIRITUALITY

Contents

Translator's Preface

The appearance of this English translation of Raymond Deville's book on the French School of the seventeenth century is the result of a dream, a project, and a great deal of perseverance and patience.

The dream began shortly after the summer of 1987, when a Congress on the French School was held for the first time on the North American continent. Congress participants represented 25 religious congregations whose foundation, charism, or spirituality could be traced, more or less directly, to the tradition that had come from Bérulle and those associated with him.

At the time, membership of these congregations numbered about 45,000 with houses in Africa, Asia, Europe, North America, South America and Oceania. The international dimension of the Congress, along with the enthusiasm generated by the conferences and other activities, pointed to the need to rediscover and own the rich heritage of a tradition too little known and too frequently misunderstood.

In July 1992, a second Congress on the French School of Spirituality was held in Montréal, Canada. Twenty-eight religious congregations were represented. Between

the two meetings, many of the congregations had initiated or developed programs of renewal based on the
teachings of Bérulle and his followers. One of the tools
at their disposal was *L'école française de spiritualité*
(Desclée, 1987), a work already cited as a major resource
at the 1987 Congress. The absence of an English translation of Deville's book had inspired my dream to find a
comparable work for the sisters of our American province, as I pursued my own research for initial and ongoing formation programs in our congregation.

My dream became a project, thanks to Father Gerald L.
Brown, S.S., provincial superior of the Priests of St.
Sulpice in the United States, who knew of my interest. A
request from Father Deville, himself, began a process
that was to take several years of perseverance and patience. At the 1992 Congress, Father Deville was able to
verify the "rumors" that a translation of his work was to
be made available to English-speaking members of congregations who traced their roots to the French School.

Perseverance and patience were necessary at many
stages as the project progressed. A willing publisher, suf-
ficient financial support, and a realistic calendar were the
first challenges to be met. Permission for an English
translation was not available until fall 1992. By that
time, I was on a year-long assignment in France, with
other responsibilities and deadlines to meet. Verification
of documents already in translation and the preparation
of a manuscript from the other side of the ocean were
difficulties to be faced, as well. The present volume is
the result of a dream fulfilled, a project realized, perseverance and patience rewarded.

This English translation is, in general, faithful to the
original French work. Chapters and subsections follow
the organization of the original book, similar to that
found in other volumes of the series in which this
work first appeared (*Bibliothèque d'Histoire du Christia-
nisme*). At times, I have omitted, adapted, or added head-
ings, as that seemed appropriate for an English-speaking

audience. Tables and timelines are reproduced almost without change. Representative documents correspond to those in the French edition, although a limited number of substitutions have been made, when similar, recently published texts became available. I have translated most of the documents included in the English version. Others were already to be found in publications dating from another era. Since these texts were already familiar to many readers, I chose to include them. They will be readily recognizable and are well identified.

I have tried to render Father Deville's engaging, pedagogical style in a comparable English version. In many instances I have made additions to the text, in order to clarify a term or an expression that would have had no equivalent in English. In the same way, I have tried to foresee brief explanations that might be necessary for readers unfamiliar with the history of seventeenth century France.

Footnotes in the volume have been rendered in English, except for works that exist only in French. Wherever possible, English publications of any works are cited. References for further study, found at the end of each chapter in the French edition, have been arranged into a bibliography of works in English at the end of the present volume. Two additional features in this book are the chapter, by Father Deville, on the role of women in the French School and a map prepared by one of the sisters in our French province, Sister Martine Dumant, SSCM, of Amiens. To both of them I owe a special work of thanks for their willing response to my requests.

Other thanks are due to the members of my own congregation who supported and encouraged me in this project. In a special way, I am grateful to Sister Françoise Lainé and the sisters of Montgeron, France, who provided interest in everything I was doing and warmth of every kind during my stay in France.

The manuscript might still not be finished, if it had not been for Barbara Hansen and her ability to resolve a

crisis with calm and competence. A final word of gratitude must be offered to John Dowds who is, surely, the
most persevering, patient editor I could have hoped to
find. To him and to all at Duquesne University Press,
especially, to Susan Wadsworth-Booth, who guided me
through the final stages of this project, I owe sincere
thanks.

I do not claim that my work is perfect. Scholars and
careful readers may differ with choices I have made in
the preparation of this volume. I do believe this translation will meet a real need, as a well-organized, comprehensive, interesting introduction to the "School" which
has reached beyond its own time and place to influence
the spiritual, theological, liturgical and pastoral life of
the Church in ways that have still to be adequately measured. I would hope to have contributed in some small
way to that appreciation.

SISTER AGNES CUNNINGHAM, SSCM

FRENCH PROVINCES
IN THE XVII AND XVIII CENTURIES

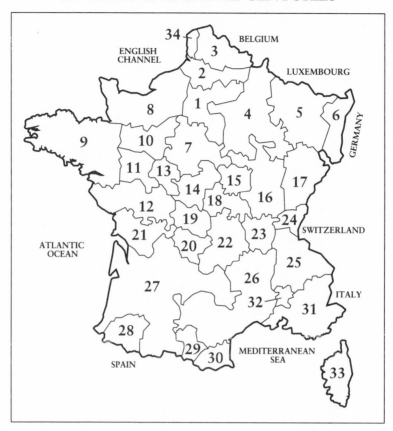

1. Ile-de-France	13. Touraine	25. Dauphiné
2. Picardie	14. Berry	26. Languedoc
3. Artois/Flandre	15. Nivernais	27. Guyenne et
4. Champagne/Brie	16. Bourgogne	Gascogne
5. Lorraine	17. Franche Comté	28. Béarn
6. Alsace	18. Bourbonnais	29. Comté de Foix
7. Orléanais	19. Marche	30. Roussillon
8. Normandie	20. Limousin	31. Provence
9. Bretagne	21. Aunis et	32. Comtat
10. Maine	Saintonge	Venaissin
11. Anjou	22. Auvergne	33. Corse
12. Poltou	23. Lyonnais	34. Boulonnais
	24. Dombes	

CHAPTER ONE

Definition of Terms

The Great Century of the Soul

L ike the sixteenth century in Spain, the seventeenth
century in France was "great," not only in terms of
politics, literature and art. It was also, like its Spanish
counterpart, "the century of saints."[1]

In spite of a number of studies and other publications,
this period of French history is, relatively speaking, little
known—except by professional historians, a few special-
ists, and one or another religious family or society. Nevertheless, it was an extremely important time. Some of
its ideas continue to have a noteworthy impact not only
in France, but throughout the world.

Think, for example, of the influence of the Daughters
of Charity, the Brothers of the Christian Schools, the

---

[1] Daniel-Rops, H., *The Church in the Seventeenth Century*, 69.

1

Eudists, the Sulpicians, the congregations founded by Grignion de Montfort. How many people know that Bérulle introduced the Carmel of Teresa of Jesus into France and was responsible for the foundation of 43 monasteries in 25 years? Again, who knows that the evangelization of Canada was due, in large part, to missionaries who left France for the New World in the seventeenth century? Not to be overlooked, either, is the influential role of the laity in this period: Madame Acarie, Gaston de Renty, Jean de Bernières, Jérôme le Royer de la Dauversière, Jeanne Mance. The last two were instrumental in the foundation of a religious congregation dedicated to the service of faith and charity in Montreal. Still other laypersons exercised roles of major importance in society at large or in favor of contemplative orders.

Within the constellation of great spiritual leaders—all of whom, in one way or another, were missionaries—a certain number shared the same *spirituality*. Bremond was the first to use the expression which, ordinarily, refers to this group: *the French School*. More recently, another title has been introduced, that is, *the Bérulle School*. This name seems preferable when reference is made to the obvious master, Bérulle, and his principal disciples: Condren, Olier and John Eudes, the *four great masters* of the French School. In this work, both titles will be used interchangeably, although *the Bérulle School* seems more appropriate.

This tradition of spirituality, marked by several easily recognizable major emphases, embraces other spiritual leaders. Two of them, St. John-Baptist de la Salle and St. Louis-Marie Grignion de Montfort, had been students at Saint-Sulpice toward the end of the seventeenth century. Still later, other significant writers, among them Bishop Gay, became witnesses to this tradition. The same spirituality can be found in the writings of Dom Marmion and Elizabeth of the Trinity in a less direct, but nonetheless authentic manner. Traces of the characteristics of the French School can also be recognized in selected texts of the Second Vatican Council.

At the heart of the seventeenth century, there were other women and men who often had a close relationship with one of the four great masters, although their teachings are marked by theological and spiritual characteristics that differ from those of the French School. Strictly speaking, they do not represent this school of spirituality, even though they were influenced, like many others, by the spirit and the doctrine of Bérulle. Among these men and women we count Vincent de Paul, Bourdoise, Fénelon and, in a certain sense, Jesuits such as Louis Lallement, Saint-Jure and Hayneuve.

The present volume is devoted to the most widely recognized masters of the French School: Bérulle, Condren, Olier and John Eudes, along with John-Baptist de la Salle and Grignion de Montfort. Other great spiritual leaders of the seventeenth century will be referred to, but it seems preferable to limit this work to Bérulle and those who are identified as his disciples, in the strictest sense of the word. Thus, this study will not allow for consideration of Vincent de Paul, with his outstanding teachings and achievements, nor of Saint-Cyran, another truly great spiritual master. Neither Bossuet nor Fénelon will be included, and the absence of certain influential Oratorians will be evident: Bourgoing, Gibieuf, Metezeau. These choices are not due to negligence or lack of appreciation, but rather to the nature of the work itself, and to a concern for clarity of thought and presentation.

Following a general overview (chapter 2), each of the four great masters of the Bérulle School will be presented in detail (chapters 3, 4, 5 and 6). In chapter 7, an attempt will be made to arrive at a synthesis of the major elements of their doctrine. Two of the principal heirs of the four masters, John-Baptist de la Salle and Grignion de Montfort, will be discussed in chapters 8 and 9. Chapter 10 will address the role of women in the French School, while the final chapter (11) will suggest a few reflections on the significance of this spirituality for us today.

Knowledge of the masters of the French School is not a matter of historical interest only. Like every encounter with a past age that has helped to shape us, it includes an aspect of contemporary significance that is all the more important because it is less evident. The differences and distances that exist between one era and another allow us to grasp more effectively the values and challenges that were both yesterday's experience and the difficulties we face today.

There is a paradox worthy of note to be considered concerning the French School. A good deal of blame and many criticisms have been leveled against it for several reasons: its pessimistic view of the human person, that "cesspool of iniquity"; what seems, at times, an exclusive christocentrism; an uncritical concept of the priest as "God's religious."

At the same time, we find a renewal of interest in increasing numbers as laypersons discover Bérulle, and religious seek to retrieve the original inspiration of their founders. Priests express the need for a new French School today, a desire to return to solid theological foundations and a longing for authentic spiritual renewal.

Over half a century ago, Emile Mersch consecrated a long chapter in his historical theological study on the Mystical Body of Christ to Bérulle and his followers. At the end of the chapter he wrote, "Yet, there are some things concerning our incorporation in Christ that can be learned best only from their lips."[2] Moreover, in these words, Mersch touches on the very heart of the mystical experience and the teaching of these spiritual leaders: the Christian life understood as communion with Jesus Christ. However, to paraphrase Montaigne, if we are to

---

[2] *The Whole Christ.* Trans. John R. Kelly, S.J. (Milwaukee: The Bruce Publishing Company, 1938), 555.

know them better, it is important to follow them down a long road, with great curiosity of mind. The following chapters are meant to be both an introduction and a guide to further reading for this very purpose.

The documents cited in the following pages are presented simply to illustrate and complete this introduction. The choice of texts was difficult and, certainly, is debatable: Bérulle and his disciples were prolific writers. Perhaps what is presented here will encourage and inspire the reader to seek to know these authors and their works more fully.

At the end of the book, a short bibliography is suggested. It is not meant to be exhaustive and presents only a few works for further study.

The texts included ordinarily represent, on the one hand, the best known editions of the authors cited and, on the other, works that are most easily accessible in English.

DOCUMENTS FOR CHAPTER 1

1.1 The Youth of the Church in the Seventeenth Century

Has it been sufficiently appreciated that the first 60 years of the seventeenth century stand out as a period of strength within the Church, an epoch of rare beauty and fruitfulness, certainly as rich as the greatest moments in the history of medieval Christianity? Has it been really appreciated that this was an era of youthful bloom and dazzling revival?

There stood Monsieur Vincent, dominating the age with his worn silhouette, his keen gaze bubbling over with kindness. Around him in their dozens rise those who, as history agrees, mirrored his achievements, tilling the same soil, ploughing other furrows, yet all gathering the same harvest of souls—men whose lives were perfectly ordered in God, and whose works had no other end than that of advancing His kingdom. There have been few centuries in the life of the Church which can muster so many great souls. (. . .)

Notwithstanding all this, it was France that was destined to lead the Catholic Reformation for over half a century. Her faithful were no better than those of other Churches; it contained just as many abuses and scandals as existed elsewhere. However, in the midst of it all there was a renewal of faith; basic principles found new methods of application; charity asserted itself in countless works. And what an atmosphere of holiness! That was the essential requirement. What gave rise to this amazing surge of revival had nothing to do with ministerial or royal commands—although Louis XIII and Richelieu were won over to these purposes; there were no parliamentary decrees, nor even resolutions voted in the Assemblée du Clergé. In this spiritual springtide the sap which welled forth everywhere rose from that good earth on which generations of good Christians had lived for centuries. Teams of men and women were already there, goaded by a purely interior urgency; men and women who longed with all their being to bear witness and to radiate the Word. Why were they so numerous in this place and in this age? But why did Renaissance Italy number so many great artists? There are no answers to these questions. The historian can surmise the work of Providence in the facts before him, but the purposes of Providence remain hidden. The historian sees only that this first upward movement of the seventeenth century makes it indeed the century of saints; and France was the home of saints.

> H. Daniel-Rops, *The Church in the Seventeenth Century* (History of the Church of Christ, 6) London: J.M. Dent & Sons, LTD; New York: E.P. Dutton & Co., Inc., 1963–53.

1.2

We have to thank Henri Bremond for shedding a ray of light on the long-forgotten French School. He more than anyone else demonstrated its originality and its riches. It was a school of the interior life, of eminent spirituality based on dogma, and especially on the Incarnation. During the whole of the seventeenth century, and up to the time of the Regency, it left a profound impression on the French mind, and even outside France. There is no doubt that its teachers contributed more than any others to the laying of the foundations of that modern Catholic spirituality which is still practiced today.

> Daniel-Rops, *The Church in the Seventeenth Century*, 57.

1.3 The French School

The French School—hitherto, whenever by chance this forgotten group of thinkers came to be mentioned, it was termed
the Oratorian School, although several of its representatives
did not belong to the Oratory. The French School is a happier
phrase. Of course, in one sense, all the schools discussed in the
present work can be called by this name, but there is nothing
in the other writers, as regards either doctrine or method, that
can be declared specifically French. The Jesuit Lallemant could
as well be Spanish, François de Sales Italian, and Jean de Bernières Flemish; whereas Bérulle, Condren and their indisput-
able disciple, Jacques-Bénigne Bossuet, are French to the back-
bone. I confess, however, that views of this kind, always open
to question, are unimportant, and I shall not pause to defend
them. Suffice it that this school is incontestably the richest,
the most original and fertile, of any born in the Golden Age of
our religious history, meriting on this score alone the proud
name henceforth assigned to it in these pages—the French
School *par excellence*. I may add that the term School is here
to be taken in its strict sense; none of the groups to be studied
later presents so perfect a cohesion of such unanimity. From
Bérulle, born under Henri III, to Grignion de Montfort, who
died under the Regency, all alike hold together, showing a
united front, though many of the units were very diverse, and
one is surprised to find them in the same line of tradition.
Nevertheless, all remained unswervingly faithful to the original tradition, content to work out the implications of the magnificent premises set forth by Cardinal de Bérulle. Truly a
School, not of theology, but of the interior life and the highest
spirituality.

Its vaunted intellect, its apparent subtlety, bow before the
inspiration of mystics often of the simplest type. Bérulle is directed by Madeleine de Saint-Joseph and the frail Catherine de
Jésus; Père Eudes by a woman of the people, Marie des Vallées;
M. de Renty by Marguérite de Beaune; M. Olier by Agnès de
Langeac together with Marie Rousseau and several others. It
is, I repeat, the French School: I will not call it Gallican. The
Church Universal approved and consecrated it, canonizing one
of its pupils, Vincent de Paul, and beatifying two of its leaders,

Jean Eudes and Louis Grignion de Montfort. [These last two were canonized; in 1925 and 1947, respectively.]

Bremond, *A Literary History of Religious Thought in France* 3:1–2.

1.4 The French School? The Bérulle School?

[The success accorded the title "French School," must not lead us to forget the great variety of spiritual movements current in France in the seventeenth century. The following text reflects André Ragez's view of this fact].

New schools of spirituality, most of which were then in their full development or growth, arose alongside the ancient traditions which continued to flourish or thrive: Benedictine, Carthusian, Cistercian, Augustinian, Franciscan, Dominican, and others. Without trying to draw up a complete list of "winners," we have only to call several facts to mind. In France, as in the West as a whole, the seventeenth century was the golden age of Capuchin spirituality. The Ignatian school took shape in a manner all its own, with members of outstanding spiritual worth. Thanks to numerous editions of the works and biography of St. Francis de Sales, the Salesian tradition knew such a rapid, considerable growth that many of its themes were taken up by other schools. The fame and influence of Carmelite spirituality kept pace with the translations of the works and the biographies of the great reformers, St. Teresa of Avila and St. John of the Cross. The relationship between Carmelite doctrine and other movements has already been pointed out, especially in regard to the doctrine of contemplation. Moreover, the movement of the Carmelites of the reform of Touraine seems indeed to have taken place in complete independence, even in regard to the Spanish Carmelite reform—with the exception of Leo of St. John (1600–1671) who was a "passionate disciple of Bérulle."

There were spiritual movements in which the laity could be involved in the seventeenth century, for mission, works of charity, and apostolic service. They, too, existed without any specific or exclusive ties to a school of spirituality, in the strict

sense of the term. An exception, perhaps, could be work for
Third Order members of Mission Congregations.

. . . In the presence of the splendid flowering of spirituality
in France during the seventeenth century, we think spontane-
ously of all that Spain had known in its golden age. We know
that we, too, can repeat Henri Bremond's own experience and
speak of "the *golden age* of our religious history," or, more
specifically, of our spirituality. Among all the jewels which
adorn that era, there is the magnificent *Bérulle School*, perhaps the most unique of the century.

The Bérulle School, "French spirituality of the seventeenth
century," golden age of French spirituality: all these are contained in Bremond's expression, "the French School."

In a word, there is not, in the strict sense of the term, a
"French School" of spirituality in the seventeenth century.
The seventeenth century is the *golden age* of spirituality in
France.

> A. Rayez, *Dictionnaire de Spiritualité*, art.,
> Française (école), Col. 783–84.

1.5 Toward a Definition of the French School

In a general sense, the French School can be defined as the
powerful christological movement made possible by Bérulle's
victory. Thus, it embraces laypersons like Bernières and Renty;
Jesuits like Saint-Jure, Lallemant and their followers; Dominicans like Chardon and Piny; like the Ursuline, Marie de
l'Incarnation, or venerable Mechtilde, foundress of the Benedictines of the Blessed Sacrament. *In a strict sense*, the French
School includes only the disciples of Bérulle, those who were
aware of the original character of his teaching and who took
up the major characteristics of his doctrines.

The characteristic themes of Bérulle's teaching, apparently,
can be limited to four: the spirit of religion and theocentrism;
mystical christocentrism; his keen awareness of the sovereignty of the Mother of God; his exaltation of the priesthood.

> P. Cochois, *Bérulle et l'Ecole Française*; Paris:
> Seuil, 1963; 146.

CHAPTER TWO

The Church in Seventeenth Century France

A Century, A Nation, A People

More than a few pages would be needed to sketch a complete picture of the Church in seventeenth century French society. However, it is important to consider a few of the main features that characterize this period, if we are to understand the role played by the artisans of Catholic renewal in this great century. Moreover, these persons were often closely involved with the political and social life of their time. In the opening pages of André Dodin's volume on St. Vincent de Paul and his works of charity, we read:

11

Born in 1581, during the reign of Henry III, at Pouy, Landes, Vincent de Paul very likely saw Henry IV in Paris, between 1608 and 1610. He knew Richelieu well and ministered to Louis XIII on his deathbed. He was at home in the company of Anne of Austria, of Mazarin, and of Chancellor Séquier. He knew everyone who cared for and watched over Louis XIV in his infancy and youth. M. Vincent left this world on 27 September 1660, when the great King took the destiny of France into his hands.[1]

This rich, troubled period in the history of France was also a time of outstanding vitality and activity in the sphere of religion. The era was dominated by a few great men, among whom were Bérulle and his disciples, reformers who restored and revitalized the church in France. They stood as one with the generation to which they belonged, living examples of Lacordaire's words: "Great hearts know how to discover the principal need of the times in which they live and dedicate themselves to it."[2]

The present work is concerned with the leading representatives of the Bérulle School, not all of whom were as closely involved as Monsieur Vincent with the political and social life of France.

Nonetheless, it is important to recall several circumstances that marked their life and action. None of them was a solitary meteor in the heavens. They knew one another, were keenly aware of the experiences of the people of their time, and all of them desired to renew their lives as Christians. Completely immersed as they were in the age in which they lived, they strove to transform it. In so doing, they fulfilled their own personal mission, long before the philosopher, Ortega y Gasset, wrote his famous words: "I am myself and the circumstances that are mine (*yo soy mi y mi circunstancia*) and if I do not save them, I do not save myself, either.".[3]

Political and Economic Situation

In comparison with its neighbors, the political situation in France had begun to improve as early as the first years of the seventeenth century. Following the Wars of Religion and thanks to Henry IV, France gradually recovered and found a second wind. With 20 million inhabitants, it had one of the largest populations and was one of the richest countries in Europe. Henry IV had tried to bring about religious peace through the Edict of Nantes (1598), which granted a status of tolerance to Protestants. He also sought to strengthen his own authority with the nobility and the clergy.

The House of Austria had been established as strongly in Spain, in the Low Countries, and in Franche-Comté as in the Empire itself (Germany, Austria, Bohemia and elsewhere). It was a threatening rival, in spite of attempts at agreement through marriage, as for example, between Louis XIII and Anne of Austria.

Frontier regions, like Lorraine or Picardy, were frequently invaded and, thus, impoverished. Beginning in 1639, Vincent de Paul intervened actively to bring aid to the inhabitants of Lorraine who had been victimized by the three scourges of war, the plague and famine. From 1650 on, he undertook efforts to assist other devastated areas: Picardy, Champagne and the Ile-de-France. It is difficult to imagine the precarious material and economic conditions of French peasants during this period. Richelieu did much not only to restrict the demands of the nobility, but also to develop commerce and external relations, thanks particularly to the Navy.

Moreover, a large part of society was on the way to becoming bourgeois, and there were already signs of what would later be called the *middle classes*. Many of the seventeenth century reformers belonged to this social milieu, close to the nobility, but distinct from it.

Seventeenth Century Christians

It would be inaccurate to claim that renewal of the Christian life in France began with the seventeenth century. Although the decrees of the Council of Trent (1545–1563) were not "received" by the Assembly of the Clergy until 1615, a vigorous reform movement had begun well before the Council. "From Gerson to Clichtove, a demanding pastoral ideal was affirmed, describing the 'new priests' and the new faithful who would be proposed as models by the Tridentine canons."[4] One example of the beginnings of pastoral reform, clearly evident among both religious and the secular clergy, can be found in Guillaume Briçonnet, the bishop of Meaux (1516–1534).[5]

It is nonetheless true that we can speak of the pitiful state of the Church of France at the beginning of the seventeenth century. *Bishops* scarcely ever resided in their diocese, but frequented the royal court or passed their time absorbed with temporal matters. Referring to the bishop of Rennes, Madame de Sévigné remarked, "Death had to take aim at the right moment, to reach him in his diocese." Some few bishop-reformers can be identified, but they were few and exceptions to the rule.

The *clergy* were often ignorant, lazy, and sometimes corrupt. There were too many of them in the cities; they had received no formation whatsoever and were concerned only about money. According to St. Vincent de Paul, it was the priests who were the cause of "all the disorders we see in the world." Bérulle and his disciples were to be obsessed by the "restoration of the priesthood." Every historian of this period emphasizes the need for an indepth renewal in this area.

One obstacle encountered by those who would bring about a clergy reform was the disastrous custom of the benefice, which was, at times, bestowed without the obligation of residence. Whether in presbyteries, monasteries or bishoprics, many clerics strove to gain a title that would dispense them from pastoral ministry, but assure them a comfortable living. The effect of this system was that young men were drawn to priestly ministry for purely human motives, without having a true vocation. All reformers insisted on the urgent necessity of what came to be called a *right intention*. According to Olier, "One must enter this state by the door of a vocation."

> The state of the *regular clergy* was not much better. Monasteries of both men and women served, most frequently, as places of refuge for a youngest son unable to be a soldier or for daughters without a dowry. The majority of monks and nuns were assigned to the cloister by the will of their families. They had neither the slightest hint of a vocation nor the least sign of a desire for spiritual things. In most convents, life crawled along in intellectual, moral, and often material mediocrity. The lion's share of the revenues went to the absentee benefice-holder, so that religious were left with the scantest possible portion. This drab, colorless background was enlivened by a number of scandals, fewer perhaps than is sometimes claimed, but nonetheless clearly present. On the whole, then, this was a most serious situation, marked by a decadence that had only worsened from what it had been in medieval times. Its gravity can be measured by the fact that some time later, the devout French population considered this state of affairs virtually beyond reform.[6]

Reform, however, was to take place rather quickly. The Jesuits were to return to France from exile in 1603; the Teresian Carmelites would be introduced into France in 1604, thanks to Madame Acarie and Father Bérulle, and their foundations would multiply rapidly; beginning in 1609, the reform of Port-Royal-des-Champs would be introduced.

Practically speaking, all the great religious orders of both men and women would experience a significant reform and development during this era. There were

Benedictines (the reform of Sainte-Vanne, then of Saint-Maur); Cistercians (*Feuillants*, then Trappists); Carthusians who carried a significant influence; men and women Dominicans, especially in the south; Franciscans (Recollects); Capuchins; Carmelites (the reform of Touraine-Brittany and the foundation of the Discalced Carmelites); Friars Minor (with the influence of Nicolas Barré, toward the end of the century). The phrase evoked by Bremond regarding the spiritual women and men of this age is appropriate here: they were, indeed, a *"turba magna"*—an immense crowd that could not be numbered.

Bérulle and his disciples found in this renewal of religious life a stimulus for reform of the clergy, which they considered to be the Order of Jesus Christ himself.

It must be emphasized that, as a result of these reform movements and new foundations, the very idea of religious life came to be purified and refined. Madame Acarie, whom we will discuss in chapter 10, bears witness to this in some of her writings.

On the whole, the *Christian faithful* were ignorant and superstitious. Cases of sorcery abounded and gave rise to multiple rumors. It is easy to understand why the reformers attached such importance to missions among the people. Following St. Vincent de Paul, all the leaders of the Bérulle School were to be parish missionaries, especially in rural areas.

Parish Missions

According to the most reliable historians, parish missions—which were to bear such fruit in seventeenth century France—had their origins in two sources:

> itinerant preaching in the sixteenth century and missions in Protestant countries (exemplified by St. Francis de Sales). However, at the beginning of the seventeenth century, this movement underwent a decisive evolution

which gave it a unique expression which was to have re-
percussions down through the centuries.[7]

New priestly or religious families gave themselves
energetically to this movement. We find among them:
Monsieur Vincent's Priests of the Mission; the Oratorians of Bérulle, Condren, and above all, Bourgoing; the
Doctrinarians; the Barnabites. There were also Jesuits
(with J. Maunoir, V. Huby and others) and Capuchins (especially, Honoré de Cannes). Small communities were
founded to organize and preach missions in regions other
than the capital: Nantes, Rodez, Bordeaux, Périgueux,
Aix, Lyons, Carpentras. Furthermore, a great number of
secular priests devoted themselves to this ministry. The
best known among them are Michel Le Nobletz and
Jean-Jacques Olier, a disciple of both Monsieur Vincent
and Father de Condren. Moreover, Olier would draw on
his missionary experience as one of the reasons for the
foundation of his seminary,[8] which would allow and prepare for the reform and the renewal of the whole Church.

A Major Pastoral Reform

During the first part of the seventeenth century, a serious reform movement was launched in an effort to remedy the shortcomings and miseries of the era.[9] This movement was pastoral, missionary and deeply spiritual in
nature. The greatest missionaries and the most effective
pastors were some we now know as saints. The century
was, at one and the same time, mystical and apostolic.

To speak of the renewal of the Church in the seventeenth century is to think, first of all, of the many achievements that marked it: renewal of parish life (with Adrien
Bourdoise at Saint-Nicolas du Chardonnet, and Olier at
Saint-Sulpice); catechetical organization; restoration of
liturgical prayer; development and increasing influence
of secondary and higher education (Jesuits, Oratorians,

and others); the multiplication of grade schools for poor children, a service to which countless women and men consecrated their lives as educators; the establishment of "exercises for those to be ordained," and then of seminaries. This list is impressive and far from complete. We might add the missionary movement toward Canada, the Near East and the Far East. In this area, the outstanding societies were the Recollects, the Jesuits, the Capuchins, and the Society for Foreign Missions.

A certain number of organizations, some of them of great importance, arose to support and encourage all this renewal. Above all, however, strong spiritual inspiration moved these men and women; they came together as much to pray and deepen their Christian life as to plan ecclesial renewal.

Madame Acarie's salon was one of these centers of spirituality. Bérulle, as a young man, frequented it, and Francis de Sales spent considerable time there, when he was in Paris. Together, the group read spiritual writers, such as the Rheno-Flemish mystics, and discovered the works of Teresa of Jesus. It was, in fact, Madame Acarie who would prepare the way for the coming of Carmel to France. Discussions centered on monastic reform and the foundation of new orders. Cochois was able to identify this center as a headquarters for Catholic reform and renewal.

Madame Acarie's circle, however, was only one of the outstanding signs of Christian fervor in Paris. The Carthusian monastery of Vauvert, the Visitation monasteries, and the monastery of the Benedictines at Montmartre had a wide influence, as did Port-Royal and, later, the Benedictines of the Blessed Sacrament. Another intellectual and spiritual center was the Abbey of Saint-Germain-des-Prés, with Dom Mabillon and Claude Martin, the son of Marie de l'Incarnation.

The Company of the Blessed Sacrament was another one of these organizations. Founded in Paris in 1627 by the Duke of Ventadour, it brought together laypersons, especially, but also priests, like Olier, Vincent de Paul and, later, Bossuet. In time, it would spread into other parts of the country.

> Its aim was not only to engage in works of piety and charity (service of the sick, the poor, prisoners), but also to defend Christian morality through discreet contacts with magistrates and officers. Duelists, blasphemers, libertines, and Protestants were closely watched and denounced. The secrecy with which this society was surrounded and the questionable character of some of its activities brought upon it the mistrust of both secular and ecclesiastical authorities, and aroused strong enmities. In 1660, it was banned by Mazarin, who would not forgive some of its members for their participation in the opposition's political party known as the Fronde. After several years of survival, the Company disappeared definitively, about 1667.[10]

For a number of years, the director of the Company of the Blessed Sacrament was Gaston de Renty (1611–1649), a married gentleman and father of a family. He is still considered one of the great spiritual leaders of his time.[11] He maintained close personal relations with Jean-Jacques Olier and John Eudes. Through him, they established contact with the Carmel of Beaune and Marguerite du Saint-Sacrement. They were all instrumental in spreading devotion to the infancy of Christ.[12]

The *Tuesday Conferences* also played a very important role during this period. This Tuesday assembly was a meeting of churchmen who came together every week at the Priory of Saint-Lazare, under the direction of Saint Vincent de Paul, to "discuss the virtues and responsibilities of their state of life." In 1633, Monsieur Vincent drew up a rule of life for an association of priests. Before long, the elite of the clergy of Paris had become members. During St. Vincent's lifetime, it is estimated that more than 250 priests attended these meetings regularly.

Among them were about 20 who became bishops, including Godeau, Pavillon and Jacques-Bénigne Bossuet. The Tuesday group members also worked in missions in Paris, at Saint-Germain-en-Laye and in Metz. On several occasions, Olier wrote to the "ecclesiastics of the Saint-Lazare Conference, in Paris" to give an account of his missions and to invite them to join him in this ministry: "Sirs, do not refuse to help Jesus in this way. . . . Paris, Paris, you hold back those who could convert many worlds. . . . Here, a single word preaches and nothing at all seems useless. . . ."[13]

Authentic Mystical Inspiration

At the heart of all these activities and organizations, we must recognize the presence of an authentically mystical inspiration. The Tridentine reform had been launched in Italy by St. Borromeo, St. Philip Neri and other great spiritual leaders. The same phenomenon had taken place in Spain through other saints: Peter of Alcantara, Teresa of Jesus, John of the Cross and among the clergy, John of Avila. Savoy had been transformed by Francis de Sales, whose influence extended to Paris and into all of France. The heritage of this great saint, however, did not prevent the emergence in seventeenth century France of its own constellation of saints.

From the beginning of the century, forces were set in motion. In referring to the visit of Francis de Sales to Paris in 1602, Bremond did not hesitate to note that there he met "saints, a great many, true saints, everywhere."[14]

This quest for the spiritual was, at times, ambiguous and would be mocked by Molière in the person of two falsely pious characters in *Tartuffe*. Nevertheless, it must be emphasized that, fundamentally, this attitude sprang from a desire for prayer—"methods of meditation flashed out everywhere,"[15] it was said—and a concern for evangelization. Moreover, if the situation in Paris is more readily known to us, it seems just as certain that the same major mystical current was found in the rest of the country as well.

> We remain poorly informed regarding the spiritual life of the French regions and provinces at the beginning of the seventeenth century. Nonetheless, all the information we do possess leads us to suspect that it was intense. The possibility and the means for souls to arrive at mystical union with God, were, without a doubt, a subject of intense preoccupation, even in the most remote areas. Almost everywhere, there were priests and religious who had read the ascetical and mystical writers. Thus, there were gradually created waves of compatibility which often found a center in the newly founded monasteries. This is one aspect of religious life in France during the period still scarcely explored: bonds of friendship, networks of prayer and mutual support, with all their ramifications. . . ."[16]

Many of these great spiritual leaders and missionaries maintained bonds of friendship with one another. For one of his works on Francis de Sales and Vincent de Paul, Father A. Dodin chose the subtitle, *Two Friends*.[17] In this work, he describes not only the meeting of the two saints in December 1618, but also the profound influence that Francis de Sales had on Monsieur Vincent. Bérulle and Olier also knew Francis de Sales. Vincent de Paul knew Bérulle, Bourdoise, Olier and John Eudes. The last two shared deep sympathies. Still other bonds of spiritual friendship were woven among the men and women of this century.

Like every dynamic era, the seventeenth century in France gave artistic expression to the spiritual movements by which it was marked. Jean Simard's volume, *Une iconographie du clergé français au XVIIe siècle [Iconography of Clergy in Seventeenth Century France]* (Quebec: Laval University, 1976) is a study whose contents far surpass its title. Unfortunately, works of this kind are still too rare. In 1982–83, a remarkable exhibit was presented at the Petit-Palais in Paris: *L'art du XVIIe siècle dans les Carmels de France [Seventeenth-Century Art in the Carmelite Monasteries of France].*

In the domain of sacred music, many contributions were made by Marc-Antoine Charpentier (1636–1704) and Michel Richard Delalande (1657–1726) among others. Their compositions reflect and nourish the sense of God's grandeur and the spirit of adoration so characteristic of this century.

This chapter began with a recital of the shadows that marked the seventeenth century. Gradually, light replaced the darkness, without, however, completely conquering it. This rapid portrayal of such striking contrasts is necessary to describe the context within which the Bérulle School was to emerge. Bérulle and his disciples were part of this social and religious milieu. They were to contribute to the renewal of the Church in ways so unique that they merit our most serious attention.

DOCUMENTS FOR CHAPTER 2

2.1 The Desolation of France

[In contrast to the progress taking place in society, the poverty of certain areas of the country and, even, of Paris, at one time or another, cannot be overlooked. A letter written on 28 June 1652 by Angélique Arnaud, Abbess of Port-Royal, gives a most dismal picture of the full fury of the revolution in Paris, following the lamentable battle of Estampes]:

France is in total desolation: every corner of every province is touched by suffering. Paris and the surrounding regions are the most ill-treated. The villages in the area are all totally deserted, and the inhabitants who are left have fled to the woods, while others have died of hunger or have been beaten to death by the soldiers. . . . It was necessary to open the Saint-Louis Hospital to receive the wounded brought in from the troops that were terribly defeated at Estampes. All the regions there are in an incomparable state of destruction and devastation, because all the wheat is lost, the vines have been uprooted and the villages, burned. . . . Flour is so scarce in Paris that bread, even black bread, already costs ten *sols* a pound. We have enough for only five days. We have wheat, but it can be ground only with great difficulty, because the soldiers are robbing the mills.

In F. Lebrun, Le *XVIIᵉ siècle*, Paris, A. Colin, 1967;
120.

2.2 Racine and the Bishops

The following verse, composed by the author of *Andromaque*, was making the rounds in Paris, about 1682:

> Yesterday, an order came from Saint-Germain,
> For a meeting.
> Tomorrow, they'll be seating
> Our archbishop and fifty-two others,
> Successors of the Apostles, brothers
> Altogether.
> The case they'll set down in history
> Is still a mystery:
> Let me point out—
> Fifty-two prelates not in residence:
> About that, there's no doubt.

> In M. D. Poinsenet, *France religreise du XVII*^e
> *siéle*, Paris: Casterman, 1952; 27.

2.3

We wonder if all the troubles we see in the world ought not be attributed to priests. This statement might scandalize some people, but the subject demands that I point out the importance of a remedy by showing the magnitude of the evil. We have had several conferences on this topic, addressing it thoroughly, so as to discover the source of so many misfortunes. The conclusion has been that priests are the Church's worst enemies. They have been the cause of heresies, as we see in the heretics, Luther and Calvin, who were priests. It is because of priests that heretics have succeeded, that vice has reigned, and that ignorance has established its throne among the poor. All this has come about through their disorderly life and their failure to oppose with all their power, in fidelity to their duties, these three flood waters that have inundated the earth.

What sacrifice, Gentlemen, would you not offer to God in order to work for the reform of the clergy, so that they could live according to the exalted dignity of their state. By means of this effort, the Church would be able to rise out of the opprobrium and desolation in which she finds herself!

St. Vincent de Paul, *Entretiens Spirituels*, éd.
Dodin. Paris: Seuil, 1960; 501–02. Conference, 6
December 1658.

2.4 The Clergy and Benefices

[The disgraceful situation of the French clergy in the seventeenth century was due, in great part, to a total lack of formation, as well as to methods of recruitment and the benefice system].

The priesthood is looked upon as the easiest of all professions. It attracts candidates by the material advantages it easily provides. The great number of church properties, foundations, and other sources of revenue assure to any pastor, chaplain, or especially, bishop holding the title of a function or a benefice, resources for a more or less comfortable life. This offers possibilities in particular, to the youngest son in a family, who cannot take up the father's profession or for all those who are not capable of doing so.

How are benefices awarded? In the case of important appointments, nobility counts and the favor of the king is the deciding factor. Political considerations have led him more than once to choose as bishops candidates of questionable, if not scandalous reputation, for example, Harlay de Champvallon, in Paris. Family settlements and relations carry great weight: Benefices pass from uncle to nephew. Thus, the Gondi family held the bishopric of Paris for a century (during which time it became an archbishopric). Fortunately, we are tempted to say, the title holder often passed his responsibilities on to a man who was more competent or available, a curate whom he reimbursed more or less meagerly. Moreover, the "minimum wage" was specified by royal authority. This system allowed a good number of benefice holders to take advantage of the goods of the church, even as they actively led the life of a layperson.

In order to receive a benefice, the clerical state was required, unless an exception was granted. In other words, in that era, one had to receive the tonsure. However, one could always find a bishop who would confer this order, so that the number of clerics seeking benefices was countless. The Council of

Bordeaux, in 1624, bemoaned this state of affairs: *ingens et egens clericorum turba.*

One had to be a priest for the exercise of certain functions, particularly to administer the sacraments and, eventually, to claim the proper allowance. It was as easy to find a bishop who would ordain you a priest as to give you the tonsure. However, you had to wait a few years more. Jean-Jacques Olier received the tonsure at the age of 12 in order to claim the Bazainville Priory. He was only ordained a priest 19 years later. Vincent de Paul was tonsured at the age of 19. . . . Furthermore, priests were more numerous both than minor clergy and than the number of positions available to them.

That is the reason why so many of them rusted out through inactivity or stagnated in misery. Since misery is an evil counselor, a good number of them went begging the faithful for an offering in exchange for the conferral of the sacraments. Others resorted to a more preferable choice, exercising a profession incomparable with their state.

Such a situation scandalized the faithful much less than can be imagined. They were no longer surprised by a state of affairs that had existed for decades. Some were quite understanding, even indulgent, toward priests who were married or living in concubinage.

In fact, priests themselves, let alone some bishops, were strongly opposed to any reform that would deprive them of certain resources or impose obligations that they had not foreseen when they presented themselves for ordination. If a man's private life did not affect the validity of the sacraments, why oblige him to lead a blameless existence? It was more important to know the ritual and have the necessary power to baptize, celebrate Mass, bless and exorcise, than to live a monastic life. . . .

M. Dupuy, *Se laisser à l'Esprit*, Paris: Cerf, 1982;
21–23.

2.5 Religious Vocations Come From God

In an era when entrance into religious life was often far from spontaneous, because attached to family interests, Madame Acarie directed her children with prudence and broadmindedness. She condemned vocations that were the result of force or, even, of simple persuasion. "If I had only one child, she would say, "and were the queen of the entire universe; if that child were my sole heir and God called that child to the religious life, in no way would I attempt to prevent response to that call. But, if I had one hundred children and no means of providing for them, I would not, on my own, send one to religious life. A vocation must come from God alone. The religious life is such an exalted state that everyone in the world, working together, could not produce one good religious, if God had not called that person. It is better to be a layperson through the divine will than a religious through human design."

> A. R. Salmon-Malebranche, *Madame Acarie.*
> Carmel de Pontoise, 1977; 26–27.

2.6

For several years, a number of us have been together, after having worked with people in missions and parishes. Our experience led us to recognize the futility of any efforts with the people, if we had not previously purified the source of their sanctification, that is, their priests. Thus, these companions withdrew in order to cultivate the new plants entrusted to their care, those who seemed to be called to the priesthood.

> Olier, *Divers Écrits* 1:71.

Now I see that we need a great number of pastors, in nearly the whole church, who desire to be reformed. . . . They make up the Order of Jesus Christ, the first Pastor of souls, and this order must now be reformed, to bring about the renewal of the universal Church.

> Olier, *Mémoires* 2:332–33.

2.7 Madame Acarie's *Salon*

Having lived with the Bérulle family during her husband's exile, Madame Acarie returned to her residence on the rue des

Juifs, in the Marais district of Paris. There, she opened her home to a great number of people.

Bérulle came nearly every day. There, he met his master from the Sorbonne, André Duval; reformed Cistercians or Feuillants: Eustache de Saint-Paul and Sans de Sainte-Catherine; the Capuchins: Ange de Joyeuse, the former Leaguer and Marshal of France, and Benoît de Canfeld, whose *Règle de perfection* was being circulated in manuscript form; another English refugee, Archange de Pembroke; saintly priests: Jean de Quintanadoine de Brétigny, a great admirer of the Teresian reform, and his friend, Gallemant; devout laymen: Michael de Marillac who would become Keeper of the Seals, René Gautier, lawyer of the Great Council and future translator of John of the Cross; and great ladies: the Marquise de Maignelay, sister of the bishop of Paris, Madame de Sainte-Beuve who would found the Ursulines, the Marquise de Bréauté, a future Carmelite.... The Jesuits were still in exile, but on their return (1603), the famous Father Coton joined the group at the Hôtel Acarie.

What did they all do there? Father Duval gives one answer: "A lady came to see me and said, 'Father, what things everyone is saying about Madame Acarie! Everyone in town is talking of nothing but her. Is everything they say true?' When I asked her what was being said, she answered: 'They say she has revelations, that she leads a miraculous life, that she is so learned that her house is filled with people who want to consult her; preachers and doctors (theologians) go to seek her advice on many things!' Everything this good woman said was true and there was much more that she had not said." Indeed, spiritual subjects were discussed at the Acarie home, but it was less a gathering for devotion than a "center" of Catholic renewal. Never had mysticism been involved so concretely in human endeavors. There, the group discussed monastic reform and the foundation of new religious orders; they studied the painful problem of the reform of the secular clergy and determined the position to be taken regarding the religious policies of Henry IV.

P. Cochois, *Bérulle et l'École française,* Paris: Seuil, Maîtres spirituels, 1960; 10–11.

CHAPTER THREE

Pierre de Berulle

The Leader of the School

Pierre de Bérulle (1575–1629) is, unquestionably, the first and the best representative of what is known as the French School. He is rightly considered its originator, whose insights and doctrines were popularized and adopted by three disciples who were heavily influenced by them: Condren, Olier and John Eudes. We may not share fully Bremond's opinion that Bérulle brought about an absolute revolution in the realm of spirituality, by putting God back into the center of the Christian life in place of the human person. Still, we must recognize the major role he played in any number of areas. All historians willingly agree with Dagens: "Without Bérulle, something essential would be missing from the spiritual life in France and from Christian thought."[1]

There has been a marked renewal of studies devoted to Bérulle in recent years. We are now able to retrace both the stages of his very active life and the evolution of his intellectual and spiritual development.[2] Nevertheless, the depth of his thought and the cumbersome style in which he wrote make his teaching difficult to grasp. One or another of his disciples, for example, Olier or John Eudes, allows us to understand Bérulle with greater ease.

We must point out the relatively short life of this man, who died at the age of 54 (Vincent de Paul lived to be 79). Still, Bérulle was closely involved with the major political and religious events that marked the beginning of the seventeenth century. He was in touch with Marie de Médicis and Richelieu, had diplomatic missions in England for the marriage of Henriette of France, and dealt in controversies with the followers of the Protestant Reformation. Bérulle introduced the Teresian Carmel into France, and provided spiritual guidance to the 49 monasteries he helped to establish, in spite of countless difficulties, between 1604 and 1629. He was the founder of the Oratory in France, the spiritual director of its communities, and founded the seminary of Saint-Magloire. He also published a number of works, maintained a voluminous correspondence, and traveled extensively in France, Spain, Italy and England. Most importantly, this intensely active life represents the deep spirituality and vigorous theological reflection found in his writings.

Bérulle was born in 1575, in the family mansion of Cérilly, not far from Troyes. He was the eldest of four children in a Catholic family that belonged to the gentry and the magistrature. Following the death of her husband in 1582, Madame de Bérulle left for Paris with the children. If Bérulle's birthplace had felt the unsettling disturbances of the Reformation, Paris did not provide much more tranquility.

Henry III, assassinated in 1589, had not been able to settle the conflict between the Protestants and the League, an organization of Catholics united against the Calvinists. Henry IV brought Paris to a state of starvation. Several members of Bérulle's family were imprisoned or sent into exile.

Following his classical studies, Pierre took up philosophy at the College of Clermont (today, the Lycée Louis-le-Grand) and then began to study theology. Since the Jesuits had been expelled from France in 1595 by Henry IV, Bérulle began his studies at the Sorbonne. He was, very probably, Duval's student. It is interesting to note that, before the Jesuits left Paris, they entrusted to this 20-year old student the mission of examining and accepting potential candidates for the Society of Jesus.

While pursuing his theological studies, Bérulle frequently had the opportunity to meet, discuss and argue with a number of Protestants whom he often saw return to the Catholic faith. Like Francis de Sales, but in another way, his whole life would be marked by much controversy. One of his "converts," Mademoiselle de Raconis, would enter Carmel. Later, he would publish his "Controversial Discourses" (1609). In 1600, he had been present at a debate between Du Perron and Du Plessis Mornay; in 1608, he, himself, took part in a similar debate with Pastor Du Moulin. Bérulle, born three years after the St. Bartholomew's Day Massacre (24 August 1572) and ordained to the priesthood in the year following the Edict of Nantes (13 April 1598), played a major role in this sad period.

Bérulle's years of study were also—perhaps, especially—marked by frequent contact with his cousin, Barbe Avrillot (Madame Acarie), Dom Beaucousin, and the group that met with Madame Acarie. Beginning in 1594, this cousin lived for several years in the Bérulle mansion, after her husband, a League member, had been exiled by Henry IV. Young Pierre became her confidante and was a witness to her deeply spiritual life, her mystical experiences and her solid, good sense of balance. With her, he took as his spiritual director Dom Beaucousin, the master of novices and vicar of the Carthusians of Vauvert. This relationship lasted until 1604, even after Madame Acarie's return home, following her husband's amnesty.

Dom Beaucousin asked Bérulle to study and adapt in French an Italian treatise of spirituality written by Isabelle Bellinzaga, a directee of the Jesuit Gagliardi. Thus, in 1597, Bérulle published the *Bref Discours de l'abnégation intérieure*. This book became very successful, as did the summary of Christian perfection written by the Italian mystic. The doctrine presented in this work was classic in every way, insisting on absolute detachment for union with God. However, no mention was made of the person of Jesus.

Dom Beaucousin introduced Madame Acarie and Bérulle to the Rheno-Flemish mystics: especially Tauler, Ruysbroek and Harphius, along with Louis de Blois. It has been demonstrated that these readings had a decisive effect on the young theologian. The transcendence, holiness and absolute nature of God on which these mystical writers insisted so strongly contributed in great part to Bérulle's sense of the grandeur of God and the spirit of adoration that characterized his faith. What is ordinarily called the *theocentrism* of Bérulle (and of the French School) became the inspiration of a fundamental attitude of adoration and true religion: "We must, first and foremost, look at God and not at self. . . ."

Priestly Ordination and Spiritual Development

On 5 June 1599, Bérulle was ordained to the priesthood in Paris, following a long, 40-day retreat with the Capuchins. Although he was not yet aware of it, this priesthood would henceforth be at the heart of his life and his mission. Gradually, and with increasing depth of insight, he came to perceive the grandeur, the dignity and the responsibilities carried by "the priests of Jesus." This intuition led him, later, to seek to "restore the priesthood" and to renew "the Order of Jesus Christ." Still later, he would explain his thought to the Oratorians:

> Through the sacrifice of Christ, we put on the person of Christ and we act in his name and in his place (*in persona Christi*): thus, our person is taken up, in a wonderful manner, by Christ, so that we can accomplish Christ's marvelous deeds.[3]

In addition to the long hours he passed in prayer and study, the events of daily life dictated Bérulle's activities. At the end of 1599, in spite of a ban issued by the king and the prohibition of a certain Doctor Marescot, Bérulle wrote and published a *Traité des Energumènes*,[4] following the case of a woman, Marthe Brossier, exorcised from diabolic possession by the Capuchins. For Bérulle, diabolic possessions were a sort of blasphemous caricature that stood in opposition to God's possession of the soul. In a phrase that is certainly characteristic of his thought, we can already see the beginning of Bérulle's christocentrism:

> (Satan), that ape of God, takes pleasure in being united to that (human) nature by an act of possession which is the shadow and illusion of the astounding possession of our humanity which God assumed in Jesus Christ.[5]

The young priest still had much to learn. The year 1602 was to be a decisive time for him. The desire for perfection and integrity in his personal life had been with him for many years. Now, he began to consider religious life. He knew and admired the Carthusians, the Capuchins, the Jesuits. He even thought of entering the Society of Jesus. In August, under the guidance of Father Maggio, he made a retreat in view of a decision. At this time, he received the definitive light he sought. The lengthy pages he wrote at the end of this retreat, confirmed by Father Maggio's recently discovered notes, reflect an astounding spiritual depth.

First, through an analysis of his feelings, he perceived that God was not calling him to change his way of life, but to "prepare himself for certain exalted interior dispositions." His surrender to God was total and complete, expressed in terms that were both concrete and poetic. He felt that grace alone could bring about this entire abdication and commitment into the hands of God. He wrote, "I have longed for and I still long through my desires to realize these dispositions."

The other fruit of this retreat, it would seem, was a clearly christocentric orientation:

> Jesus Christ alone is the end and the way to the end. . . .
> We ought to bind ourselves to him as the goal of our life
> and to make use of him as the means to the goal.

He saw in the humiliation of the Incarnate Word "the model of the annihilation of the human self and of that submission to God toward which the self aspires."[6] Jesus is the true fulfillment of our very being.

Several Jesuits played a similar role in the spiritual development of Teresa of Jesus. It is very possible that she owed to them, at least in part, her intense devotion to the humanity of Jesus.[7]

Introduction of Carmel into France

Despite the tensions that existed between France and Spain, spiritual leaders in France, for some time, had been fascinated by Spanish mysticism. This influence would extend through the entire seventeenth century.

In 1601, a priest of Rouen, of Spanish origin, Jean de Quintanadoine de Brétigny, had translated and published, at his own expense, the works of Teresa of Jesus. This priest, who was a frequent visitor to Madame Acarie's salon, awakened in her and her friends a desire to introduce Carmel into France. What Brétigny alone could never have done became possible through the influential connections of the Acarie group and above all, through the untiring energy of Bérulle. He overcame many difficulties, including, especially, the resistance of the persons in authority of Carmel in Spain.

On 15 October 1604, the feast of Teresa of Jesus, an impressive number of priests and laypersons were able to persuade and accompany a group of six Spanish Carmelite nuns to Paris. Two of them were already known as great friends of the saintly foundress: Anne of Jesus, the "queen of prioresses" to whom John of the Cross had dedicated the "Spiritual Canticle," and Anne of St. Bartholomew, St. Teresa's nurse. Thus, 15 October 1604 is recognized as the foundation date of Carmel in France. Its beginnings were marked by much light and by many shadows. Bérulle's personality was responsible in large part for both.

The arrival of the Carmelites, along with the many foundations that followed, was a response to the need and the desire for renewal of religious life. Between 1604 and 1660, there were 62 Carmelite monasteries founded in France alone, and other foundations were made in Flanders. At the same time, Francis de Sales, in Savoy, was presenting Teresa of Jesus as the model of a reformer to be imitated. Carmel played a leading role in religious reform at this time: in 1609, Port-Royal; in 1604, the Benedictines of Sainte-Vanne; and in 1618, the Benedictines of Saint-Maur, among many others. The initiator of it all was Bérulle.

But, as mentioned above, light often went hand-in-hand with darkness. The French postulants formed by Madame Acarie possessed an *intellectual* piety that astounded the Spanish. Anne of Jesus, among others, was scarcely able to appreciate what seemed to her to be neglect of the *humanity* of Jesus. She could not get Bérulle to understand her. He, on the contrary, greatly admired the humble Anne of St. Bartholomew. These fundamental differences were joined to a multitude of misunderstandings in matters of food, devotions, pronunciation of Latin, and so on. Things were not easy on either side and were to become more difficult still. Much to the displeasure of the Spanish Carmelite friars who were banned from France by the king until 1610, Bérulle, Gallemant and Duval were named ecclesiastical superiors of the Carmelite nuns. The vow of servitude that Bérulle imposed on them in 1615 was to be a source of endless controversy.[8]

No matter what is said about these difficulties, however, Bérulle's merit cannot be denied. He would have the great joy of seeing his own mother enter the Carmel of the Incarnation in Paris, on 14 August 1605. Madame Acarie's three daughters also entered Carmel, as she, herself, did after her husband's death. Madame Acarie—in religion, Marie of the Incarnation—died in the Carmel of Pontoise on 18 April 1618; she was attended by André Duval, the theologian, the superior and the friend of her early years.

Mystical Christocentrism

During the retreat at Verdun in 1602, Bérulle's attention was drawn to the person of Jesus, Incarnate Word. He was not less influenced by the abstract mysticism of the northern spiritual writers, so that his evolution toward an authentic christocentrism took place only gradually. It is most likely that the Carmelites, as much as his Jesuit friend, Father Coton, were also influential in this development. In 1607, he experienced what he characterized as an authentic mystical grace, which gave definite and permanent form to the tendencies already in him and set his future in an irreversible direction. This grace has been compared to Descartes' "Night of Illumination" or to Pascal's "Night of Fire." Bérulle had been invited to accept the role of tutor to the Dauphin. Under the influence, probably, of the Carmelites and of the Acarie group, he refused. He then understood his true vocation in a new light that left no doubt in his mind: he was not destined to the court of King Henry IV, but to the court of Jesus Christ, "to proclaim to nations and to peoples the design and the will of God." Bérulle would later describe this grace as one of the most significant that he had ever received in his life. From this time on, the person of the Incarnate Word was to be at the heart of his existence, his thought, his teaching and all his writings. Thus, he became, as Pope Urban VIII named him, *the apostle of the Incarnate Word.*

Here, we are at the heart of Bérulle's spiritual experience and of his mystical teaching, properly so called. The human person finds fulfillment only through union with God in adoration and love. But it is Jesus alone who, through the unity of the two natures in his person is, *by his very state,* the perfect adorer. Bérulle's thought was to find "one of the bases of its stability and one of its best expressions," as Cognet remarked, only in 1623, in the *Discourse on the State and the Glories of Jesus.* All of this existed already, in seed, in 1607. This "mysticism of essences" would gradually give way to an adoring, loving contemplation of Jesus, without any neglect of theology on Bérulle's part. In the midst of the lyrical elevations found in the *Discourse,* other considerations, metaphysical in nature, appear:

> If the person of the Word is united to this humanity, the essence and the subsistence of the Word are also one with it. This humanity of Jesus Christ Our Lord bears and receives in itself not only the personal being, but also the essential being of God. For the Word is God, God is man, and man is God, according to the best and most commonly known concepts of faith. The Word is God through this divine essence and God is man through this humanity.[9]

Bérulle adored the divinized humanity of Jesus:

The person of the Word is divine and infinite. Thus, it has a completely extraordinary and unspeakable application to the human nature. The latter, without its own subsistence, needs that of the eternal Word which, we might say, activates and penetrates this humanity in its essence, its powers, and in all its parts.[10]

According to Cognet, the contemplation of Jesus gave rise in Bérulle to lengthy considerations of the "states and mysteries" of the Incarnate Word.

Each circumstance in the life of the Son of God is a mystery and a corresponding state of the Incarnate Word, a state which takes its value from the Incarnation. . . . A state, at least as Bérulle conceived it beginning in 1615, is the interior attitude of Jesus in every circumstance of his earthly or glorified life, considered as an eternal reality insofar as this life has been assumed by a divine person.[11]

Bérulle would consider "the state, the virtue and the merit of the mystery" all on the same level. These mysteries remain a source of grace, eternally: "They may be past, in terms of performance, but they are present in their virtue, which will never pass away."[12] The Christian life thus consists both in adoring Jesus in his states and mysteries, and in adhering to him in his interior attitudes. This calls for radical abnegation of one's very self.

Among the major mysteries that Bérulle proposes for consideration, the Incarnation remains at the heart of his contemplation. The same can be said of the mystery of the infancy of Jesus. For Bérulle, the state of infancy is the height of annihilation. It is the mystery of the Word, the Voice of God becoming mute (*infans*). Again, it is here that we find the roots of Bérulle's deep devotion to the Blessed Sacrament and to the Virgin Mary. The text published as the *Life of Jesus* is a prolonged meditation on the mystery of the Incarnation, with wonderfully inspiring pages on the Annunciation. It contains passages that lead us to contemplate the attitudes of Mary at the birth of Jesus and during his infancy.

The vow of servitude to Jesus and the office in honor of Jesus must be understood in light of the central position given by Bérulle to mystical christocentrism. There is a complete pedagogy here, one which was taken up in another way, later, by Jean-Jacques Olier and John Eudes. For example, Olier's method of prayer and John Eudes's midday exercise were to be centered exclusively on the person of Jesus. Both invite us to adore Jesus, to draw his Spirit within ourselves, so as to enter into communion with his dispositions and to act in this same Spirit.

Foundation of the Oratory

The foundation of the Oratory, in 1611, follows Bérulle's experience of grace in 1607. Like all true Christians of his era, he suffered from the deplorable situation of the clergy. In 1611, the nuncio, Ubaldini, bemoaned the fact that "churchmen sleep and it is impossible to awaken them." As a number of religious families (Benedictines, Carmelites, Capuchins) undertook an authentic renewal, some priests were moved to reform the clergy, also: "Well, now, what is going on? Could our Lord possibly have willed such perfection for religious orders, without requiring it for his own, the order of the priesthood?"[13]

The movement started in Italy, with Charles Borromeo in Milan and Philip Neri in Rome, while John of Avila pursued the same goal in Spain. Francis de Sales had little success with his efforts in Savoy, but it was he who encouraged Bérulle to take up the cause; it was he who introduced Bérulle to the Oratory of St. Philip Neri. Finally, at the insistence of Henri de Gondi, bishop of Paris, Bérulle launched a movement whose aim was to renew "the state of perfection among the clergy . . . without separation from its ecclesiastical body."[14] If religious orders were to be reformed, there was all the more reason for the Order of Jesus Christ, the priests, to be renewed, according to the decrees of the Council of Trent, but still more basically, in fidelity to the will of Jesus, the "founder" of the Order of the Priesthood.

Bérulle sought to live this ideal of the priesthood himself, and to give authentic witness to it. On 11 November 1611, the feast of St. Martin, he established a community with five companions in a house on rue Saint-Jacques, not far from Carmel. They celebrated the Office together in choir and attracted many people who came to hear the beauty of their chant. They spent long hours in prayer, pastoral ministry, and study of the Bible, the church fathers and theology.

Oratorians, while leading a life in common, desire to remain diocesan priests in every way. Bérulle had even thought of imposing on his priests a vow of obedience to the bishop. The Bull of Approbation granted on 10 May 1613 did not retain this point. The pope, however, did ask the Oratorians to accept the responsibility of secondary education. In 1615, the group pronounced the vow of servitude to Jesus, acknowledging him as the first and highest superior. In this same year, the Assembly of the Clergy "received" the decrees of the Council of Trent. The Oratory had already begun to develop in France, beginning in 1611. The members did not accept any ecclesiastical benefices, which were more often than not highly ambiguous. They dedicated themselves, however, to every kind of ministry: preaching, confessions, catechetics and missions. Later, many of them would devote themselves to teaching in colleges or at the Sorbonne. Most naturally, they were invited to take on the formation of priests. Sébastien Zamet, the remarkable bishop of Langres, entrusted his seminary to them in 1619. In 1624, they took charge of the Seminary of Saint-Magloire in Paris.

These "seminaries" consisted of times of retreat along with periods of spiritual and pastoral formation, meant to prepare future priests for ordination. St. Vincent de Paul, directed for several years by Bérulle, was able to organize "exercises" for those to be ordained at Saint-Lazare, beginning in 1631. There were only about 14 students at the Seminary of Saint-Magloire in 1642, but the seminary in Langres was more successful, and the momentum was underway. Bérulle and his first group at the Oratory brought a concern for organization to the priestly renewal movement, but, even more, a mystical and ecclesial conviction regarding the glory and the dignity of Jesus' priests.

Bérulle, the Oratory, the Carmelites

Bérulle continued to direct his communities of the Oratory, initiating them to a truly mystical life. On 8 September 1614, he had the members pronounce a vow of servitude to the Virgin. Then, on 28 February 1615, in the course of a celebration of the Solemnity of Jesus, they made the vow of servitude to Jesus and to his divinized humanity.

In 1614, Pope Paul V appointed Bérulle as the visitor of Carmel in perpetuity, despite the requests of the first Discalced friars who had come from Italy in 1610. From the beginning, Bérulle had been superior of the Carmelite nuns, along with Duval, a theologian at the Sorbonne, and Gallemant, a pastor at Aumale. From 1614 on, however, Bérulle discovered in himself an authentic vocation to initiate the Carmelite nuns to the mystical life. His intuitions and his psychology did not correspond entirely to those of the foundress, still less to the ideas of the Carmelite friars. In June 1615, he proposed that the Carmelite nuns of Chalon-sur-Saône pronounce the vow of servitude to the Virgin. This was the beginning of painful tensions between Bérulle and Duval, and even of misunderstandings with Madame Acarie.

Between 1619 and 1623, one storm succeeded another. If difficulties appeared, initially, with the arrival of the Spanish Carmelite friars in 1610, the Papal Brief of 1614 served only to increase their resentment and bitterness. The Carmelite, Father Denis of the Mother of God, fomented a violent opposition among the nuns of Bordeaux and of Saintes. Father Coton was to write, "Aside from heresy, I have never seen anything like this for shrewishness!" Bérulle's appointment was to be confirmed, however, by Paul V in 1620, by Gregory XV in 1621, and by Urban VIII in 1623.

In 1620, an erroneous copy of the vows of servitude was submitted to the Universities of Louvain and Douay by some of Bérulle's enemies. At first, the celebrated Jesuit theologian Lessius was taken in. Then he advised Bérulle to defend himself. This affair unleashed a veritable war of anonymous, libelous notes.

All of this, which appears as highly dishonorable conduct today, led to the writing of Bérulle's masterpiece: the *Discourse on the State and Glories of Jesus*, published in 1623. Bérulle had worked carefully in order to justify in a detailed and fundamental way the strictly theological intention that had led to the writing of the vows of servitude, in direct fidelity to baptismal commitments. The reading of this difficult work calls for sustained attention. It is not simply a polemic, written in response to the accusations of his opponents, but a demonstration of Bérulle's theology and mystical fervor.

In the preparation of the *Discourse*, Bérulle had sought the help of Jean Duvergier de Hauranne, a priest of Saint-Cyran, who was universally recognized as a scholar in patristic and scholastic studies. Several years later, this priest was to undertake the defense of Jansenius's *Augustinus* and would, himself, join the Jansenist movement.

Bérulle, the Diplomat

On several occasions, Bérulle was called on to intervene in sensitive diplomatic missions. He facilitated the reconciliation of Louis XIII and Marie de Médicis in

1619. He was actively involved, in 1624 and 1625, in the negotiations preparing for the marriage of Henriette of France, the sister of Louis XIII, and Charles Stuart, heir to the crown of England. The political and religious stakes were high in this matter. On the one hand, Spain was proposing another suitor; on the other hand, the union between a French Catholic and a Protestant king might be a guarantee for persecuted English Catholics.

Bérulle was not satisfied with bringing matters to completion in Rome and Paris. With 25 priests, 12 of whom were Oratorians, he accompanied the new queen to England. There, in the presence of Henriette, he preached on St. Mary Magdalene. This discourse occasioned the *Elevation on St. Mary Magdalene*, one of his better writings. Despite many difficulties and the relative failure of his efforts, he nonetheless continued from Paris to encourage the young queen. Bérulle was also involved in many other negotiations, especially those to prepare the treaty with Spain in 1626.

Bérulle's attitude in the domain of diplomacy and political affairs has been compared with that of Richelieu. If Bérulle proved to be naive, obstinate and little suited to political intrigue, he acted always out of religious motivation and his idealism commanded respect. The relationship between Bérulle and Richelieu had its own history. After a beginning marked by mutual respect, differences of temperament and of goals grew progressively more marked. Eventually, Richelieu was able to bring about Bérulle's fall into disfavor on 15 September 1629, two weeks before the great master's death and one year before Richelieu was to receive in full the powers he coveted.

The Final Years

At the request of Louis XIII, motivated perhaps by the services he had received, Urban VIII named Bérulle a cardinal of the Consistory on 30 August 1627. The red hat added nothing to Bérulle's personal value, but it did bear witness to the pope's confidence in him.

Although his humility suffered from the promotion, Bérulle willingly accepted the new missions entrusted to him by the pope. This time the mandate was specifically religious. Bérulle was active in bringing about the union of the Benedictines of Brittany with the Congregation of Saint-Maur. He worked for the reform of the Premonstratentians of the Abbey of Ardenne, then for that of the Augustinians in Paris.

Worn out by these labors and suffering from an illness of the eyes which was a source of great distress to him, Bérulle died, prematurely, while celebrating Mass, on 2 October 1629.

Bérulle's spiritual and apostolic heritage was not to be limited to his writings, which would not be widely read, nor even to the Congregation of the Oratory. His influence would extend much further, and his immediate disciples, Condren and John Eudes, or others, like Olier, would continue to spread his spirit. In his preface to the *Œuvres complètes* of Bérulle, Bourgoing does not hesitate to describe the dimensions of the renewal brought about by Bérulle in the Church:

> Through the means which God gave him, our most esteemed Father brought about in the Church a renewal of the spirit of religion and the supreme worship of adoration and reverence due to God. ... This is the spirit he so ardently desired to establish among us, a spirit with which he was penetrated and exalted, a spirit we find in all his writings. ... They are filled with what he has to say about the honor, adoration, and other essential duties we owe to the divine majesty. ... Indeed, many people are drawn to God because of his goodness, but few, through adoration of his grandeur and holiness. Affectionate or timid persons are uplifted more by the sweetness of devotion, in a kind of liberty or familiarity with

God, than through abasement and holy fear (that is, respect, the spirit of religion). Here (at Bérulle's School), we are taught to be true Christians, to be faithful to the primitive religion we professed at our baptism. We learn to adore the divine grandeurs, perfections, designs, will, and judgements of God, along with the mysteries of his Son. There was very little of this, before Bérulle; there can never be too much of it now.

This sense of God, of adoration, of Bérulle's "mystical christocentrism," along with his loving devotion to Mary and concern for the holiness of priests, constitutes the essence of the heritage that comes from the founder and leader of the French School.

Documents for Chapter 3

3.1 Bérulle and His Spirituality

Because of their great influence, both direct and indirect, Bérulle (1575–1629) and his work constitute one of the monuments of our spiritual history. No one denies this importance. Nevertheless, reactions to Bérulle and his spirituality have been varied, divided, and longstanding. Bérulle was never uncontested, neither during his lifetime nor after his death. We cannot enter, here, into the details of his complex life story which, to a certain degree, determined his spirituality and its interpretation. However, one fact must be noted: Bérulle never dreamed of being only a contemplative. Following his preferences and the ideas of his era as of his social class, he chose to be not only a founder, but also a political figure and a diplomat. As a result, he provoked obstinate hostility which has, at times, continued down through the ages. For example, the opposition of the Carmelites or the Jesuits has lasted almost to our own days. Only recently, studies devoted to Bérulle seem to have reached a stage of serene, scientific objectivity. Only since then has it been possible to render full justice to Bérulle's memory, even while striving to temper the enthusiasm aroused forty-five years ago by the rediscovery of his work.

L. Cognet, *La Spiritualité Moderne*. Paris: Aubier;
310–11.

3.2 Major Stages in Bérulle's Life

BÉRULLE		POLITICAL AND RELIGIOUS HISTORY
	1572	St. Barthomew's Day Massacre
Birth, in Cérilly	1575	
	1581	Birth of Vincent de Paul
His father's death	1582	
Begins studies at Clermont College	1592	
Madame Acarie lives with the Bérulle family	1594	Henry IV enters Paris
Brief Discourse on Interior Abregation		
	1598	Edict of Nantes
Ordination to the priesthood	1599	
Traité des énergumènes		The Martha Brossier affair
Retreat, at Verdun	1602	
Trip to Spain Introduction of Carmelite nuns into France	1604	
Light regarding his vocation	1607	*Introduction to the Devout Life*
Controversial discourse	1609	Reform of Port-Royal

	1610	Assassination of Henry IV
Foundation of the Oratory	1611	
Permanent ecclesiastical visitor of Carmelite nuns	1614	Louis XIII comes of age
Vow of servitude to Jesus at the Oratory	1615	The Council of Trent "received"
Attacks against Bérulle	1616	*Treatise on the Love of God*
Mission in favor of Marie de Médicis	1619	The Peace of Angoulême (Louis XIII and Marie de Médicis)
Decree of Praise of Paul V	1620	
Preparation of the *Glories of Jesus*	1622	Richelieu becomes cardinal Death of St. Francis de Sales
The State and the Glories of Jesus	1623	John Eudes enters the Oratory
Negotiations for the marriage of Henriette of France	1624	
Elevation on St. Mary Magdalene	1625	Opposition from Richelieu
Negotiations with Spain	1626	Treaty of Monçon

Bérulle becomes cardinal	1627	
Vie de JESUS	1629	Bérulle dies on 20 October

3.3 Bérulle and the Virtue of Religion

He (Bérulle) is the one who has lifted up in our days this virtue which was dead and buried; he has awakened our century to an enthusiastic remembrance of its most ancient duty. . . .

True, there may never be as many Nazarenes as we have seen; as many persons who are as courageous as Samson, as enlightened as Samuel, as austere as St. John. . . . But it is certain that, in this century, when so much sanctity abounds, we find more persons who are familiar with God then respectful of him; there are many Christians who love God, but few who revere him.

In the midst of an infinite number of good people who practice every kind of virtue, *nothing is as rare as the virtue of religion.* Everyone willingly dedicates himself to works of charity, there are large numbers of penitents, people are impelled to fulfill every kind of holy activity. However, anyone who looks into the depths of such persons will have to admit that respect for God is scarcely acknowledged. Children are reared not in profound adoration of God's grandeur, but in a spirit of liberty toward him. The result of this is neglect of the holy Sacrifice, esteem for the appearances of austerity, and contempt for those given to ascetical practices.

Amelote, *Vie du P. Charles de Condren.* Paris; 1643; 2:80–81.

3.4 The Mystery of the Incarnation

One of the first and most important lessons that we are taught in this school of wisdom and salvation, which was founded and made available to the world, is the holy mystery of the Incarnation. This mystery is so exalted that is surpasses the loftiest thoughts of men and angels. It is so excellent that it contains and includes both God and the world in itself. This mystery is so deep that it is hidden from all eternity in the most secret thoughts of the Ancient of Days and in the very bosom of the eternal Father, in such an exalted and ineffable manner that the Apostle speaks rightly of it in various places as: *the mysterious design which for all ages was hidden in God, the Creator of all* (Eph. 3.9).

Nevertheless this mystery, which is so exalted and excellent, so deep and so hidden, is at the same time quite public. It is realized in the fullness of time, in the center of the earth, so as to be seen by both earth and heaven. Its purpose here is to become the object of faith for all people, the anchor of their hope, the cause of their salvation and the fulfillment of the glory of God in the universe. For it is through this mystery that heaven is opened, earth is made holy and God is adored. This adoration is new. It is ineffable and was unknown to earth and heaven even in former times. For although heaven previously had adoring spirits and an adored God, it had not as yet an adoring God.

It is through this mystery that God is on earth hiding his greatness in humility. He is covered with our weaknesses and clothed with our mortality. He himself accomplishes the salvation of the world in our midst just as if he were one of us. Through this mystery earth is a heaven. It is a new heaven where God dwells in a manner that is loftier and more august, holier and more divine than the way in which he dwelt previously in the highest heavens. It is with faith, love and homage toward this sacred mystery that God himself, rather than through angels and servants, established a religion on earth. This religion will never be changed or removed from the earth. He saved it for the end times since this mystery also bears within it the final manifestations of his power, his love and his eternal wisdom.

The church should be caught up in this mystery in a holy and divine way. It should be the focus for the devotion of the most advanced souls, transfixed with wonder and admiration as they contemplate this object where they discover and perceive in an unspeakable fashion the majesty of the divine essence, the distinction of its persons and the depth of its designs as well as the exalted, rare and unheard of way in which God chose to exist in this masterwork. For everything that is great, holy and worthy of admiration is there. It is like a résumé and a summary of all that the oracles of faith reveal and teach us about God and his works. This divine mystery is like the center of the created and uncreated world. It is the only place where God chose once and for all to contain and reduce to our level both the world and himself, that is, his own infiniteness and the immensity of the whole universe. (. . .)

For Jesus is a world, a splendid world, according to authentic theology, and this is true for many more reasons than philosophy ever knew when referring to the human person as a world in miniature, as we will say later. Furthermore, we adore in Jesus the unity of a divine Person, subsisting in two different natures, who, divinely and unspeakably, proclaims, honors and serves the supreme unity of the divine essence. O supreme unity, how lovable and admirable you are in the divinity and in the most divine of its works! How adorable you are, because God himself honors you through the unity of his Word in two related natures! He honors you forever because you are eternal and everlasting!

> "Discourse on the State and Grandeurs of Jesus"
> (1, 2) in *Bérulle and the French School*. The
> Classics of Western Spirituality. Trans., Lowell M.
> Glendon, S.S., intro. and ed., William M.
> Thompson. New York/Mahwah: Paulist Press,
> 1989; 109–12.

3.5 Three Births of Jesus

We find in the book of life three wondrous births of Jesus, who is the life of God and men. They are his birth in the womb of his Father in eternity, his birth in the womb of the Virgin in time, and his birth in the tomb to immortality. These three births are accompanied by wonders, worthy of Jesus and worthy of his source and origin in these three different lives.

For in his birth in divine and uncreated life, there is a twofold wonder: that God engenders and that God is engendered. In his birth in the human and incarnate life, there is a twofold wonder: that a Virgin gives birth and that God becomes incarnate. In his birth or rather his rebirth to the heavenly and glorious life, it is marvelous that a tomb becomes the source of life and that a place of death becomes the source of life without end. Thus God, who is admirable in himself, his works and his saints, is also admirable in his only Son, who is another self; and in his masterwork, which is the Incarnation; and in the holy of holies, who is Jesus Christ, our Lord, foretold and given this name by one of the prophets. (. . .)

Allow me to contemplate and adore you in these three lives and in the three moments when you enter these three lives. They are the three lives to which all human and angelic life should be dedicated. They are the three precious moments to which every moment of our mortality and our eternity should be consecrated.

There is the moment of the Incarnation, when Jesus begins to be Jesus and to live with an uncreated life. The Word begins a new and incarnate life, a divine and human life, a divinely human and humanly divine life. There is the moment of his pilgrimage and life of merit, when the soul of Jesus is united to a body capable of suffering and to the life of glory at the same time. Through this arrangement Jesus possesses a new type of life. It is a life that is his alone, a life that is the origin of our eternal life! It is a life of glory and suffering! It is a life that unites and joins two very distinct states in the same soul, through a miracle performed in Jesus Christ by Jesus Christ himself. It is accomplished in him alone and continues for thirty-four years on earth!

There is the moment of his celestial and fully glorious life when Jesus is victorious in life, glory, and immortality. It is a life without suffering and without mortality! It is life that is nothing but life and nothing but glory! It is a life that will last eternally! From these three moments originate three lives. These three lives have three distinct dwelling places, in which we must adore the sacred humanity of Jesus. O moment! O dwelling places! O adorable life! This should occupy our thoughts and be the center of our activities. It will be the object of our eternity. (. . .)

O divine gaze! O eternal gaze! O gaze full of love and honor! O gaze that should draw our gaze, our love and our homage toward that humanity, which God beholds eternally and unceasingly as his own, and which we should look upon as our own. It is ours through a gift of the Father, through the activity of the Holy Spirit, through the subsistence of the Son, which was given him so that he might accomplish our salvation. Finally it is ours through the power of the cross and his death, which consumed him for us in sacrifice and holocaust.

Bérulle and the French School; 150, 156–57.

3.6 Mary and Jesus

. . . Let us see what [the Son of God] is and what he does in his Blessed Mother. For she is the one who is the closest and the most united to him by the state of this new mystery accomplished in her and through her. This is the first period of Jesus' stay in the Virgin. These are two subjects important enough to be considered. Therefore let us say that strictly speaking, after the divine Persons, there is no other person to whom the Son of God is more closely bound than to the Virgin.

Moreover this bond imitates and adores the bond he has with the divine Persons. He is united to his Father through birth and nature, and he is united to the Virgin through nature and birth. He is joined to the Holy Spirit as to its origin since he is its source in eternity. He is united to the Virgin through production and the infusion of a Spirit in her spirit, which is the life of her life and the soul of her soul. He is the source of her grace. For all grace in the Virgin originates from the highest grace and the mysteries of Jesus. Thus he is joined to her through both nature and grace.

The bond that he has with the divine Persons is eternal. The one he has with the Virgin is new and quite recent. However, it will be for all eternity. This holy Virgin is and will be always the Mother of Jesus. She will possess that attribute in heaven as well as on earth, and he will honor her eternally in her condition as Mother of God. However, we see tangibly that in this present state she is closer and more united to him while he is in her and is a part of her; while she lives for him he lives through her; while he is in a constant state of dependence and even neediness toward her.

He is in her in a variety of ways according to his various attributes. It is pleasant to consider them more than once. The period of this mystery invites us to reflect carefully on it often. For it is the period when he is and will be nine months in the Virgin. He is in her as a son is in his mother, drawing his life from her. He is in her as her son and her God, giving life to her as he receives life from her. He is in her as in his earthly paradise. For everything in the Virgin is holy and delightful. Even the darkness of sin is not there and never was.

Jesus finds in her his peace and his delight. Outside of her he meets only sinners and sin. Being in her is like being in heaven. For he experiences life and glory, seeing God and enjoying his divine Essence. He is in her as in a temple where he praises and adores God; where he offers his respects to the eternal Father, not only for himself but for every creature. It is a holy and sacred temple where Jesus dwells, the true ark of the true covenant.

It is the first and holiest temple of Jesus. The heart of the Virgin is the first altar on which Jesus offered his heart, body and spirit as a host of perpetual praise; and where Jesus offers his first sacrifice, making the first and perpetual oblation of himself, through which, as we have said, we are all made holy. Thus Jesus is in the Virgin. In her he finds his peace, his paradise, his highest heaven, his temple, his mother.

Bérulle and the French School; 160–61.

3.7 Magdalene at the Tomb

There [in the Scriptures] I discover that the first person you visited in your new life and in your state of glory was the Magdalene. There I discover that the first word you uttered in that blessed state was addressed to her and concerned her tears and her grief. *Woman, why are you weeping?* (Jn. 20.15). There I find that the first name your sacred lips pronounced in your glory was her name, that sweet name of Mary, which enlightens her, which makes her recognize her Lord, which makes her fall at his feet, which restores life to her and fills her with joy and with new love.

When you were born in Bethlehem, Lord, indeed it was your

holy Mother whom your mortal eyes first beheld. However, you did not speak to her. You did not at all utter her name, which is the same name, Mary, even though this name, in her, was dedicated to innocence, to divine Motherhood and to an eminent grace that has never had any equal. Nevertheless, you did not utter it, and you remained in the sacred silence and powerlessness of your infancy.

When you were reborn, Lord, from the tomb into your life of glory, the first gaze and the first view of your immortal eyes, glorious and as brilliant as the sun, was of the Magdalene. Your first words were to Magdalene. The first name you pronounced was her name, the name Mary, the name dedicated, in her, to love and penance. The first commission you gave and, if I can speak this way, the first Bull and Patent that you officially issued in your state of glory and power, was to her, making her an apostle, but an apostle of life, glory and love, and an apostle to your apostles. You had made them apostles some time before, but it was during your mortal life. You made them twelve in number but you made them your apostles to the world to proclaim your Cross and your death. In this case, you make Magdalene your apostle in your state of glory. In this new state you make her alone an apostle, an apostle of your life only, for she will proclaim and make public only your life, power and glory. You make her an apostle not to the world, but to the very apostles of the world and to the universal pastors of your church because you are so pleased to highlight the honor and the love of her soul.

Bérulle and the French School; 178–79.

3.8 Vow of Servitude (Ancient Formula)

I make to God the vow of perpetual servitude to Jesus Christ; to his divinized humanity and to his humanized divinity, according to the intention of our Reverend Father Superior. Thus, by this way, in honor of the *unity* of the Son with the Father and the Holy Spirit, and of the *union* of this same Son with this human nature which he took and joined to his own Person, I bind my being to Jesus and to his divinized humanity, by the bond of perpetual servitude. And I make this bond with my whole being and with all my power; I beg him to give me more power to bind myself to him more fully and more closely, in honor of the holy and sacred bonds that he wishes to have with us on earth and in heaven, in the life of Jesus and the life of glory.

I reverence and I adore the life and the annihilation of the divinity in this humanity; and the life, the subsistence and the divinization of this humanity in the divinity; all the humanly divine and divinely human actions which have preceded from this new and mutual life of the man–God in his twofold essence—external and temporal, divine and human. But I dedicate and consecrate to him my life and my actions, both of nature and of grace, as the life and actions of his slave for ever. . . .

O great and admirable Jesus! I give myself to be forever your slave and the slave of your adorable humanity. In honor of the *state and form of servitude* which you assumed and to which you willed to reduce your *divinity* into humanity, and your humanity into the state and *form of life* lived upon earth; and I place my soul, my state and my life in a relation of dependency and servitude to you and to your divinized *humanity* but I will that my life of nature and of grace and all my actions belong to this humanity as something that belongs to it, through my state and condition of servitude towards it, which I vow at this time.

Thus, O Jesus, I offer my life and my actions to honor and glorify your sacred humanity. I offer them as the life and actions of your slave, through the most humble and intense relationship that I know, the relationship of servitude. And I make this offering as something that is due or much to the grandeur of the actual state to which your humanity has been raised by the hypostatic union, as to the extreme and voluntary abasement to which it has been reduced for my salvation and my glory. And I thus offer my life and my actions in honor of your life, hidden from and unknown even by the angels and all created nature, outside the manifestation of glory. I make my offering (in honor) of all the actions depending on this twofold hidden life of divinity in this humanity and this humanity in divinity. And, I will that, by reason of the present intention, each moment of my life and each of my actions might belong to you, O Jesus, and to your sacred humanity, as if I offered each of them individually. (. . .)

I beg the holy soul of Jesus to deign itself to take the power over myself that I am unable to give you. Make me your slave in the way you know, a way I do not know. May this holy soul make me its own that I may serve it not only by my actions, but still more by the *state* and condition of my whole being and my life, interior and exterior. And I plead with this holy soul to keep me and treat me on earth as its slave who has surrendered all its desires and all its possessions to the sovereign rule over all that belongs to it.

Archives of the Oratory, carton 11, text quoted in Dupuy, *Pierre de Bérulle*. Paris: Bloud et Gay, 1964; 11–15.

CHAPTER FOUR

Charles de Condren

T he immediate successor to Bérulle as superior of the
Oratory was Charles de Condren, a great spiritual
master and a true mystic. He was to have a significant
influence on the Church in France during his lifetime,
primarily through spiritual conferences and with the
many persons who consulted him for guidance. J. Delu-
meau claimed that, "Between 1630 and 1640, he was the
spiritual director of all the saints in Paris."[1] Condren
is the one who encouraged Olier in the founding of
seminaries; also, Olier's spiritual doctrine was influenced
to a great degree by Condren, his director and spiritual
master.

Unlike Bérulle, Condren wrote little. However, we do
have a good critical edition of his letters.[2] They reveal a
man who was both a spiritual guide and a community
leader. What we know of his life is due, above all, to a
psychological biography by Denis Amelote, his closest

disciple. Amelote entered the Oratory only in 1650, after having belonged for many years to a group of priests closely associated with Condren. In 1643, he published, in Paris, *La vie du Père Charles de Condren*. The historical value of this very enthusiastic work needs to be verified in more than one instance, especially since the second edition (1657) differs somewhat from the first.

Many of Condren's contemporaries praised his human qualities, his theological insight, and the excellence of his spiritual guidance to a point of emulation. He has been described as "the most noble human mind created by God, after Saint Augustine." Bremond speaks both of the "subtle genius and the refined consciousness" of Condren as well as of his "curious psychology."[3] In fact, he was at one and the same time an excellent theologian and a poor administrator, slow in making decisions, but enthusiastic in his mysticism. Amelote presents him as "the greatest wonder that I can imagine . . . a living image of Jesus Christ."[4] Father Louis Quinet, abbot of Barbery, writing from the school of the Bernardines in Paris, along with his approval of Amelote's work, expressed his appreciation of Condren: "a true Christian . . . an apostolic man . . . a perfect priest of Jesus Christ."[5]

Early Years and Activities

Charles de Condren was born in Vaubuin near Soissons, on 15 December 1588, of a noble family. His father, a convert from Protestantism, was governor of the royal palace of Monceaux, not far from Meaux. Charles was destined for a military career, but his preferences led him, rather, to study and prayer. After successful completion of studies at Harcourt College in Paris, he obtained his father's permission to pursue a vocation in the church. At the Sorbonne, he studied with the well-known theologians André Duval and Philippe de Gamaches. For one year, he taught philosophy, undertaking a long preparation for ordination to the priesthood, which he received on 14 September 1614. At this time, he renounced his birthright and his family inheritance. In 1615, he was received as a doctor at the Sorbonne. During the course of 1614–15, he was the Advent preacher at Saint-Nicolas-du-Chardonnet, where Bourdoise (1584–1655) was beginning his priestly ministry. That same year, he was the Lenten preacher at Saint-Honoré, a church belonging to the Oratory, and he preached the Octave of the Blessed Sacrament, at Saint-Médard. Like many of his contemporaries, he felt drawn to the life of the Carthusians and to that of the followers of Saint Francis, probably the Capuchins who were so active at this time. In spite of Duval's hopes that Condren would become a professor, he chose to follow another path and entered the Oratory in 1617.

In writing of this early period of Condren's life, Amelote highlights not only his "frequent infirmities," but above all, his precocious genius and his prodigious memory. Condren himself, it would seem, claimed that he "had not forgotten anything since he was 18 months old" and that he knew "a great many things that he had never intended to remember." In the realm of philosophy, he had "a most open mind and a quite extraordinary facility of intelligence," along with "such an insatiable desire" that he passed days and nights in study. He was interested in every area of human knowledge: mathematics, chemistry, astrology, history and poetry. He was refined and charming, and possessed a great facility of expression, and a taste for cordial relationships.

Even more outstanding than these exceptional qualities, so often pointed out by his contemporaries, was another characteristic discussed by Amelote. This was the apparently decisive spiritual experience that marked Charles at the age of 12:

> In the flash of a moment, he found his mind surrounded by a wonderful light, in whose brightness the divine

Majesty appeared so immense and so infinite, that it seemed to him that nothing but this pure being could subsist and that the entire universe ought to be destroyed for its glory. [6]

This passage deserves to be considered seriously. It is possible that Denis Amelot exaggerated the presentation of this authentic "vocation story" in light of his master's doctrine and in comparison with certain biblical texts. However, we find in these words the seeds of the essence of Condren's spiritual experience and teaching: the grandeur of God can be glorified only through destruction of the creature. This stark affirmation is one that can give rise to simplistic interpretations, unless it is understood within the context of the total sacrifice that leads to union with God and to the glory of God, by passing through death and the death of the Cross.

Amelote's text continues in a manner that is not less revelatory, introducing us from the outset to the interplay of forces at the heart of Condren's life and mission. He was, according to Amelote, well ahead of his time, a true disciple of Bérulle:

With this insight and with this love of the beauty of the sacrifice of Jesus Christ, God placed in his mind two very different dispositions, one of which was to prevail over the other. The first was an incomparable esteem for the priesthood, with a conviction of his unworthiness to be admitted to it. The second was a brilliant light, by which he knew with certainty that God willed to give him this grace. He then heard a powerful interior voice which said to him: *I will that you be a priest and that you serve me in my Church.* This spiritual voice was more striking and more convincing than any human word that his ears might have heard. It filled him with such delight in and love for the priesthood and the Church that his great humility was lost in an overflowing joy and he was conquered by the obvious grace of God's will. Immediately, he fell prostrate to the ground, offering himself to God

with so firm a resolution to obey the divine Will, that he
never after hesitated or wavered from it.[7]

Early Ministry in the Oratory

Bérulle had the greatest admiration for Condren,
whom he chose as his confessor. Amelote tells us that
"when he (Bérulle) passed his (Condren's) room, he knelt
down to kiss the traces of his footsteps." At first, Bérulle
assigned Condren to preaching and giving conferences
against the "heretics." Condren also devoted himself to
the spiritual direction of one or another of the Carmelite
nuns entrusted to him by Bérulle. He was the confessor
of Gaston d'Orléans, the king's brother. This latter task
was often a heavy one for him, but he was able to bring
about a reconciliation between the two brothers at
Troyes on 18 April 1630. Condren was the director of
Gaston de Renty, with whom he worked to develop the
Company of the Blessed Sacrament. The list of those
who consulted him and whom he was able to help is
long: M. Bernard, known as the Poor Priest; Balthasar
Brandon, the abbot of Bassancourt who would be one of
Olier's associates for a period of time; Father de Saint-Pé,
and many others. Condren would also play an important
role in the conversion of countless Protestants.

In 1618, Bérulle sent Condren to open a house of the
Oratory in Nevers, then one in Langres (1619) and in
Poitiers (1621). In 1624, he became director of the Seminary of Saint-Magloire, before being recalled to the
motherhouse on rue Saint-Honoré in 1625.

Superior General

Condren was with Gaston d'Orléans in Nancy when
Bérulle died on 2 October 1629. The process for election
of a successor took place quickly, beginning on 30 October, most likely in order to avoid any intervention by
Richelieu. Condren accepted this new responsibility only

after a long delay (21 November) and then, half-heartedly. He began by refusing to continue as ecclesiastical visitor of the Carmelite nuns, partly because of his conviction that the purpose of the Oratory "was to work to reestablish an ecclesiastical spirit among the clergy." He then undertook to free his priests from giving spiritual direction to religious, so that they might be more available for parish missions and seminaries.

In 1631 always hoping to resign, he convoked a new assembly of the 71 houses of the Oratory. His election was confirmed and the characteristics of the Oratory were reaffirmed: the fathers are not "bound by the ordinary vows of religion"; this is "a congregation that is exclusively ecclesiastical and priestly." The members desire to be "the religious of God," as Condren insisted in a commentary on the Bull of Institution of the Oratory. As vicar-general, Condren chose Father Bourgoing, the oldest Oratorian, who had presided over the assembly of October 1629. Bourgoing would later publish the works of Bérulle, for which he wrote an outstanding preface.

Other assemblies followed, in 1634 and 1638, during which Condren sought to resign, even if it meant trying to run away in 1634, and accepting, in 1638, only because his confessor threatened to refuse him absolution. Despite his protestations of humility, he served the Oratory with all his strength, clarified its purpose and organization, opened nine new residences, two parishes and six schools, including one in Juilly, in 1639. He showed a constant concern for the missions and maintained a voluminous correspondence.

Condren died on 7 January 1641.

Condren and Olier

Shortly before his death, and as a kind of testament, Condren convinced Olier and his companions that they were to found a seminary. Beginning in 1634, Condren had become Olier's director, following the wish and the urging of Mother Agnès de Langeac. It was Condren who turned Olier and du Ferrier away from the episcopacy, stating that "Our Lord has willed to use them for a great project." Moreover, Condren convinced Vincent de Paul that his Congregation of the Mission was to take on the responsibility of seminaries, also. As superior general, Condren maintained great discretion concerning the "great design" for Olier and du Ferrier, asserting "The affairs of God are preserved in the secret of the Spirit." He saw the need for a period of growth in spiritual and apostolic maturity on their part before discussing this "secret."

In fact, Condren was, first of all, to exercise a profound spiritual influence on the founder of Saint-Sulpice, introducing Olier to the spirit of Bérulle and, in particular, to devotion to the Blessed Sacrament. He gave Olier his "little prayer": "Come, Lord Jesus, and live in your servant." Olier loved this prayer and modified it. Also, Condren sent Olier as a missionary into a number of rural parishes, but always with the seminary in mind. He insisted on the need to continue the missions before doing something of still greater value. The missions continued, sometimes with Olier joining the disciples of Vincent de Paul, and always without any clarification on Condren's part of his project.

Not until the last days of his life did Condren feel moved to speak of the foundation of the seminaries, as du Ferrier testifies in his *Mémoires* (134–37). In a sense, this is his true testament as an apostle: Olier and Saint-Sulpice recognized Father de Condren as the originator and father of their seminary.

Spiritual Doctrine

Condren's heritage also includes a whole *corpus* of spiritual doctrine that corresponds with both his own mystical experience and his teaching. The writings of

John Eudes and Olier took up this doctrine and popularized it. We are aware, even, of two passages in John Eudes *Life and Kingdom of Jesus* that reproduce, in part, a letter addressed by Condren to the future founder of the Eudists.[8]

In addition to his letters, we have little written by Condren except the work in which Father Quesnel, first in 1677 and again in 1697, presented the ideas and a few texts from Condren on *L'idée du sacerdoce et du Sacrifice de Jésus-Christ*. Other editors, much later, published the *Considérations sur les mystères de Jésus-Christ* and several conferences. A limited number of texts or copies remain unpublished.

Such a situation makes it difficult for us to determine the specific elements of Condren's theological insights and spiritual doctrine. It is, however, possible to identify in his teaching several important points that have not always been well understood.

In Condren, we find the theocentrism of Bérulle: God is the all-holy, infinitely transcendent in relation to the created world and to sinful humanity. But, for Condren, adoration is expressed through sacrifice, immolation, the victim state of the Host. He speaks frequently of annihilation. Where Bérulle proposes "elevations" and invests adoration with enthusiastic praise, Condren places before us the total sacrifice of adoration, that is, consummation.

So, too, Bérulle's mystical christocentrism, for Condren, is found in the victim state. Nothing is worthy of God, except the one and only sacrifice of Jesus. That is why Condren speaks more often than Bérulle of the Mass. There, Jesus finds "the way to continue the same sacrifice down through the centuries and to multiply his offering, every day, on his altars."[9] Condren's doctrine of the priesthood and the sacrifice of Jesus has been popularized and carried into the twentieth century in any number of theological and spiritual works by authors such as de la Taille, Mersch, Giraud and Grimal.

Condren's doctrine has often been accused of pessimism. It is not enough for us to try to modify his vocabulary. He speaks often of death and annihilation. It does seem, however, that, like John of the Cross and other mystics, he was so keenly aware of the grandeur of God and the absolute dependency of the creature that for him, creatures could find their true meaning only in a total offering of self as a sacrifice of love and praise, as a living victim-host. Some of Condren's expressions startle us: "You must desire to renounce your nature, to deny yourself, completely; we should be totally occupied with God alone."[10] Condren is very close, here, to John of the Cross and his *Todo y nada* (All and nothing).

Condren's pedagogy is centered on adoration and on communion with Jesus Christ:

> You must seek and find in Jesus Christ the spirit and grace that God wills to give you, so that you may carry this out . . . adore Jesus, give yourself entirely to him. . . . Hold on to the intention to renounce everything you are; surrender yourself into his hands, so that you no longer live in your own spirit, but in his; no longer according to your own will, intentions and inclinations, but only in his divine and adorable dispositions.[11]

These are words Olier will use later when he speaks about prayer.

When Condren presents the examination of conscience, which he would have liked to see practiced three times a day, he focuses this exercise on the adoration of Jesus as judge, head, priest, and source of our life and all our actions. We must, he writes, "first of all, give ourselves to the Son of God and consecrate all our exercises of piety to him. . . ." [12]

Following Bérulle and preceding Olier and John Eudes, Condren professed a profound concept of the Church, the Body of Christ. Thus, he insisted strongly, as we have seen, on communion with Christ's mysteries and intentions for all Christians and even more so for priests, especially when they celebrate the sacrifice of the Mass.

Other great Oratorians who were contemporaries of Condren contributed to the extension of Bérulle's thought, although with slightly different accents. Among them we find François Bourgoing (1585–1662), Guillaume Gibieuf (1591–1650), Metezeau, and Louis Thomassin (1619–1695). Later still, Nicolas Malebranche (1638–1715), a philosopher as well as spiritual writer, would continue the tradition.

However, most historians identify Jean-Jacques Olier and John Eudes as the authentic heirs of Charles de Condren. While the Oratory turned toward theological, biblical and other studies in view of taking on the responsibilities of higher education, Olier was to contribute to the realization of the dream cherished by Bérulle and de Condren: the restoration of the priestly state.

DOCUMENTS FOR CHAPTER 4

4.1 Chronology of Charles de Condren's Life.

1588	–	15 December: Birth, near Soissons.
1600	–	Intense spiritual experience of God's grandeur.
1603–1605	–	Studies at Harcourt College.
1605–1607	–	Illness; return to his family.
1613	–	Admission to the house and society of the Sorbonne.
1614	–	Ordination to the priesthood.
1615	–	Doctorate from the Sorbonne.
1617	–	Entrance into the Oratory, rue St-Honoré.
1618	–	Foundation of a house of the Oratory in Nevers.
1619	–	Zamet takes him, with three other Oratorians, to found a seminary in Langres.
		In September, named Vicar-General of Langres.
1620	–	Return to Paris. Foundation in Poitiers.
1624	–	Foundation of St-Magloire. Condren named superior.

1625	–	Return to rue St-Honoré.
1627	–	Becomes confessor of Gaston d'Orléans, the king's brother.
1629	–	Following the death of Bérulle (2 October), Condren becomes superior general of the Oratory (30 October).
1631	–	August: First General Assembly at St-Honoré.
1634	–	From Spring through Summer: visit of the houses in Burgundy and Lyons.
		8 September – 2 October: Second General Assembly. Flight and attempt to resign.
1638	–	6 – 22 May: Third General Assembly at Saumur (Notre-Dame des Ardilliers).
1641	–	7 January: Death.

4.2 A Man to be Admired

Writing of Condren in his *Mémoires*, Nicoles Goulas exclaims: "Imagine the most lofty spirit and the most noble soul in the whole world. He possessed all the arts and all the sciences, knowing their most hidden secrets; he knew everything possible to the human mind about the mysteries of nature. He reasoned like Solomon and knew everything from the cedar to the hyssop. He spoke well, and with ease, and wrote the same way. . . . "

Amelote, for his part, insisted that "he had such a pleasant spirit that nothing was more attractive than his conversation. He knew a thousand interesting details that he recounted just to prepare his hearers for serious matters. . . . I notice now that he ordinarily took delight in ordinary conversation, but he did so with such simplicity that neither he nor those with whom he spoke ever became dissipated. On the contrary, his simple, unaffected gaiety, like that of children, opened the minds of everyone present and unconsciously disposed them to devotion."

Along the same line, Nicolas Goulas wrote, on another

occasion, "His conversation was so mild and pleasant that one left his presence charmed. He loved to laugh during recreation time, and if, at such times, he did not speak directly about God, he still lifted people up from the earth. When he spoke about devotional or religious matters, it seemed as if he had been taught by the angels."

> *Lettres du Père Charles de Condren*, ed. Auvray et Jouffrey. Paris: Cerf, 1943; introduction, 19–20.

4.3 Sacrifice and Annihilation

We need only let it be known that his greatest grace, the one which especially marked the path by which God led his most pure soul, was the grace of sacrifice, love of the sanctity and purity of God, desire for his own annihilation so as to glorify the divine perfections, the spirit of death to Adam's life and world, the constant virtue of religion, and the company of Jesus Christ, host and victim. He was such even at his conception and birth, that God destined him to share in this way in the sacrifice of his son.

> Amelote, *La vie du Père Charles de Condren*; 1643, 1:43–44.

4.4 Devotion to the Mysteries of the Life of our Lord Jesus Christ

You cannot too often realize and reflect on the truth that the mysteries of the life of Christ have not yet reached their full perfection and completeness. Although they are perfect and complete in Christ's own Person, they are not yet completed in you who are His members, nor in Holy Mother Church, which is His Mystical Body. It is the plan of the Son of God that His whole Church should participate in and actually be, as it were, the continuation and extension of the mystery of His Incarnation, birth, Childhood, hidden life, public life of teaching and of labor, His Passion and His death, by the graces He desires to impart to you, and by the effects He wishes to accomplish in you through these same mysteries. By this means, He desires to fulfil His mysteries in you.

Therefore, St. Paul says that Jesus Christ is fulfilled in His Church (Eph. 1.22–23) and that we all come together in His perfection and His maturity (Eph. 4.13), which means, as I have said, His mystical Body, which is a maturity that will not be complete until the Day of Judgment. And St. Paul again speaks elsewhere of the same fullness of God which is accomplished in you, and of the growth and increase of God in you (Eph. 3, 19). And in another place he says that He fills up in His body the Passion of Jesus Christ (Col. I, 24). Now what he says of the fulfillment of the mystery of the Passion may also be said of the other mysteries of the life of Jesus Christ.

So the Son of God plans to perfect and complete in you all His states and mysteries. He intends to fulfill in you the divine life which has been His for all eternity in the bosom of His Father, imparting a participation in that life, and making you live, with Him, a life entirely pure and holy.

It is His design to complete in you the mystery of His Incarnation, birth and hidden life, by taking flesh in you and being born in your souls, as it were, through the Sacraments of Holy Baptism and the Blessed Eucharist, causing you to live by a spiritual and inward life, a life hidden with Him in God.

It is His design to perfect in you the mystery of His Passion, death and Resurrection, by causing you to suffer, to die and to rise again with Him and in Him. It is His design to fulfill His glorious immortal life in heaven, by causing you to live, in Him and with Him, a glorious and immortal life after death. He likewise intends to perfect and accomplish in you and in His Church all the other mysteries of His life by the communication and participation granted to you by His holy will, through the continuation and extension of these mysteries operating in you.

This universal plan of the Son of God will not be completed until the Day of Judgment. The ranks of the saints will not be filled up until the consummation of the time God has allotted to men for their sanctification. Therefore, the mysteries of Jesus will not be complete until the end of the time determined by Jesus Christ Himself for their consummation in you and in His Church, that is, until the end of the world.

Now the life you have here on earth was given to you only for the accomplishment of the infinite designs of Jesus Christ for humankind. Hence, you should employ all your time, your days, your years, in cooperating with Jesus Christ in the divine task of consummating His mysteries in yourself. You must cooperate in this by good works and prayer, by frequent application of mind and heart to the contemplation, adoration and veneration of the sacred mysteries of His life according to the different seasons of the year, so that, by these very mysteries, He may work in you all He desires to accomplish for His pure glory.

Sacrifice According to Condren

Sacrifice is a response . . . to all that God is. It is an essential aspect of the duty of religion, just as religion towards God is the obligation of a spiritual creature who carries it inscribed in the depth of his being. Even the angels are not dispensed from this duty, although by their very nature, they seem far removed from those matters that ordinarily are necessary for sacrifice. (. . .)

Sacrifice was instituted, first of all, to adore God, to acknowledge his grandeur, and to render homage to his divine perfections. . . . It proclaims that the creature is not worthy that God look upon it. In the presence of such holiness, she is destroyed and consumed. . . . Secondly, sacrifice is meant to honor God's sovereignty and dominion not only over life and death, but also over the creature's very being. God alone is the author of being. . . . In the third place, sacrifice exists to acknowledge and honor the fullness of God, that is, God's self-sufficiency, for no creature is necessary to him.

Jesus Christ offers himself to the most Holy Trinity and, with himself, all his members; the saints also offer themselves and Jesus Christ, their head, making their offering through Jesus Christ with Jesus Christ and in Jesus Christ. . . .

It is he [Christ] who offers himself to God as a whole and perfect holocaust, totally consumed in the burning furnace of divinity.

We must be entirely . . . for God, united to Jesus Christ's will and intention, so that he might completely consume us in his own being. We must be willing to lose all that we are, above all, everything that belongs to the old Adam. . . .

Charles de Condren, *L'idée du sacerdoce et du Sacrifice de Jésus Christ*. Paris; éd. 1901; 35, 41–79. *Considérations sur les mystères*. Paris, 1882; 75.

4.6 To a New Priest

Give yourself to him (Jesus Christ) afterwards, not only to offer him in sacrifice according to his will and in his spirit, but also in his name and person. We must annihilate ourselves in this action and be pure members of Jesus Christ, offering what he offers and doing what he does as if we were no longer ourselves. We will never know how to forget ourselves enough in this holy ministry, nor to say with enough simplicity in Jesus Christ: *Hoc est Corpus meum*. In the third place, make this offering to the divine majesty in honor of all he is; in thanksgiving for all the blessings given to the Church, and even, to every creature; in satisfaction for all her offenses, so that she might receive in Jesus Christ the homage and the worship due to his infinite perfections, the gratitude worthy of his charity and the reparation due to his offended honor. Offer this sacrifice, again, as the prayer of the Church and your own prayer, for Jesus is and has all that we can desire and ask of God. Our most perfect and fervent prayer ought to be that this be accomplished in us and in others. Jesus is all our virtue in the perfection we ought to ask for. In him God's holiest intentions reside along with our own. You must remember that the sacrifice you offer is not only the sacrifice of God's Son, but the sacrifice of the head and the members, of Jesus Christ, fulfilled by all that is in his Church. For he communicates the priesthood to her and she offers it with him, as he, through her.

Letter 38, eds. Auvray and Jouffrey; 126–27.

4.7 The Ideal of the Oratory

[Before the Revolution, out of concern to maintain institutional flexibility, the Oratory had no other "Constitutions" than the texts of its founders and the decision of its Assemblies. Initial emphasis was placed on the restoration of the priesthood by enriching the spiritual life of priests. Father de

Condren refers to this in his commentary on the Oratory's Bull of Institution.]

The houses of the Oratory of Jesus must be for other priests what monasteries are for the laity. Just as God inspired some of the laity to seek retreat and solitude at a time of decadence and lack of fervor in early Christianity, God impelled St. Philip Neri in Italy and Cardinal de Bérulle in France to form a Congregation of priests. In the first instance, monasteries were founded to serve as refuges for penitent sinners, but also for the faithful laity. There, they were able to preserve the purity of Christian faith, religion and morals, while inspiring imperfect members of the laity by their examples. In a similar way, the priests of the Oratory not only make profession to seek priestly perfection, but also to renounce everything that could lead them from this quest at a time when the priestly state, in many places, has fallen from its first fervor. Thus, they are to be for other priests what religious are for the laity.

Living in and like Jesus Christ, we shall truly be his religious. Without being bound by any solemn or particular vow, we shall live in a religious manner. We must not try to hide from ourselves the fact that obedience must be prompt and exact in a Congregation where love ought to command and love ought to obey; that purity must be unsullied there where everything is consecrated to divine purity; that the spirit of poverty must reign among us, if it is true that our heart is attached to Jesus Christ alone and that we reject everything that is not God. In other words, we must continue on earth the prayer life of the Son of God, honor by our state of life his life of religion, and make prayer our primary, continual occupation. Thus, the spirit of prayer is the true and proper spirit of the Oratory and that is what gives us our name.

Oratory Archives

4.8 St. John Eudes: An Exercise for Holy Mass

O my Saviour, in honor of and in union with Thy supreme oblation and sacrifice, I offer myself to Thee to be for ever a victim of Thy will, a victim immolated to Thy glory and to the glory of Thy Eternal Father. Unite me to Thee, O Good

Jesus. Absorb me into Thy sacrifice so that I may be sacrificed with Thee and by Thee and, since it necessary that the host of a sacrifice should be slain and consumed by fire, make me die to myself, that is, to my vices and passions and to all that displeases Thee. Consume me utterly in the sacred fire of Thy divine love, and grant that henceforth my whole life may be a continual sacrifice of praise, glory and love of Thy Father and Thyself.

Chapter Five

Olier: Missionary, Mystic, Pastor, Reformer

J ean-Jacques Olier (1608–1657) is much better known than Condren. His works speak for him: on the one hand, we have the Seminary of Saint-Sulpice, the society of priests he founded, and their formation of priests for over 300 years. On the other hand, his writings allow us to know him well, especially his letters and *Mémoires*. As Dupuy has remarked, they reveal "his personal experience with an extraordinary precision."[1] A few shadows, however, prevent us from appreciating at his just value this man who was, at one and the same time, a missionary, a pastor, a founder and a spiritual master whose influence was widespread and noteworthy.

His printed works, intended for the parishioners of Saint-Sulpice, included four small books, published in the three years that preceded his death. In spite of their spiritual depth, they are marked by two limitations: the style is often quite heavy, and above all, the spiritual doctrine seems filled with an excessive pessimism. These two characteristics are much less evident in the letters, which reveal Olier as an excellent spiritual director. Unfortunately, they are not widely known.

Olier's *Traité des Saints Ordres* has been read and studied by countless generations of future priests and, thus, has exercised a significant influence in the church. We now know how this text came to be composed. Eighteen years after Olier's death, Louis Tronson took a number of his master's writings and published them as one complete text, in which some of the main aspects of Olier's thought seem to have been abbreviated or distorted. Despite these limitations, Olier is still one of the best representatives of the French School. His influence was widespread, as much with religious and the laity as with priests and seminarians.

Olier can be studied from many points of view. At the celebration of the third centennial of his death, in 1957, he was hailed as the pastor of the church of Saint-Sulpice by Cardinal Feltin; as the founder of the seminary by Bishop Lallier; as a spiritual master by Bishop Chappoulie.[2] Olier was all of that, and more: a missionary, a reformer of religious communities, a spiritual guide, the originator of the evangelization of Canada. Thanks to his *Mémoires* in eight volumes, totaling nearly 3,000 pages, the task of retracing his own spiritual journey has been made possible.[3]

Olier was not the greatest theologian of the French School, as was Bérulle; nor the greatest mystic, as was Condren; his language was not as clear as that of John Eudes. Still, beyond any doubt, he was the one who best popularized Bérulle's doctrine. Bremond did not hesitate to devote an entire chapter to "the excellence of M. Olier," stating: "He alone presents the common teaching, in the full extent of its principles and applications."[4]

Olier was deeply influenced by Bérulle's thought, above all, through a man he admired greatly, Father de Condren, his spiritual director from 1635 to 1641. Nevertheless, it was from his own personal, spiritual and apostolic experience, along with constant meditation on the Scriptures—especially, the writings of St. Paul and St. John—that he drew the dynamic, vital convictions that directed him throughout his brief, but fruitful priestly existence.

Early Years

Jean-Jacques Olier was born the fourth of eight children, on the rue du Roi de Sicile, in the Marais district of Paris, on 20 September 1608. He was baptized the same day in St. Paul's church. His father was a council member of the Parliament of Paris. The year of Olier's birth was the very year when Francis de Sales, at the age of 41, published his *Introduction to the Devout Life* and Champlain founded Quebec. This twofold coincidence was to have a double resonance in Olier's life. In the first place, he always had a great respect for the bishop of Geneva, who frequently visited the Olier family in Lyons between 1618 and 1622. Jean-Jacques was to develop a deep veneration for Francis de Sales. Secondly, up to the time of his death, New France was to hold a place of privilege in Olier's missionary concerns.

When Jean-Jacques's father was appointed minister of justice in Lyons, the family went to live in that city (1617–1624). Young Jean-Jacques studied at the Jesuit College. His parents dreamed of an ecclesiastical career for him, so he received tonsure when he was 11 years old.

His first benefice was the Priory of Bazainville, in the diocese of Chartres, with others to follow later in Clission, Pébrac and elsewhere.

After the nomination of his father as State Councillor, the family returned to Paris. Jean-Jacques pursued his studies in philosophy at Harcourt College, followed by courses at the Sorbonne, leading in 1630 to the Baccalaureate in Theology.

After a visit to Rome, he went on pilgrimage to Loretto, where he was healed of a disease of the eyes and felt moved by "a great desire for prayer." His memory of this experience would never fade, and he was to speak of it as a true "conversion."

In 1631, Olier was recalled to Paris at the death of his father. In spite of his mother's opposition—she wanted to have him appointed as the king's chaplain—he decided to take up the ministry of parish preaching. In December 1632, he followed the "Exercises for Ordination Candidates" and took Vincent de Paul as his spiritual director. Olier was ordained to the priesthood on 21 May 1633; he celebrated his first Mass at the Carmel of the Faubourg Saint-Jacques. Like Bérulle, he considered religious life, but understood very soon that his true vocation was to be a diocesan priest.

Even before his ordination, Olier had attended the Tuesday Conferences where he met the most apostolic priests in Paris. Before long, he joined the missionaries who were being sent by Vincent de Paul into every corner of France. Between 1634 and 1641, Olier consecrated much of his time to these missions, which had a profound effect on him. He would always look on them as the means of renewing the Christian spirit, and the most necessary ministry in the years following the Wars of Religion.

Olier's first missions were in Auvergne, in parishes dependent on his Abbey of Pébrac near Brioude (today, the department of Haute-Loire), at that time under the jurisdiction of the bishop of Saint-Flour. He attempted to reform the community at Pébrac. After negotiations with Alain de Solminihac, he united Pébrac with the Canons Regular, whom Charles Faure was organizing near Sainte-Geneviève in Paris.

During the course of his missions in Auvergne, Olier met Mother Agnès de Jésus (1602–1634), prioress of a monastery of Contemplative Dominicans at Langeac. The few hours he passed with her in the monastery parlor were decisive, it would seem, for his spiritual and apostolic future. Mother Agnès directed him to Father de Condren and revealed that "God had destined him to lay the first foundations of the seminaries in the kingdom of France."[5] She had a profound spiritual influence on him, inviting him to true intimacy with Jesus, in a kind of veritable "mystical initiation." Their meetings were to be few in number, since Agnès de Jésus died on 19 October 1634, at the age of 32.

Without severing his ties with Vincent de Paul, through rural missions and meetings of the Company of the Blessed Sacrament, Olier took Father de Condren as his spiritual director. Throughout his life, he maintained a boundless veneration for this holy priest who introduced him to Bérulle's thought, nuanced slightly by his own teaching. Above all, Condren's direction resulted in Olier founding a seminary in 1641.

Condren's first act was to dissuade Olier from accepting the bishopric of Langres as successor to Zamet, and to continue his ministry in the missions. Olier returned to Auvergne from May 1636 to September 1637. Later, between July 1638 and February 1639, he preached in the region of Nantes, not far from his Priory of Clisson. He worked for the reform of the religious of Regrippière. Moreover, he remained closely attached to this community. A number of his letters of spiritual direction are addressed to one or another of the sisters of Regrippière, as also to many Visitandines of Nantes. Olier was always perceived to be a wise director, and his advice was faithfully heeded.

In June 1639, Olier preached for missionary purposes in Picardy, at Montdidier, and from December of that year until April 1641, he took part in missions in the

diocese of Chartres. It was at this time that he under-
went a severe, interior trial that decisively affected his
spiritual development. Months passed, during which he
experienced the darkest of nights; he was totally unable
to preach or take part in missionary activities. Overcome
by guilt, he could see nothing in himself but self-love
and his own arrogance; he believed that even God ac-
counted him guilty, and he was convinced that he was
damned. His condition has been described as one of an-
guished neurosis and serious imbalance. It seems clear
that the strictly psychological, if not neurotic, aspect of
this trial was real. It was, nonetheless, also a veritable
interior purification that he describes in detail in his
Mémoires. The analysis made by Dupuy of this experience is powerfully enlightening.

After he was cured, Olier acknowledged the action of
the Holy Spirit in the interior and exterior transformation he had undergone:

> I had nothing at all to do with it. On the contrary, I was
> astonished at so many changes that took place so sud-
> denly in me: so much light, instead of darkness; such
> clarity of thought, instead of confusion; such freedom to
> speak, in place of stammering; so many good results from
> my words, instead of the great dryness I had experienced
> in myself and caused in others; such feelings and trans-
> ports of love for God, in place of that hateful, unhappy
> preoccupation with myself. I was forced to admit: It is
> the divine Spirit.[6]

This experience marks Olier's thought and spiritual
pedagogy. He assigns the first place in the Christian life
to the Holy Spirit. If the Christian is, indeed, "one in
whom the Spirit of Jesus Christ dwells," then "we must
abandon all to the Holy Spirit; we must let the Spirit act
in us." It seems that Olier was freed from his trial in
Chartres while the missionaries, under the leadership of
Denis Amelote, were attempting to found a seminary.

During these years, most precisely beginning in 1638,

Olier developed a profound spiritual relationship with Marie Rousseau. This mystic, whom Condren respected deeply and who was in touch with many priests and Christian laypersons, lived in the Saint-Germain section of Paris. She was able to assist Olier greatly in the years that followed, especially during the beginnings of his seminary. Olier's friendship with Marie Rousseau has sometimes been interpreted in a negative way. She certainly held "a major place in his religious universe," as Noye has remarked. This influence was to diminish, however, in the last years of his life.

The Evangelization of New France

Jean-Jacques Olier had the soul of a missionary; he was always concerned about proclaiming the Gospel to distant peoples. At this time there was a great deal of discussion in France about the evangelization of Canada, already begun by the Recollect friars and the Jesuits. The Jesuit "Relations" were widely read at the beginning of the seventeenth century, stirring the imaginations of many and giving rise to countless missionary vocations. On 2 February 1636, as Olier was praying at Notre-Dame, the singing of the *"Lumen ad revelationem gentium"* aroused in him the desire to carry the Gospel to some faraway land. It seems that, a year earlier, he had met a layman from the Jesuit College of La Flèche, Jérôme Le Royer de la Dauversière, who dreamed of founding a general hospital in Montreal.[7] Their meeting led to the decision to found the *Société des Associés de Notre-Dame de Montréal*, to which the two new friends planned to give much of their time and their money. Other persons joined them, among the best known, Gaston de Renty, superior of the Company of the Blessed Sacrament. The association purchased the island of Montreal from the former New France Company. As the year passed, projects were clarified with the principal aim being "to promote the instruction of poor savages in the knowledge of God and to draw them to a civilized life." In view of this objective, a school and hospital were to be founded, with the latter entrusted to the Hospitallers of St. Joseph, founded at La Flèche in 1636. On 27 February 1642, the members of the association met at Notre-Dame in Paris and gave their projected foundation the name of Ville-Marie.

The first group of missionaries left from La Rochelle in the summer of 1641, under the leadership of M. de Maisonneuve. Jeanne Mance, a woman from Langres, was part of the group.[8] After a brief winter spent in Quebec, the group arrived at Ville-Marie on 18 May 1642, and the first Mass was celebrated there.

Jean-Jacques Olier carried a concern for Canada in his heart until his death. He maintained close relations with Jeanne Mance, who deeply respected and often visited him on her return trips to France. Before his death, he designated four priests of his community who were to leave for Montreal some time later, in May 1657. Olier and the Society of Saint-Sulpice have always been counted among the founders of Ville-Marie, along with Jeanne Mance and St. Marguerite Bourgeoys, just as Marie de l'Incarnation and Catherine of St. Augustine are considered the foundresses of Quebec, with Bishop François de Montmorency-Laval, the first bishop of that city.

Saint-Sulpice: The Seminary, The Parish

At this time, priests were the major concern and topic of conversation everywhere in France. There were too many of them, without formation or spiritual life, totally absorbed in self-seeking. The picture was sober, indeed. Attempts at reform had had little success, through lack of planning or collaboration. One of the solutions ought to have been the institution of seminaries, but a good number of steps had to be taken. One of the originators in Paris and Beauvais was Adrien Bourdoise (1584–1655), who established a community of priests in the parish of Saint-Nicolas-du-Chardonnet. From 1631 on, this center became a sort of seminary, where newly ordained priests of the diocese of Paris came to learn, along with "rubrics and ceremonies," the meaning of their pastoral mission, in a lifestyle of community and prayer. Unfortunately, Bourdoise's eccentricities interfered with the survival of this institution.

Vincent de Paul, for his part, had laid a solid, indepth foundation for what was to come. His "Exercises for Ordination Candidates" were retreats preparatory to the reception of Orders. They would gradually become obligatory for those who desired the priesthood. The Tuesday Conferences were also a sort of continued, ongoing formation program, well ahead of their time. Besides, in 1642, Vincent de Paul was to found the Seminary of the *Bons Enfants*. The Oratorians had tried several experiences along this line, as early as 1613, but with only moderate success.

These achievements allow us to situate Olier's work and to grasp its meaning. He has given us his own, most basic explanation, drawn from his personal experience as a missionary:

> For several years now, a number of persons have come together with us, after having worked in missions and parishes. We recognize the futility of our efforts, if we have not first labored to purify the source from which the holiness of the people comes, that is, priests. As a result, these former missionaries have come to cultivate the new plants placed in their hands, namely, those who seem to be called to the priesthood.[9]

We must not, however, forget what Mother Agnès de Langeac had said to Olier in 1634, or what Father de Condren expressed as his last wish, shortly before his death in 1641.

Then events began to happen more quickly. On 29 December 1641, Olier, Caulet and du Ferrier settled at Vaugirard, at the time a town southwest of Paris, where they were joined by several disciples. Their intention was to begin a real "seminary." They were encouraged in the venture by Bourdoise as well as by Richelieu—who wanted, moreover, to control them.

> The destiny of this little community suddenly took a new turn. On 25 June 1642, Jean-Jacques Olier obtained the benefice of the parish of Saint-Sulpice, through personal transaction, not by nomination. The community moved to Paris, took up residence in the parish and thus became the "seminary of Saint-Suplice." Olier was to take care of everything at once: the acquisition of buildings to establish the seminary near the rectory; the spiritual formation of the seminarians; renewal of parish life; plans for the expansion of the church; reform of the many communities of priests employed in the parish. At the same time, he continued to be the most active supporter of the recent foundation in Montreal, meant to be a missionary outpost under the name of Ville-Marie.[10]

Olier also continued to try to submit to God's action in his life. Condren's death had led him to consult two of the Benedictines at Saint-Germain-des-Prés, Dom Tarrisse and later, Dom Bataille. His spiritual development did not lessen in intensity. On 11 January 1642, he pronounced the vow of servitude to Jesus. On 11 January 1643, a year and several months after his installation as pastor, he made a vow of servitude to souls. These commitments fell in line with fidelity to his baptism and to the apostolic mission entrusted to him by God. They were crowned, on 31 March 1644, by his vow as a victim-host. Careful examination of this progressive development shows us the degree to which Olier sought to correspond with the inspiration he had received, with the mission entrusted to him, following his deepest aspirations and the practices proposed by Bérulle.

Between 1642 and 1652, Olier was to be both a model pastor, bringing about interior renewal of his parish, and the founder of a seminary. In the parish, he organized liturgical prayer, especially eucharistic devotion, along with catechetical teaching and works of charity. In the space of ten years, he transformed a huge parish that was, for all practical purposes, nearly dead, into a center of Christian and apostolic life that was renowned in all of Paris.

Olier had to face countless conflicts in his activity, including a violent riot from which he escaped, in 1645, thanks to Vincent de Paul and the protection of Princess Anne of Austria. Far from diminishing his zeal, the antagonism of libertines, Huguenots and later, Jansenists, served only to increase his spiritual enthusiasm. Olier's ten years of pastoral ministry are still valued as an outstanding example in the religious history of Paris. Nearly 50 priests served in his parish, which today would be equal in size to six or seven. He undertook the renewal of these ministers, even as he gave special attention to the development of the seminary. This seminary, as he saw it, was to be an "apostolic house," a community of priests and future priests, sharing the same life, in preparation for receiving or renewing the apostolic Spirit in their hearts.

> The Seminary of Saint-Sulpice is consecrated and dedicated to Jesus Christ our Lord, in order to honor him not only as Sovereign Priest and the great Apostle of his Father, but also to venerate him living in the College of Apostles. This seminary daily prays that the apostolic spirit be given to its community and to the entire Church, so that the love of Jesus Christ and the worship of his Father might be renewed in her. Above all, it intercedes for the renewal of the clergy as the source of that holiness which must be brought by them to all people everywhere.[11]

The seminarians were to carry the spirit of the gospel to the Sorbonne, where they studied theology. They received a solid spiritual formation at the seminary, thanks to authentic spiritual teaching and guidance, for the disciples of Jean-Jacques Olier are, first and foremost, spiritual *directors*. The seminary program lasted one or two years. It was Olier's wish that the priests who spent some time at the seminary would come "to realize who they are in GOD'S Church and what is the grace of their state . . . so as to apply it faithfully in their holy ministry."

This last citation is an extract from a text presented in 1651 by Olier to the Assembly of the Clergy of France:[12] *"Projet de l'établissement d'un séminaire pour un diocèse."* This is a text of great interest, although it is incomplete. In it, we find a theology of the bishop, father of his people, but above all, of his priests; the notion of a seminary as an "apostolic house," composed of seminarians, their directors—"ministers of direction"—priests seeking spiritual renewal, and "missionaries," available for service as their bishop saw fit. It is interesting to note that at the very time Olier was presenting this project to the Assembly of the Clergy, St. John Eudes was preaching a major mission in the parish of Saint-Sulpice. Certainly, their discussions centered on the problems of priestly formation. John Eudes had founded a seminary at Caen in 1643; in 1648, he had presented a proposal to the Assembly of the Clergy to devote himself to the service of priestly formation in France. He and Olier shared the same lofty ideas of the Church and of apostolic grace.

Actually, Olier agreed to send, either temporarily or definitively, several of his priests to serve one or another bishop in the foundation of a seminary or for missions: Nantes (1649), Saint-Flour (1651), Magnac (1651), Le Puy (1652), Clermont (1656), Amiens (1657). The movement was to continue, as it does even today. The principal mission of the Society of St. Sulpice throughout the world is to be "at the service of those ordained to the presbyterial ministry . . . with a concern for education to the 'interior life' and the formation of an 'apostolic spirit'."[13]

Last Years and Death

In June 1652, Olier fell gravely ill. He resigned from his benefice, entrusting the parish to a disciple, de Bretonvilliers. Still, his final years were filled with every kind of activity. In 1653, he undertook a series of conferences with Charles III of England, in view of the monarch's conversion to Catholicism. That same year, he met Father Alexander de Rhodes, a missionary in Tonkin, to whom he offered himself for work in the Far East. In 1654, he established the Community of Daughters of the Interior Life of Mary. Above all, despite partial paralysis, he continued to labor for the seminary, and dedicated much of his time to spiritual direction. During these later years, also, he published several works of spirituality, in which we find the essence of his thought on the Christian life: in 1655, the *Catechism of an Interior Life* and the *Introduction à la vie et aux vertus chrétiennes*; in 1657, the *Explication des cérémonies de la grande messe de paroisse.*

One of Olier's last acts was to name the four priests of his community whom he wished to send to Montreal. They left France after his death and reached Canada on 29 July 1657. Jean-Jacques Olier died on Easter Monday, 2 April 1657; he had the consolation of a last visit with Vincent de Paul.

Olier's heritage includes not only a parish that was totally renewed, a flourishing seminary, and a society of priests actively engaged in many dioceses, but also a personal witness and a spiritual doctrine of highest quality. His teaching deserves to be continued and made known, so as to bear as much fruit as possible, in seminaries and religious communities. In Olier, we find a mystic, a man of prayer who was totally abandoned to God, and a missionary, a "man of fire," wholly surrendered to the apostolic Spirit. He was one of greatest servants of the Church in the seventeenth century.

Documents for Chapter 5

5.1 The Excellence of M. Olier

His especial grace and mission was, not exact [sic] to popularise Bérullism, but to present it with such limpidity, richness of imagination and fervor that its apparently somewhat difficult metaphysics are placed invitingly in the reach of most readers. If he does popularise it, it is in the highest sense of the word, that is to say after the manner of poets, as a man for whom the exterior world exists and who never separates feeling from comprehension. "General notions," he observes in the preface to the most exquisite of his books, "are not enough; one must come down to the particular, to gather the fruit of what has been seen or read." He could not better have defined his own particular excellence and the unique value of his work. Bérulle was certainly no abstract genius; he too can realize and feel passionately, yet, slow and massive, he lacks variety and suppleness, Condren is not more abstract than Plato, but the "particular" to which he comes down is yet so lofty, in trying to follow him, many will find only abstractions. P. Saint-Jure and P. Eudes cannot be taxed with giving way to pure speculation, their intellects, to my mind, are less curious and less sublime than M. Olier's; but it is rather oratorical amplification that dominates the eloquence of both, and this quality, in spite of its incontestable advantages, must

90

cede the palm to poetry. May I be forgiven for so often repeating this word, since, in the face of obdurate ignorance, I cannot too frequently repeat that M. Olier has the right to figure in that royal pageant in which eloquence alone may not take part, common among us though it is.

> Bremond, *A Literary History of Religious Thought in France* 3:393.

5.2 A Spiritual and Apostolic Journey

Preparation (1608–1634)

1608	20 September, Birth in Paris; years in Lyons (1617–1624)
1622	Blessed by St. Francis de Sales
1625–1630	Philosophy at Harcourt College, then Theology at the Sorbonne. Received several benefices.
1630	Rome and Loretto; "a great desire for prayer"
1633	21 May, Ordination to priesthood. Directed by St. Vincent de Paul, then by Father de Condren.
	Attends the "Tuesday Conferences"

First Missions; the Great Trial (1634–1641)

1634–1641	Rural missions
1634	Meeting with Agnès de Langeac
1635	Chooses Father de Condren as director
1636–1638	Important retreats
1638	First contacts with religious communities; beginning of relationship with Marie Rousseau.
1639	July to July, 1641: The great trial. Refusal of a second episcopal nomination (Langres, in 1634; then Châlons).

Major Apostolic Accomplishments (1641–1651)

1641	January: Death of Father de Condren.

	29 December: beginning of the seminary at Vaugirard.
1642	11 January: Vow of servitude to Jesus. Dom Tarisse then, Dom Bataille became his director; begins writing his memoirs.
	27 February: Meeting of the "Company of Notre-Dame de Montréal" at Notre-Dame, in Paris.
	June: Olier becomes pastor of Saint-Sulpice. He establishes the seminary in the parish.
1643	11 January: Vow of servitude to souls.
1644	31 March: Vow as victim-host.
1647	First missioning of confreres to two provincial dioceses.
1648	Beginning of Olier's action against Jansenism.
1649	Seminary in Nantes; 1650, seminary in Viviers.
1651	Proposal to the French Assembly of the Clergy of a "Project for the Establishment of a Seminary."
	15 August: Blessing of seminary buildings.

Trials and Final Activities (1652–1657)

1652	June: Serious illness. Olier resigns as pastor.
1653	26 September: partial paralysis
1654–1657	Negotiations to found seminaries in Le Puy, Clermont, and Montréal.

Publications (1652–1657)

1655	*The Christian Day*
1656	*Catéchism chrétien*
1657	*Introduction à la vie et aux vertus chrétiennes*
	2 April: Death in Paris, at age 48.

29 July: Arrival in Quebec of the first
four Sulpicians named by Olier.

5.3 Condren and Olier at Prayer

Condren's "Little Prayer"
Come, Lord Jesus,
and live in your servants,
in the fullness of your virtue,
in the perfection of your ways,
and in the holiness of your Spirit,
and dominate every enemy power
in the strength of your Spirit
for the glory of your Father.

Olier, *Mémoires* 11:120

Olier's Prayer
O Jesus, living in Mary,
come and live in your
servants,
in your Spirit of holiness,
in the fullness of your
power,
in the perfection of your
ways,
in the communion of
your mysteries;
dominate every hostile
force,
in your SPIRIT,
or the glory of the
FATHER.

Journée chrétienne. Paris, 1655.

Another Form of Olier's Prayer
JESUS, you who live in Mary,
    in the beauty of your virtues,
    in the fullness of your power,
    in the splendor of your divine,
        eternal riches,
give us some share in this holiness
    which belongs only to God;
Let us communicate with the zeal
    of this holiness for the Church;
finally, clothe us with yourself so totally
    that we may be nothing in ourselves,
    and so live only in
        and like your SPIRIT,
    for the glory of your FATHER.

Autograph text. St. Sulpice Archives.

1. Note the Marian dimension in Olier's prayers.
2. The first (shorter) of Olier's prayers follows the Latin text and is the one ordinarily used. The formula from the *Journée chrétienne* is slightly different (cf. éd Amiot. Paris, 1954; 178).
3. Cf. I. Noye, *La prière à Jésus vivant en Marie*, in "Cahiers marials," n. 123, 15 June 1988; 173–79.

5.4 The Christian Life

Christian life strictly speaking is the Christian person living interiorly, through the operation of the Spirit, in the same way Jesus Christ lived. Without this there can be neither the unity nor the perfect conformity to which our Lord does call us. He wishes that, through the operation of the Holy Spirit, we live with him a life that is truly one, just as the Father and Son live with one another. For they have only one life, one sentiment, one desire, one love, one light, because they are but one God living in the two persons.

This is why the Spirit of God is poured forth in Christians, as in the members of the same body, to enliven them with the same life and to have in them the same operations he produced in Jesus Christ, thus dilating his occupations, dispositions, loves and movements. It is like a drop of oil on a piece of white satin, which at first covers only a small corner of the material, but spreads out quickly over the whole piece. In the same way the Spirit of God, who lived in the heart of Jesus Christ, with time and the passage of the years during which the faithful have been united to Jesus Christ, has spread out in all, guaranteeing that everyone is made to share in the same taste and the same smell and finally in the same sentiments.

It is the same Spirit in all, producing the same effects in everyone. Having been transformed and reformed in this way by the Spirit in Jesus Christ at the depth of their souls, they are no longer distinct by the individual sentiments of their flesh and their self-love, which normally rule in everyone differently according to their various temperaments and distinct caprices. Rather, they are all one through the unity of the same Spirit, who rules in them and penetrates their hearts. They are no longer distinct through the diversity of religions: *There is no Gentile nor Jew, circumcised nor uncircumcised* (Col. 3.11); no Jew nor Greek (Gal. 3.28) nor through the distinction of climates, nations, nor the opposition of temperaments and barbaric customs: *Barbarian nor Scythian* (Col. 3.11); nor through the distinction of social condition: Slave nor freeman; nor through sexual distinction: *Neither male nor female,* because they are all the same in Jesus Christ: *You are all the same in Christ Jesus* (Gal. 3.28); and Jesus Christ is all things in all, *Sed omnia et in omnibus Christus* (Col. 3.11).

Furthermore, the Spirit fills them not only with the general dispositions of his heart, such as a horror for sin, self-annihilation, profound adoration and reverence for his Father, and perfect love of neighbor, but also with the particular dispositions that he had in his mysteries. Because every holy disposition in the soul of Jesus pleased the Father and caused him joy, thus the Holy Spirit, who seeks only to please the Father in everything, gladly pours himself out in the same way through his holy operations in those souls prepared to let him act in them.

This is what he accomplishes for the glory of God, especially in those souls who, because they are at peace and emptied of all things, give him the opportunity. And above all he desires to do this in those souls who are chosen to represent Jesus Christ on earth and to continue his life as Head and Shepherd for others, his life as a supplement for others, which is the life of the priest. It is the priest who takes the place of Jesus Christ in order to make up what is lacking in the religion of men, and therefore to be the universal religious of the church, praying, praising, loving on behalf of everyone, accepting and fulfilling the duties of all, the one who makes amends for the omissions of all.

This, then, was the plan of the Son of God, as he came on earth. He wished to continue in Christians the holiness of both his exterior and interior mysteries and establish in them these two conformities, which create a perfect likeness between the members and the head.

God's way of carrying out this very sublime work is in accord with the way he acts in the natural order, where nothing changes suddenly. In fact, each thing grows little by little and achieves imperceptibly the perfection to which the holy providence of God wishes to elevate it in the natural order. Thus we must be children before we become fully adults. Trees must have buds, leaves and flowers before bringing forth fruit. It is the same in the spiritual life. First we must begin, then advance before being brought to completion. For the height of the Christian state consists in the participation and the blessed communion in Jesus Christ, our Lord, risen, ascended in heaven and consumed in God his Father. Moreover, we must first pass through his first state, which is that of mortification, suffering, the cross, humiliation and death to everything.

In order for Christians to live their true vocation, which is to reproduce Jesus Christ in themselves, they must express all these holy states in their life in the same order in which they occurred in Jesus Christ. Therefore, as our sacred model Jesus Christ first suffered all sorts of disgrace, scourgings and gibbets, then died and was buried before rising and entering into his glory. *It was necessary for the Christ to suffer and then enter into his glory* (Lk. 24.26), in the same way Christians must bear in their lives all these states of humiliation before being able to share in his grandeur and state of exaltation.

Christian life has two parts: death and life. The first is the foundation for the second. This is repeated in the writings of Saint Paul and especially in the sixth chapter to the Romans: *Are you not aware that having been baptized in Christ Jesus, we were also baptized into his death? For we were buried with him in death through baptism, so that, as he is risen from the dead, we might also walk in the newness of life* (vv. 3–4). And afterward he adds: *Consider yourselves dead to sin and living for God in Jesus Christ* (v. 11). And in a thousand other places he repeats these two elements of the Christian life. Therefore, as we have said, death must always precede life. This death is nothing other than our complete downfall, so that as everything in us opposed to God is destroyed, his Spirit may dwell in us in the purity and holiness of his ways.

It is therefore through death that we enter into the Christian life. But we must know how this death comes about and how the Spirit of God works in us. To do this we must be aware of the difference between the Spirit of God and the Spirit of Jesus Christ. Even though the Spirit of God and that of Jesus Christ is one, nevertheless, due to the diverse operations that the

Spirit produces, at times he is called Spirit of God and other times Spirit of Jesus Christ.

When the Holy Spirit acts in us and establishes within us the virtues of fortitude, vigor and power and gives us a share in the perfections and attributes of God, which contain in themselves no abasement, then this divine Spirit is called Spirit of God, because God as God has only grandeur and majesty in him. However, when this same Spirit produces in us the virtues of Jesus Christ, which are the Christian virtues containing abasement and humiliation, such as love of the cross, of humility, of poverty, of disdain, then this holy Spirit is called the Spirit of Jesus Christ. We have pointed out this difference so that, in what follows, the reader can distinguish between these ways of speaking. Thus it is this Spirit of Jesus Christ who introduces us into death to sin. By sin I mean all the life of the flesh, which Saint Paul normally calls sin. He brings about this death in us by placing in the depth of our soul the virtues of Jesus Christ; that is, the virtues that he produced in Jesus Christ in his first state, which was one of abasement and humiliation.

Thus it is by these holy virtues that the Spirit of Jesus Christ crucifies our flesh and causes it to die to itself; knowing full well that if anyone tried to build the spiritual life on any other foundation, it would be only an illusion and a deceit. It would never be solid, but constantly wavering and would fall with the first wind of temptation and contradiction. Holy mortification, which flows from an authentic practice of virtues, is the firm rock on which we should build and without which there can be no guarantee.

Bérulle and the French School, 224–27.

5.5 On Seeing the Sun

My God, I adore you in this beautiful star, where you dwell as in your tabernacle. *He made the sun to be his tabernacle* (Ps. 19.5).

In it I adore and conceive some small idea of what you are in yourself.

In yourself you are one. You are very simple in your life and substance. Nevertheless, my God, you give life to a countless multitude of creatures, all distinct and different, which subsist and have life through you.

Have you not expressed, my God, this wonder? Have you not shown in the sun, which is unique and simple in its substance, that the lives of creatures depend on a single reality?

If it traverses the whole world, is it not to proclaim this truth: that you are the Father of every creature and the source of life in all that subsists?

When this sun brings creatures to the fullness and perfection of life, which they receive from you, you show us that you possess in yourself alone, in unity and eminent perfection, the life that is poured out in creatures. You have placed yourself in it, as in a throne, from which you enliven all the dead and all the creatures that languish in the graves of earth, where they possessed only the seed of life, which you furnish them through this star.

O my God, my possession and my life, everything depends on you. If for a moment you would cease giving existence and life to creatures, we would see everything perish.

You teach us this truth through this beautiful star, for when it undergoes an eclipse and is prevented from lavishing its effects on the earth, it leaves everything to languish.

O my God, you use the rays of the sun to bring life and energy to everything on earth. Through the absence of their effects, you make us realize that it is through them that you operate in the world.

You wish, O my possession, that while we see creatures rejoicing at its rising, turning themselves toward it and opening themselves to it in order to receive life; you wish, I was saying, that we adore you in it and that we fix our *gaze* on you, proclaiming with a spirit of religion that it serves only as a covering for you and as a channel to bring your life into the world, for there is nothing in us that does not come from you.

Also it is you, O my God, that all creatures behold. They give homage to you as their sovereign, and in this star they recognize you as the king and source of their life.

In it all creatures are your slaves. They all render homage to you. From them you receive adoration and the unspoken reverence of the work of your hands.

However, O great all-encompassing One, this veneration is quite lowly and very unworthy of your sovereign majesty. Jesus Christ came to offer you the homage of all creatures. He is the one who should animate them, who, through them, should adore you as the author and the source of everything and who should give you thanks for all your lavish generosity.

O Lord, O the love of our hearts, you who are yourself a sun, do for us what you do for your nonrational creatures. Thank your Father for us, since you cannot tolerate that he remain without honor and gratitude for all the good he does. Do this both for them and for us at the same time. For we are indebted to God for all the good that he does for us through them.

We are overwhelmed with blessings. Through both grace and nature, he gives us everything we could think of and more than we can understand. O my Lord, you alone understand everything. Be charitable and merciful enough to kindly thank him for everything.

It is not, my Lord, that we want to become lazy in offering our homage for his lavish gifts or that we want to remain ungrateful or silent because you are thanking your Father on our behalf. No, my Lord. For we want to lose ourselves, plunging into your Spirit and thus entering into your praise and thanksgiving to God.

Inasmuch as it is possible, we wish to share in your religion toward him. However, since we know practically nothing of the gifts he gives us, and since we have nothing in us that is pleasing or acceptable to him, we need to approach you and seek in you what we need to satisfy him.

O Lord, be our only supplement. And you, who alone are worth more than all things, be our unique offering and present to God.

> "The Christian Day," in *Bérulle and the French School*, 277–79.

5.6 A Way of Meditating on the Virtues

The method that our Lord teaches his disciples is given only when the more individual attentions of the Spirit, who guides his children in prayer, are absent.

Whenever he abandons them, and they do not know which path to follow, they can become quite hindered in such a period if they are not sustained and directed by some holy method to guide them.

We are suggesting an easy method here, which also is in keeping with the very plan of God the Father, expressed formerly in the Law. It consists in having our Lord before our eyes, in our heart and in our hands. Following the command of God, this is the way in which the Jews were supposed to carry the Law with them. *Let these words be in your heart. Bind them to your hand as a sign and let them hang and swing between your eyes* (Dt. 6.6,8).

Christianity consists in these three points, and the whole method of prayer is contained therein; that is, to look at Jesus, to unite ourselves to Jesus, and to act in Jesus. The first point leads us to acts of respect and religion. The second leads to union and unity with him. The third leads to action, which is not isolated but rather united to the power of Jesus Christ, whom we have drawn to us through prayer. The first is called adoration; the second, communion; the third, cooperation.

So that you can easily apply this exercise to any virtue, we will give now an example of this method applied to the virtue of penance.

FIRST POINT

Let Us Place Our Lord Before Our Eyes

That is to say, let us respectfully look at Jesus Christ, doing penance for our sins. Let us honor in him the holy Spirit of penance, which animated him all the days of his life and which subsequently filled the hearts of all those who have done penance in the church.

Let us remain reverent and respectful before such a holy and divine reality. After our heart has expressed freely its love, praise and other duties, let us remain for a while in silence before him, with these same dispositions and religious sentiments in the depth of our soul.

SECOND POINT

Let Us Have Our Lord In Our Hearts

After having considered in this way Jesus Christ and his holy Spirit of penance, we will spend some time longing for this divine Spirit. We will pray to this Spirit, who alone can create a new heart and fashion a penitential soul. We will ask him to please come into us. Using all the wiles of love we will plead with him to enter our soul to make us like Jesus Christ, the penitent one. We are called to carry on in ourselves the same penitential spirit that the Spirit began in him. We need to experience the amount of suffering appropriate for a body, such as ours, which is filled with sins.

We will give ourselves over to him in order to be possessed and in silence to allow ourselves to be saturated interiorly with his divine balm, so that he may bring us, when appropriate, to whatever practice of mortification is pleasing to him.

THIRD POINT

Let Us Hold Our Lord In Our Hands

The third point of this prayer is to have our Lord in our hands, that is to say, to wish that his divine will may be accomplished in us, who are his members. We must be submissive to him who is our head and should experience no other movement than that prompted in us by Jesus Christ, who is our life and our all. Filling our soul with his Spirit, his power and his strength, he should be accomplishing all that he desires in and through us.

In pastors, he is *the* Pastor; in priests, *the* Priest; in religious, *the* Religious; in penitents, *the* Penitent. Through them he accomplishes the works of their vocation. Thus he should produce in us the effects of penance. We should always dwell in that Spirit, in faithful cooperation with all that he wants to do in us and accomplish through us. Thus, in this third point, we will give ourselves over to this Spirit, whom we have drawn to ourselves in the second point. This is so that we may produce through him all day long the works of penance, wishing to live in him constantly, since this is the reason we have sought him in our prayer. We will give ourselves over to that divine Spirit in order to produce through him works of penance, since without this union with him there can be none. Furthermore, we will abandon ourselves completely to him so that he can accomplish in us and with us all that he wishes in order to satisfy God. (. . .)

Our Lord has dilated himself by dilating the body of his

church. Furthermore, he bears the suffering of his members since he is inserted and enfleshed in them through his Spirit. He gives life to their souls. He gives strength to their spirits and to their hearts by his presence and his power. Thus he is more the penitent in them than they are in themselves. It is the Spirit of Jesus Christ, the penitent, in their souls that makes penitents of them.

Bérulle and the French School, 228–31.

5.7 Living Sacraments

Apostolic men, like all apostles, are bearers of Jesus Christ. They carry Our Lord everywhere; they are like the sacraments that bear him, so that beneath and through them, he may glorify his Father.

Behold, this wonderful invention of Love. Formerly, he was in one place only, living in our flesh to glorify God. Now, he is in one hundred thousand places. He could preach, previously, to only one crowd at a time. Now, dwelling in his preachers, he speaks to everyone at the same time. And, since he alone is able to inspire thoughts to be expressed in a thousand tongues, because of the breadth of his knowledge and his capacities, he provides words to one hundred thousand at a single time so that God may be glorified.

Olier, Mémoires 11:314

5.8 Olier on Interior Humility

[The following text reflects themes that characterized Condren's thought and his influence on Olier.]

God is immense in himself. The infinite weight of his being should humiliate everything under him, leading us to the love of scorn and vileness. Nevertheless, we discover that our heart resists him so strongly and exercises such control over him that, instead of tending toward littleness, we tend only toward greatness, looking only for praise, esteem and applause. God, who is so powerful in all things and especially in the soul of his Son, finds himself powerless in us.

Let us study how to renounce our inner core, how to condemn it and how to surrender it to God, so that he can imprint in us what he wants and insert in us his inclinations, his sentiments and even his dispositions. We must pray much to the majesty of God that he exercise his power and immense strength in us, so that he may humiliate us in him and offer us a share in his inclinations and desires.

The most important humility is the interior one, which concerns primarily the spirit. It consists in always submitting the powers of the soul to God in complete dependence on him, so that the spirit of the Christian would never be so insolent and so proud as to exalt itself in the presence of its king and God, but rather would remain always in submission and reverence before him, waiting upon his light and his orders with patience. And thus it will never be so bold as to act or reason about things on its own and in itself, but rather it will always submit itself to God, waiting with faith upon his guidance and his command.

It is the same with our will, which being in sinful flesh and in the present state of disorder, needs, even more than our understanding, much like a queen who commands and rules, to depend on the Holy Spirit, who wishes to be king and master in us.

Our will is more affected by sin than the rest of us. Therefore, it is more haughty and arrogant. It is always ready to give orders and rarely disposed to obey. It takes great effort and continuous attention to keep it in subjection and submission. It gives commands in every situation and pays no attention to the orders, movements and guidance of the Holy Spirit and to his love, which alone should rule over us and lead us smoothly toward those things that God desires.

Therefore, true and perfect interior humility consists in the submission of the will to God, along with our understanding, which should act as if it were dead and wait very faithfully, submitting itself to the divine impressions and to those lights that God promises to his children. Thus the soul will be truly humble in spirit and truth, in deed and in perfect sacrifice. For the soul in this state protests that it is worth nothing, that it cannot act in justice and holiness, but that everything comes from God and depends on him and that everything in us should be accomplished by him.

To be aware that we are worth nothing, that we know nothing and that we can do nothing, and to take pleasure in this insight and knowledge, is the first point of humility.

Bérulle and the French School, 236–37

Chapter Six

John Eudes: The Saint of the French School

T he reputation of the French who come from Normandy is as ambiguous as the phrase used to describe them in the rest of France: a Norman never answers a question directly, but "maybe yes, maybe no" ("*peut-être que oui, peut-être que non*)! John Eudes, however, was a Norman who always said, yes. This is not the only characteristic that makes him unique among the four great masters of the French School. For one thing, he is the easiest of all to read and understand. For another, he is the only one of the four to have been canonized. We know John Eudes through his writings and through the religious congregations who claim him, directly or indirectly, as their founder. The Eudists, Religious of Our Lady of Charity and of the Good Shepherd, the Little Sisters of the Poor, Religious of the Sacred Hearts of Jesus and Mary, the Religious of Paramé: all continue his missionary action, engage in priestly formation and commit themselves to service of the poor.

In his lifetime, John Eudes saw most of the seventeenth century. He was born in 1601, at Ri, Normandy, near Argentan; he died on Monday, 19 August 1680, at "three hours after noon" in Caen. Like Bérulle and Olier, he traveled and conducted missions extensively during the course of these years. He spent time in Paris, in the regions and provinces of France and, even, at the royal court.

Our knowledge of John Eudes comes to us from his first disciples and through his own writings. The most notable of these is his *Mémorial des bienfaits de Dieu*, a kind of spiritual journal he wrote toward the end of his life to record the graces he had received. More than 250 of his letters have been preserved. They help us to see him as a man of action, extremely sensitive, easily given to authoritarianism, immersed in matters of every kind, but wholly centered on the will of God and overflowing with authentic charity toward others. We do not possess for John Eudes, as we do for Olier, an abundant collection of *Memoirs*, enabling us to follow his spiritual development. Nevertheless, it is still possible to pinpoint several major stages in his spiritual and apostolic itinerary.

Infancy and Youth

The early life of John Eudes was influenced by his deeply Christian, well-to-do family and by his first educators: a priest who taught him Latin, the Jesuits at Mont College in Caen, where he studied the humanities and began his philosophy courses. Somewhat like Teresa of Jesus and Therese of the Child Jesus, he recalls these early years in his *Mémorial*:

> About the age of 12 (I began) to know God, through a special grace of the divine goodness, and after having made a general confession, I received Holy Communion every

month. . . . God also gave me the grace . . . to consecrate my body to him through a vow of chastity, for which I forever bless him.[1]

Among his Jesuit teachers, he does not hesitate to mention "Father Robin . . . who often spoke to us about God, with extraordinary fervor. This helped me more than I can say for my salvation." In 1618, when he was 17 years old, he entered the Confraternity of Our Lady; "there, Our Lord, through the mediation of his most holy Mother, granted me very great graces."

In 1620, at Sées, he received tonsure and the minor orders, in preparation for the priesthood. The arrival of the Oratorians in Caen in 1622 opened new horizons for him. Perhaps he had already heard of Father de Bérulle and the Oratory through one of Bérulle's admirers, Madame de Sacy. At any rate, he was captivated by the Oratory's ideals of reform. In spite of his family's opposition, he left for Paris where, on 25 March 1623, Bérulle himself received him "into the Congregation of the Oratory in the house of Saint-Honoré, in Paris." The spirituality of Bérulle and Condren would penetrate his thought and his writings throughout his entire life. We see this on nearly every page of his masterpiece, *The Life and Kingdom of Jesus in Christian Souls*.

The Oratory

John Eudes entered the Oratory the same year that Bérulle published the *Discours de l'Estat et des Grandeurs de Jésus*. At the age of 47, the founder had already realized his major works. The Teresian Carmel had been introduced into France in 1604 (John Eudes could have heard of the foundation of Carmel at Caen, in 1616); in 1611, the Oratory had been established and, in response to countless attacks, Bérulle had been obliged to clarify his thought and his intentions more than once. The Oratory was widely known in France. In 1623, when John Eudes joined the group, nearly 25 houses had already

been founded; Saint-Louis des Français had been entrusted to the Oratory in 1618, and the houses of the
Oratory in Provence had been united with the house in
Paris in 1619. In the company of Bérulle and Charles de
Condren, who had joined the Oratory in 1617, John
Eudes prepared for the priesthood in a climate of enthusiastic renewal, despite accompanying difficulties. He was
ordained a priest on 20 December 1625, in Paris, and celebrated his first Mass there on Christmas Day. During
the first two years of his priesthood, he suffered from a
"bodily infirmity" that prevented him from "working
outside." This extended period was to be a time of "retreat, [given] to prayer, to reading books of piety, and to
other spiritual exercises: this proved to be a very special
grace [for him] and one for which [he had] to bless and
thank the goodness of God eternally" (*Mémorial*).

In August 1627, after repeated requests, he was sent to
the Oratory in Caen. With the permission of his superiors, he intended to care for and bring spiritual comfort to
the victims of the plague in Argentan, and did so with
incredible energy. In 1631, he repeated this service of
charity in Caen, lodged in a huge barrel in the middle of
a field. His ministry was launched; in 1632, he began his
missionary work. Between that year and 1676, he was to
preach two or three "missions" a year, eventually totaling more than 100. Each mission lasted from four to
eight weeks and attracted large crowds; at times, several
thousand attended at once. The purpose of these missions was to give Christian instruction to those who had
been baptized, to provide reconciliation for them through
the Sacrament of Penance, and to encourage them to live
a renewed Christian life. On average, 12 to 15 confessors
were available, but on occasion, there could be as many
as 100.

John Eudes exercised his mission ministry especially
in Normandy, but he also preached seven or eight missions in Brittany, four in Burgundy, and three at the court

in Paris. The history of his missions is an important part of the history of the Church in France in the seventeenth century. An indepth study of this subject, one to which we can refer only in passing, has been made by Father Berthelot du Chesnay.[2] Missions flourished everywhere at this time, with Jesuits, Capuchins, disciples of Condren and of Vincent de Paul preaching in nearly all the provinces, towns and cities of France. It is true to say that this "missionary invasion" could not be separated from a "mystical invasion." They were "two complementary aspects of the movement of religious renewal of the Church in France." It is not too much to claim that renewal of religious and priestly life was prepared for and fostered by renewal of the Christian life in countless families.

In the missions, John Eudes excelled as "a great preacher . . . the wonder of his century," as Olier said, thanks to his many gifts of oratory. Like other apostles of his day, he also exercised a more hidden ministry of spiritual direction. Laypersons, priests, probably, and many religious, surely, consulted him. Without any hesitation, and from the first years of his ministry, he offered guidance to women such as Laurence de Budos, the great abbess who reformed the Benedictines of Caen. In Paris, as in Caen, he guided and offered counsel to Benedictines, Carmelites, Ursulines, Visitandines.

This double ministry of parish missions and spiritual direction would lead John Eudes to write many books. In so doing, he extended the influence of his preaching and spoken words. The list of texts he published is long, and some of them have disappeared; still others were published after his death. Here, we shall mention only a few, taken from his years as an Oratorian (1623–1643):

1. 1636: *l'Exercice de piété.* A manual for living the Christian life on a daily basis, there were several editions of this work.
2. 1637: *The Life and Kingdom of Jesus in Christian*

Souls. This contains the essence of John Eudes's message. It was frequently republished, with about 20 editions in the seventeenth century alone. The edition of 1670 is considered definitive. The work was dedicated to Madame de Budos and addressed to all Christians who seek to serve God in spirit and in truth: "it is one and the same thing, to be a Christian and to be holy." This book can be considered the Eudist parallel to the two masterpieces of Francis de Sales: *Introduction to the Devout Life* (1607) and *Treatise on the Love of God* (1616). John Eudes's work is more prolific and less well structured than that of Francis de Sales, but it is more explicitly biblical and theological, centered more directly on communion with Jesus: the Christian life is "the continuation and the fulfillment of the life of Jesus in us." Jesus comes to live and reign in the souls of Christians. Following Bérulle and Condren, John Eudes invites all Christians to "profess Jesus Christ," to continue and fulfill the mysteries of Jesus, and to pray that he bring to completion and realize them totally in us and in his whole Church.

3. 1642: *La vie du chrétien ou le catéchisme de la mission.* Frequently republished, this contains the teaching Eudes gave to children and adults during his missions. It was a true catechism, in the format of questions and answers, intended for his confreres in the missions as well as for others.

It was also during his Oratorian years that John Eudes, at the request of Léonor de Matignon, bishop of Coutances, began his relationship with Marie des Vallées (1590–1656). Between 1641 and 1656, he both helped and was helped by her. Marie des Vallées was an uneducated, uncultured, even rude, woman, but she was known and recognized as a mystic. She was gifted with human and spiritual wisdom, apparently not diminished by the eccentric behavior and questionable phenomena that sometimes accompany mystical gifts. John Eudes took a real interest in her. He wrote *La vie admirable de Marie des*

Vallées et des choses admirables qui se sont passées en elle as well as another, shorter work, neither of which, unfortunately, has been published. It is interesting to note that Eudes gave such attention—"passionate attention," L. Cognet wrote—to the experience of the so-called "mystical marriage," where the soul experiences itself as the spouse of God. In this, he seemed to discover something of his personal spiritual experience. His own mysticism was certainly different from that of Marie des Vallées, who was influenced by the abstract mysticism of Canfeld and Catherine of Genoa. He, like Bérulle and Condren, was more explicitly christocentric, but he could not be insensitive to the truth of an authentic spiritual life. Vicious accusations were made against John Eudes, all because of his admiration for Marie des Vallées.

Still another event marked the year 1641: the foundation of Our Lady of Refuge, which was to become the Institute of Our Lady of Charity. In the course of his missions, John Eudes had met a number of women and young girls who had become prostitutes. How could they be helped to get out of this life and lead a Christian one? Some efforts had already been made, with the creation of "refuges" here and there, in Nancy, Paris and Marseille. Members of the Company of the Blessed Sacrament devoted themselves to this work. John Eudes had been made aware of this situation as early as 1634 by Jean de Bernières, and carried the concern in his heart. We know, too, about the challenge addressed to him and several friends, as they passed through a section of Caen in 1641:

> Where are you going? To visit the churches, no doubt, and to feed there on the images of the Saints; then you will think yourselves very pious. That is not where the quarry lies. Better try and establish a house for those poor girls who are being lost for want of assistance and advice![4]

John Eudes heard this cry for help. He worked energetically to overcome many difficulties and finally received permission from Rome to establish the Institute of Our Lady of Charity and to obtain approval of its well-wrought Constitution. This congregation would give birth, much later, to the Institute of Our Lady of Charity of the Good Shepherd. This was to be the work of St. Mary Euphrasia Pelletier (1796–1868) who, in 1835, united the monasteries of the Order of Our Lady of Charity founded by the house of the Good Shepherd of Angers.

Steps on a New Path

In 1643, at the age of 41, John Eudes decided to leave the Oratory to found a seminary. While all the details of this separation are not clear, he seems to have been led by deep fidelity to Bérulle's intuitions. Bérulle's whole desire had been "to restore the priestly state." Like Monsieur Vincent and Jean-Jacques Olier, John Eudes understood that the missions could bear fruit only if there were priests who could continue what the missionaries had begun. As we have seen, priests were plentiful, at this time, but they were sadly lacking in any formation. In spite of the intentions and decisions of the Council of Trent, seminaries did not exist and truly "apostolic" priests were few in number.

From 1641 on, John Eudes, like other Oratorian missionaries, had begun to hold several meetings during the course of each mission for the priests working with him. These were times for sharing and prayer, but also for true formation. Out of such experiences, John Eudes would later write several books: in 1644, *Les avertissements aux confesseurs missionnaires*; in 1666, *Le bon confesseur*. Two other works were published after his death: in 1681, *Le Mémorial de la vie ecclésiastique* and in 1685, *Le prédicateur apostolique*.

All of this still left something to be desired, however. Formation centers were necessary. In the beginning, "seminaries" for children and youth were opened, in response to the requests of the Council of Trent, following a model established by Charles Borromeo. The results of this effort were disappointing. Gradually, retreats were organized here and there for those to be ordained, followed by communities that were somewhat more stable. The attitude of Vincent de Paul was readily understood:

> These seminaries for boys ... did not give Vincent the satisfaction he had expected. ... The way to priesthod was actually easier at an older age. ... [H]e thought of two types of seminaries, one for young men and one for advanced students. ... [5]

Following this line of thought, retreats for those to be ordained were quickly followed by a number of formation communities. They emerged almost simultaneously and differed only slightly from one another: in 1641, Olier was at Vaugirard; in 1642, Vincent de Paul, at *Bons Enfants*; in 1643, John Eudes, in Caen. John Eudes, like Olier, was influenced by Father de Condren, who had been most anxious to see seminaries established in France but also very prudent and slow in making decisions. The successor to Condren, Bourgoing—for reasons that are still not clear—refused to approve the project presented by John Eudes. After Bourgoing's death in 1641, Eudes made a pilgrimage in March 1643 with several secular priests to Our Lady of La Délivrande, near Caen, to entrust the new undertaking to Mary. In a new house, known in Caen as the *Mission*, he brought together a few candidates for the priesthood and several priests. They spent several weeks or months together. There was no academic program, but time was given to periods of spiritual retreat, in preparation for ordination. There were also sessions in pastoral formation for preaching, celebration of the Sacraments, the study of cases of conscience and the like. Priests came to renew the spirit of their ordination and the exercise of their ministry. Thus, on 25 March 1643, the Company—later, the Society of Jesus and Mary, the Eudists—was born, founded for the work of seminaries and for missionary activity, especially parish "missions." John Eudes himself often signed his letters: *missionary priest.*

After the foundation of this seminary, John Eudes and his *Eudist* confreres were to take charge of seminaries in Coutances (1650), Lisieux (1653), Rouen (1659), Evreux (1667) and Rennes (1670). Like the priests of the Oratory and the Society of Saint-Sulpice, the members of the Society of Jesus and Mary did not choose to be religious: "This is an ecclesiastical society and its intention is to remain always within the order of the ecclesiastical hierarchy." Its founder is Jesus Christ and its spirit "is nothing other than the spirit of the High Priest, Jesus Christ Our Lord, which the ecclesiastics ought to possess fully, so as to spread it to others."[6]

Spiritual and Liturgical Pedagogy

In the midst of his activities as a missionary and a founder, John Eudes remained devoted to spiritual pursuits, marked by the mystical christocentrism of Bérulle and the concept of *devotion,* as taught by Francis de Sales. His goal was to live in constant loving intimacy with Jesus and Mary, and he was filled with a desire for martyrdom. Indeed, at the age of 36, he had signed, with his blood, a "vow to Jesus, offering himself as a host and a victim, to be sacrificed to the glory and the pure love of the Lord" (*Complete Works 12*). His own spiritual experience along with his entire life at the Oratory, especially, with Bérulle and de Condren, inspired him to compose prayers and liturgical offices. Thus, we have the prayer, "*Ave Cor,*" a salutation to the Heart of Jesus and Mary, written about 1640. Just as Bérulle had composed and celebrated at the Oratory an Office for the Solemnity of Jesus, John Eudes composed an Office in honor of Jesus the High Priest and all holy priests and Levites. This office was approved in 1649. It was celebrated on 13 November, so that its Octave was celebrated on 21 November, feast of the Presentation of the Virgin, the day for renewal of priestly commitments. Previously, he had composed a first office in honor of the Heart of Mary. It was celebrated for the first time in public on 8 February 1648, in Autun, with the permission of the bishop. This feast had all the earmarks of a novelty and encountered opposition more than once. Eudes would often quote the "elevation" he had learned at the Oratory: "O Heart of Jesus living in and through Mary! O Heart of Mary living in and for Jesus!" Where Jean-Jacques Olier spoke of the "interior of Mary" or the "interior of Jesus," John Eudes used the word *Heart*.

Devotion to the Heart of Mary spread throughout a number of monasteries, convents, and in certain dioceses. Confraternities of the laity, organized by John Eudes at the time of his missions, fostered the extension of this devotion. Encouraged, very likely, by the success of the office of the Heart of Mary, he later composed another, in honor of the Heart of Jesus. Official celebration began only in 1672, after its approbation, but the Office and the Mass had been composed several years earlier. This liturgy was adopted not only by the Religious of Our Lady of Charity and the Congregation of Jesus and Mary, but also by many religious communities with which John Eudes worked. That is why the Benedictines of Montmartre, since 1674, have celebrated a solemn feast in honor of the Sacred Heart. On 29 July 1672, John Eudes wrote a letter reflecting his great joy, inviting his confreres to celebrate the feast of the Heart of Jesus in their houses on 20 October of that year.

The limits of this study do not allow for a presentation of the history of devotion to the Sacred Heart and the new orientation given it by St. Margaret Mary Alacoque and the preachers who popularized the devotion. However, it is important to remember that Pius XI called John Eudes the "Father, the Doctor, and the Apostle of liturgical devotion to the Sacred Hearts of Jesus and Mary." It is also important to note that John Eudes insisted on the unity of the Heart of Jesus and of Mary, just as Olier had asked his disciples to pray to "Jesus living in Mary." John Eudes centered his prayer and the prayer of his followers on the Heart of Jesus and Mary, through the use of one word and a single symbol designed to awaken the love of Christians through contemplation of the love of Jesus and Mary.

The *spiritual pedagogy* of John Eudes included noonday prayers—that is, short texts meant as guides for a brief moment of prayer in the middle of the day. These texts consider a mystery of Christ or one of his virtues, permitting the individual to focus attention on God and on Jesus, and not on oneself. This is not meant to be a period for self-examination in view of correction; it is, rather, a time to look at Jesus, to adore and thank him, to ask his pardon and to give oneself to him so as to enter into his dispositions. This is the outline of prayer, as taught by Olier. According to the French School, it is the heart of the Christian Life.

Like Francis de Sales, John Eudes suggests other "little practices" in the ascent of "the path that we must follow if we are to walk always before God and live in the Spirit of Jesus." For example, he suggests insistently that we raise our heart to Jesus at the beginning of our actions to say:

1. That we renounce ourselves, our self-love and our own spirit, that is, all our personal dispositions and attitudes;
2. That you give yourself to him, to his holy love and to his divine Spirit, and that you desire to accomplish all your actions with the dispositions and intentions with which he accomplished his.

He then insists, vehemently, that we are not to become attached to these exercises, themselves.[7]

Last Years and Death

John Eudes encountered great opposition in his apostolic ministry, as we have seen. The Oratorians who looked on him as a renegade opposed him and his undertakings openly. The Jansenists found fault with his devotion to the Heart of Mary and, above all, with his deep respect for Marie des Vallées. As early as 1650, the authorities in Caen had sealed the door of the seminary chapel. Beginning in 1660, defamatory accusations were circulated against him. Later, when he thought of establishing the Congregation in Paris, a still more violent campaign led to an official letter expelling him from Paris and, indirectly, threatening his work. This disfavor with the royal court lasted until 1679. None of this, however, kept him from continuing to preach and to bring to conclusion the major work that had occupied him for many years: *The Admirable Heart of the Most Holy Mother of God.* John Eudes died on 19 August 1680, entrusting the leadership of his Congregation to one of his most loved disciples, Jean-Jacques Blouet de Camilly (1632–1711).

The texts presented here allow us to grasp a little of the theological richness of Eudes's spiritual doctrine, reflecting his encouragement for others to live by his own motto: to serve God and others *"corde magno et animo volenti"* "with a great heart and a magnanimous love" (cf. 2 Mac. 1.3).

DOCUMENTS FOR CHAPTER 6

6.1 Brief Chronology of John Eudes's Life

1601	Birth at Ri, near Argentan
1615	Studies with the Jesuits at Caen
1620	Tonsure and minor orders, at Sées
1623	Entrance into the Oratory, in Paris
1625	Ordination to priesthood
	Time for retreat and studies
1627	At the Oratory in Caen
	The plague in Argentan
1631	The plague in Caen
1632	First missions (there would be more than 100)
1637	First edition of *The Life and Kingdom of Jesus*
1640	Superior of the Oratory in Caen
1641	Meeting with Marie des Vallées
	Foundation of Our Lady of Refuge, in Caen
1643	19 and 25 March: foundation of the seminary in Caen and of the Congregation of Jesus and Mary
1648	First public celebration of the Feast of the Heart of Mary, in Autun
1650	Foundation of the seminary in Coutances
1651	Our Lady of Refuge becomes Our Lady of Charity
1653	Seminary and college in Lisieux
1654	*Contrat de l'homme avec Dieu par le saint baptême*

1657	Foundation of the seminary in Rouen
1666	Our Lady of Charity approved by Rome; *Le bon confesseur*
1667	Foundation of the seminary in Evreux
1670	Foundation of the seminary in Rennes
1672	First liturgical celebration of the Heart of Jesus
1673	Our Lady of Charity in Rennes
1674 *to*	
1679	In royal disfavor
1676	Our Lady of Charity in Hennebont and in Guingamp Last mission at Saint-Lô.
1680	19 August: Death
1925	31 May: Canonization

6.2 Christian Life, The Continuation and Fulfillment of the Life of Jesus

> As I am in the Father, living his life which he communicates to me, so are you also in me, living my life, and I am in you communicating it to me.
>
> St. John Eudes, *The Kingdom of Jesus*, Part 2, p. 2; O.C. 1, 161–66

Not only is Jesus, Son of God and Son of man, King of men and of angels, our God, our Savior and our sovereign Lord; he is also our Head and *we are members of his body*, as St. Paul puts it (Eph. 5.30).

It follows that we are united to him in the most intimate union possible, comparable to the link there is between members and their head. Spiritually, we are united to him by faith and by the grace he gave us in holy Baptism. Bodily, we are united to him by the union of his most holy body with ours in the Blessed Eucharist. As a necessary consequence, just as the members are animated by the spirit of the head and live of the same life, so too must we be animated by the spirit of Jesus, live of his life, walk in his ways, be clothed with his sentiments and inclinations, perform all our actions with the same dispositions and intentions with which he acted. In a word, we must continue and fulfill the life, religion and devotion which he had on earth.

This proposition is based on the sacred words of the one who is Truth itself: *I am the Life. I have come that you might have life. I live and so will you. On that day you will know that I am in my Father, and you in me and I in you* (Jn. 14.6, 10.10, 14.19–20). In other words, just as I am in my Father, living of his life that he communicates to me, so are you also in me, living of my life, and I am in you, communicating that same life to you. Thus, I live in you and you live with me and in me.

All these sacred texts teach us that Jesus Christ must live in us, that we must have no life but in him and that our life must be a continuation and expression of his.

To understand more clearly this fundamental truth about Christian life and to root it strongly in your soul, bear in mind that Jesus Christ has two kinds of body and two kinds of life.

First, there is his personal body, which he received from the Blessed Virgin, and the life which he lived in his human body while on earth. His second body is his mystical body, the Church. St. Paul, indeed, calls her *the body of Christ* (1 Cor. 12.27). His second life is the one he lives in this mystical body and in all Christians, its members.

The first kind of life, mortal and limited in time, which he lived in his natural body, was fulfilled and ended with his death. But he wills to continue living in his mystical body until the end of time in order to glorify the Father by the actions and sufferings of a mortal life of work and toil, not only during 34 years, but until the end of the world. In this way, the mortal and temporal life Jesus has in his mystical body, that is to say, in all Christians, is not yet fulfilled, but proceeds towards fulfillment day by day in each true Christian and will not be perfectly complete until the end of time.

St. Paul writes that he is fulfilling the sufferings of Jesus Christ. We can also rightly say that a true Christian, as a member of Jesus Christ united with him by grace, continues and fulfills the actions that Jesus performed while on earth by every one of the actions he performs in the spirit of Jesus. So, when a Christian prays, he continues and fulfills the prayer of Jesus; when he works, he continues and fulfills Jesus Christ's work life, and so on, in all the other actions done in a Christian manner.

So, you see what Christian life is: a continuation and fulfillment of the life of Jesus. You see that our actions must be a continuation of Jesus' actions and that we must be so many other Jesuses on earth, in order to continue here his life and work, to do and suffer everything he wants us to do and suffer in a holy and divine way, in the spirit of Jesus, that is, with the divine and holy dispositions and intentions which Jesus had in all his actions and sufferings.

> *Lectionary proper to the Congregation of Jesus and Mary*. Trans., Louis Levesque, C.J.M. Charlesbourg, 1 December 1989; 32–34.

6.3 A Letter from Mission

To Father John Blouet de Camilly, in Paris. *On the success of the Vasteville mission, in the diocese of Coutances.*

Vasteville, 23 July 1659

My dearest brother:

I cannot tell you what blessings God is bestowing on this mission. It is certainly wonderful.

I have not preached in the church for quite some time now, for although it is very large, it is nevertheless too small on this occasion. I can truthfully say that we have more than fifteen thousand people present on Sundays.

There are twelve confessors, but without exaggeration there is enough work for fifty. People come from a distance of eight or ten leagues, and their hearts are so touched that there is nothing to be seen but tears and nothing to be heard but laments from the poor penitent men and women. The results observed by the confessors in the tribunal are wonderful. But what grieves us is that we shall be able to confess only a fraction of these people. We are exhausted. The missionaries see some who have been waiting for a week without having been able to get to confession, and who cast themselves on their knees whenever they meet a priest, imploring him with suppliant hands and tears in their eyes to hear them. And yet this is already our sixth week here.

What a great blessing the missions are! And how necessary!

What a great evil it is to hinder them in any way! Oh, if those who have prevented us from giving several in this diocese only knew the harm they have done! "Father, forgive them, for they know not what they do."

Let us pray the Lord of the harvest, my dear brother, to send laborers for it, saying frequently to Him with all our hearts: "Lord of the harvest, send laborers into thy harvest." What are all those doctors and bachelors of arts doing in Paris, while souls are perishing by the thousand for want of someone to offer them a hand to withdraw them from perdition and preserve them from everlasting fire? Certainly, if I dared, I should go straight to Paris and cry out in the Sorbonne and the other colleges: Fire! Fire! The flames of hell are consuming the whole universe! Come, you doctors, bachelors and parish priests, come, all you ecclesiastics, and help to extinguish them!

> *Letters and Shorter Works.* Trans., Ruth Hauser,
> M. A. New York: P. J. Kenedy & Sons, 1948; 138–39.

6.4 To be a Christian is to Confess Jesus Christ

> Let our whole lives be a continual sacrifice of praise and love of God.
>
> St. John Eudes, The Kingdom of Jesus, Part 2, p. 38,
> Part 7, p. 13; O.C. 1, 265–69, 515

For Our Lord Jesus Christ, devotion was a matter of accomplishing with the greatest perfection, everything his eternal Father willed. It consisted in serving his heavenly Father and serving men out of love for his Father and in doing everything for the greater glory of his Father, having taken the form and lowly condition of a servant.

There were three solemn vows Jesus made from the very first moment of his Incarnation and carried out most perfectly during his lifetime and in his death.

1) At the moment of his Incarnation, he vowed to obey his Father, that is to say, never to do his own will, but rather to conform perfectly to everything willed by his Father and to find his bliss and joy therein.

2) He professed to be in his Father's service. It is the charac-

ter given to him by his Father, saying through the prophet: *You are my servant, Israel* (Is. 49.3). And it is the character he adopts himself: *assuming the condition of a slave* (Phil. 2.7), lowering himself to the state and condition of a humble and servile life with respect to his creatures, to the cruel shame and servile death of the Cross, for love of us and the glory of his Father.

3) He professed to become a host and victim entirely conse-crated and immolated to his Father's glory from the very first to the very last moment of his life.

Such was Jesus' devotion. Since Christian devotion is none other than Jesus Christ's devotion, our own must consist of similar vows of service.

Professing at the time of our Baptism to adhere to Jesus and remain in him, we make three great, holy and divine vows upon which we must often reflect.

1) With Christ we profess never to do our own will, but rather to submit to everything willed by God, to obey all kinds of people in all that is not contrary to God, and to seek our total satisfaction and paradise in doing so.

2) We profess to be of service to God and to his Son, Jesus Christ, and to all Jesus' members, according to the words of St. Paul: *We are your servants for love of Jesus* (2 Cor. 4.5). Be-cause of this profession, no Christian can call anything his own. Nor has a Christian the right to any use of the faculties of his soul, or of the members and sentiments of his body, or the powers of his soul, his life, his time, the temporal goods he possesses, except for Jesus Christ and for his members.

3) We profess to become hosts and victims continually sacri-ficed to God's glory. St. Paul says: *My brothers, think of God's mercy and worship him, I beg you, by offering your living bodies as a holy sacrifice, truly pleasing to God* (Rom. 12.1).

So, we are obliged to glorify and love God with all the pow-ers of our body and soul, to do everything possible to have him glorified and loved, to seek nothing in all our actions and in all things save his pure glory and love, and to live in such a way that our whole life be a ceaseless sacrifice of praise and love of him. Each one of us should be ready to be immolated, con-sumed and annihilated for his greater glory.

In a word: *Christian living is witnessing to the life of Christ,* says St. Gregory of Nyssa. St. Bernard assures us that Our Lord *does not admit to the ranks of those professed in his religion, anyone who does not live the life of Jesus.*

That is why we bear witness to Jesus at Baptism. We bear witness not only to his poverty or chastity or obedience, but we profess Jesus himself, that is to say, his life, his spirit, his humility, charity, purity, poverty, obedience and all the other virtues that are in him. In a word, we make the same profession he made before his Father from the first moment of his Incarnation and fulfilled perfectly during his whole lifetime. In other words, we profess never to do our own will, but to delight totally in doing all that God wills, to be as servants before God and man for love of God. We profess to adopt a constant state of host and victim sacrificed to the glory of God.

Lectionary, 80–82.

6.5 The Mysteries of Christ and the Life of the Church

> The Son of God wills to give us a share in his mysteries and somehow to extend them to us. He wills to continue them in us and in all his Church.
>
> St. John Eudes, *The Kingdom of Jesus*,
> Part 3, p. 4; O.C. 1, 310–13

We must strive to follow and fulfill in ourselves Jesus' various states as well as his mysteries, and frequently beg him in prayer to bring them to completion in us and in the whole Church. For the mysteries of Jesus are not yet completely perfected and fulfilled. In the person of Jesus they are complete, but not in us, who are his members, nor in the Church, which is his mystical body. The Son of God wills to give us a share in his mysteries and somehow to extend them to us. He wills to continue them in us and in all his Church. This is brought about first through the graces he has resolved to impart to us, and then through the works he wishes to accomplish in us by way of these mysteries.

For this reason, St. Paul says that *Christ is being brought to fulfillment in his Church,* and that *all of us contribute to this fulfillment* (Eph. 1.22–23, 4.13). Thus he achieves the fullness of life, that is to say, the mystical stature that he has in his mystical body, which will reach completion only on judgment day. And in another place St. Paul says: *I complete in my own flesh what is lacking in the sufferings of Christ* (Col. 1.24).

This is the plan by which the Son of God wants to complete and fulfill in us all his various states and mysteries. He wishes us to perfect the mystery of his Incarnation, of his birth and his hidden life, by forming himself in us and being reborn in our souls through the holy sacraments of Baptism and the Eucharist, making us live a spiritual and interior life hidden with him in God.

He intends to perfect in us the mystery of his passion, death and resurrection, by making us suffer, die and rise again with him and in him. Finally, he wishes to fulfill in us the state of his glorious and immortal heavenly life, when he will cause us to live a glorious, eternal life with him and in him in heaven.

In the same way, he wants to complete and fulfill in us and in his Church all his other states and mysteries. He wants to give us a share in them and to accomplish and continue them in us. So it is that Christ's mysteries will not be completed until the end of the time he has ordained for their completion in us and in his Church, that is to say, not until the end of time.

The life we have here on earth is given to us only for the fulfillment of Christ's infinite designs on us. That is why we must spend all our time, days and years, cooperating with Jesus in the divine task of completing his mysteries in ourselves by good works and prayer, by frequent application of mind and heart to contemplating, adoring and venerating the sacred mysteries of his life, by giving ourselves to him that he might work in us, through them, all that he wishes to accomplish for his pure glory.

Lectionary, 65–66

6.6 To the Sisters of Our Lady of Charity

[John Eudes often wrote to the sisters of Our Lady of Charity. In the following letter, written for the feast of the Assumption, he points out to them the ideal they are to pursue. This document, written before 1656, reflects the clarity with which he expressed his counsels.]

You ought to seek ways of increasing Mary's joy and glory. Here are four excellent means:

The first is to inscribe in the depth of your heart a firm resolution and a constant intention to seek only the glory of her Son and the fulfillment of his most adorable will, in all your actions, mortifications, and exercises.

The second is to be faithful and exact to your Rules and Constitutions as also in the obedience you owe your good Mother Superior. You ought to look upon and honor her as one who has taken the place and represents for you the person of the most blessed Virgin, your true Mother and your first Superior.

The third is to love and cherish one another with a sincere, simple, tender and cordial love; to banish from your thoughts, words and actions everything that is even contrary to this affection; and to atone promptly and effectively the least faults by which you might violate mutual charity.

The fourth means is to desire with all your heart to realize the aim of your holy Institute: that is, through your prayers, your example, your instructions and every other way holy obedience will direct you, to work for the salvation of the lost souls divine Providence will send you. (. . .)

Yes, my most beloved daughters, your vocation, in some way is the vocation of God's own Mother. God chose her so that his Son could be formed in her, and through her, in the heart of the faithful. So you, too, have been called to this holy community, where you are to bring her Son to live in you and to bring him back to life in the sinful souls where he is dead. (. . .)

Know this, however: this work so violently displeases the wicked spirit, who hates no one as much as those who work for the salvation of souls. He will not fail to tempt you against your vocation.

How can you be counted among his numbers and his spouses if you are not like him? Do you want a new gospel written just for yourselves? Or do you want God to send you another Messiah, a Messiah of honey and roses? Do you hope to go to Paradise by another road than the one traveled by the

Mother of God and all the saints? Or do you want to go to
heaven alone, leaving your poor sisters on the pathway to hell,
because you are so delicate that you are afraid of the effort it
would take to extend a hand toward them?

> The full text of this letter (53) can be found in:
> *Letters and Shorter Works* by Saint John Eudes.
> Trans. Ruth Hauser, M.A. New York: P. J. Kenedy
> & Sons, 1948; 90–96.

6.7 The Priests of Jesus Christ

A priest is another Christ living and walking on earth.

> St. John Eudes, *Memorial of Priestly Life*,
> Part 5, p. 10, no. 2; O.C. 3, 187–89

A priest is truly another Christ living and walking on earth.
He takes Christ's place, represents his person, acts in his name
and exercises his authority. Our blessed Lord said: *As the Father has sent me, I also am sending you* (Jn. 20.21), that is to
say, I send you to dispel the darkness of hell which covers the
face of the earth, and to illuminate the world with heavenly
light. I send you to work for the destruction of the tyranny of
sin and the establishment of the kingdom of God. I send you
to perpetuate on earth the life I led and the virtues I practiced.
I send you to continue my own office of mediator between
God and man, of judge and savior.

These three functions are the principal qualities with which
Christ has endowed priests, especially pastors.

First of all, priests are mediators between God and man,
making known his divine will. Theirs is the duty of drawing
men to God and of reconciling them with him; theirs is the
obligation of rendering to him the homage, adoration, praise
and satisfaction due to him. Between God and man they must
deal with the greatest and most important relations in heaven
and on earth, those which have to do with his glory, the salvation of the world, the completion of the sufferings of his Son
by their application to men's souls.

With the Son of God, they are judges of the world, not in
earthly and temporal things, but in things heavenly and eternal. With Christ, priests are saviors of the world. The Son of

God shares with them the heavenly prerogative of Savior, desiring that they should be associated with himself in the salvation of souls: We are *God's coadjutors* (1 Cor. 3.9). He wants them to discharge the office of saviors and be employed in the continuation and fulfillment on earth of the greatest and most divine of all his works, the redemption of the world. Towards this one end, every duty and office of the priestly life is primarily directed.

In the work of saving souls, Our Lord Jesus expended himself completely, spent every moment of his time, all his thoughts, words and actions, his works, his blood and his very life. Thus too, priests, and more so pastors, must give to this work their heart and soul, their thoughts and affections, their time, their strength and ten thousand lives if they had them to give, in order to be able to truly say with St. Paul: *I mostly gladly will spend and be spent myself totally for your souls* (2 Cor. 12.15). Otherwise, if a single soul is lost through the negligence of priests, all the wounds of Christ, his sufferings and the Blood he shed for that soul will cry vengeance against them at the hour of death: *I will require his blood at your hand* (Ez. 3.18). Truly, the priest is another Christ living and walking on earth. Consequently, our life and our conduct should be a perfect and living image, or rather a continuation of Jesus' life and conduct.

We are obliged then, to study carefully what he said and did while he was on earth, the virtues he practiced, his way of living and acting, his horror for sin, in order to express them and continue to practice them in our own lives.

Lectionary, 128–30

6.8 Ave Cor

Hail, Heart most holy,
Hail, Heart most meek,
Hail, Heart most humble,
Hail, Heart most pure,
Hail, Heart most devout,
Hail, Heart most vigilant,

Hail, Heart most wise,
Hail, Heart most patient,
Hail, Heart most obedient,
Hail, Heart most faithful,
Hail, Heart most blessed,
Hail, Heart most merciful,
Hail, most loving Heart of Jesus and Mary.

We adore you,
We praise you,
We glorify you,
We give you thanks,
We love you
With all our heart,
With all our soul,
With all our strength.

We offer you our heart,
We give it to you,
We consecrate it to you,
We sacrifice it to you,
Receive it and possess it totally,
Purify it,
Enlighten it,
Sanctify it,

That you may live and reign in it now and forever. Amen.

> *In the Footsteps of St. John Eudes* 5: *Hail, Heart
> Most Holy!*
> Trans., Louis Levesque, C. J. M., Ed., Edouard
> Boudreault, C.J. M.

6.9 The Heart of Mary

Before speaking of the phenomenal supremacy and the incomparable marvels of the admirable heart of the blessed Mother of God, according to the lights that it pleases him who is light itself and the source of all light to give me through the divine Scriptures and the writings of the holy Fathers, I will first state that the word *heart* has many meanings in sacred Scripture.

1. It signifies this material and bodily heart, which we possess in our chest. It is the most noble part of the human body, the source of life, the first to live and the last to die, the seat of love, hatred, joy, sadness, anger, fear and all the other passions of the soul. It is of his heart that the Holy Spirit speaks when he says: *Omni custodia serva cor tuum, quia ex ipso vita procedit,* "Take good care of your heart for it is the source of life" (Prov. 4.23); which is as if he said: Take great care to subdue and rule the passions of your heart. For if they are appropriately subject to reason and the Spirit of God, you will live a long and peaceful life in your body and a holy and honorable one in your soul. However, if, on the contrary, they possess and govern your heart as they wish, they will bring you temporal and eternal death through their dissipation.

2. The word *heart* is used in sacred Scripture to signify the memory. This is the meaning of these words of our Lord to his Apostles: *Ponite in cordibus vestris, non praemeditari quemadmodum respondeatis,* "Put this in your hearts," that is, remember, when they bring you before kings and judges for my name's sake, "do not worry about what you should respond" (Lk. 21.14).

3. It also denotes the understanding used for meditation, which consists in the discursive reasoning of our intellect about the things of God. This tends to persuade us and convince us of the truth of Christian teaching. It is this heart that is indicated by these words: *May the meditation of my heart be always in your sight* (Ps. 19.15). "My heart," that is, my understanding, "is forever devoted to meditating and reflecting on your grandeurs, your mysteries and your works."

4. It signifies the free will of the superior and reasonable part of the soul, which is the noblest of its powers, the queen of the other faculties, the root of good and evil and the mother of vice and virtue. It is this heart our Lord mentions when he says: *The good man out of the good treasure of his heart produces good, but the evil man out of the evil treasure produces evil* (Lk. 6.45). "A good heart," that is, the good will of the just man, "is a rich treasure out of which can come only good; but an evil heart," that is the ill will of the wicked man, "is the source of all sorts of evil."

5. It means that highest part of the soul, which the theologians call *point of the spirit*. This is the seat of contemplation, which consists in a most special gaze and an utterly simple vision of God, without discursive reasoning and the multiplicity of thoughts. The holy fathers understand that these words, which the Holy Spirit inspires in the blessed Virgin, refer to this part of the soul: *Ego dormio, et cor meum vigilat*: "I sleep and my heart is awake" (Song 5.2). According to Saint Bernardine of Siena and many others, bodily rest and sleep did not prevent her heart, that is the highest part of her spirit, from being always united to God in sublime contemplation.

6. At times it signifies the whole interior and spiritual life, according to these words of the Son of God to the faithful soul: *Pone me ut signaculum super cor tuum, ut signaculum super brachium tuum*, "Place me as a seal upon your heart and on your arm" (Song 8.6); that is, imprint, through perfect imitation, the image of my interior and exterior life in your interior and exterior, in your soul and your body.

7. It means the divine Spirit, the heart of the Father and the Son, which they wish to give us to be our spirit and our heart: *I will give you a new heart and I will place a new spirit in your midst* (Ez. 36.26).

8. The Son of God is called the heart of the eternal Father in the sacred Scriptures. For it is of this heart that the divine Father speaks to his divine spouse, the most pure Virgin, when he says to her: *You have wounded my heart, my sister, my spouse* (Song 4.9); or in the Septuagint version, *You have ravished my heart*. Also, in the same Scriptures, this Son of God is called, *The spirit of our mouth* (Lam. 4.20), "our spirit," that is, soul of our soul, heart of our heart.

All these hearts are found in the Mother of love and make up a single heart in her because all the faculties of the superior and interior part of her soul have always been perfectly united with one another. Moreover, both Jesus, who is the heart of his Father, as well as the divine Spirit, who is the heart of the Father and the Son, have been given to her to be the spirit of her spirit, the soul of her soul and the heart of her heart.

But to understand better what we mean by the heart of the blessed Virgin, we must know that just as we adore in God three hearts, which are in fact a single heart, and just as we adore in the Man-God three hearts, which are one and the same heart, so also we honor in the Mother of God three hearts, which are a single heart.

The first heart in the blessed Trinity is the Son of God, who is the heart of his Father, as we have said earlier. The second is the Holy Spirit, who is the heart of the Father and the Son. The third is divine love, one of the adorable attributes of the divine essence, which is the heart of the Father, the Son and the Holy Spirit. These three hearts are an utterly simple and unique heart with which the three eternal Persons love one another with as sublime a love as they deserve and with which they love us as well with an incomparable love.

The first heart of the Man-God is his bodily heart, which is divinized, as are all the other parts of his sacred body through their hypostatic union with the divine Person of the eternal Word. The second is his spiritual heart, that is, the superior part of his holy soul containing his memory, understanding and will, which have been divinized in a special way by the hypostatic union. The third is his divine heart, the Holy Spirit, which has always animated and enlivened his adorable humanity more than his own soul and heart ever did. These three hearts in this admirable Man-God are but a single heart, because his divine heart is the soul, the heart and the life of his spiritual and bodily heart. He grounds them in such a perfect union with himself that these three hearts are but a single unique heart, filled with an infinite love toward the blessed Trinity and an inconceivable love toward men.

The first heart of the Mother of God is the bodily heart enclosed in her virginal breast. The second is her spiritual heart, the heart of her soul, which is indicated by these words of the Holy Spirit: *Omnis gloria Filiae Regis ab intus,* "All the glory of the King's daughter originates from her interior" (see Ps. 45.14), that is, in her heart and in her inmost soul, of which we will speak more later. The third heart of this divine Virgin is the one she refers to when she says: *I sleep and my heart is awake;* that is, according to the explanation of many holy doctors, while I give my body the needed rest, my son Jesus, who is my heart and whom I love as my own heart, is always watching over me and for me.

The first of these hearts is bodily, but totally spiritualized by grace and by the Spirit of God who fills it completely.

The second is spiritual, but divinized, not by the hypostatic union like the spiritual heart of Jesus, which we just mentioned, but by an eminent participation in the divine perfections, as we shall see in the following pages.

The third is divine, indeed God himself, since it is the Son of God.

These three hearts of the Mother of God are but a single heart through the most holy and most intimate bond that ever existed or will exist, next to the hypostatic union. Referring to these three hearts, or rather to this unique heart, the Holy Spirit uttered twice these divine words: *Mary kept all these things in her heart* (Lk. 2.19,51).

First she preserved all the mysteries and marvels of her Son's life in some way in her material, bodily heart, source of life and seat of love and all the other passions, because every movement and beat of this virginal heart, all the functions of material life that flowed from it and all the activities of the aforementioned passions were at the service of Jesus and everything that occurred in him. There was love to love him; hatred to hate everything opposed to him, that is sin; joy to rejoice in his glory and splendor; sorrow to grieve over his labors and sufferings; and so on with the other passions.

Second, she preserved them in her heart, that is, in the noblest part of her soul, in the innermost recesses of her spirit. For all the faculties of the superior part of her soul were occupied unceasingly in contemplating and adoring everything that happened in the life of her Son down to the least detail.

Third, she preserved them in her heart, that is in her son Jesus, who was the spirit of her spirit and the heart of her heart. He preserved them for her, suggested them to her and recalled them to mind when it was opportune to serve as nourishment for her soul in contemplation and so that she might honor and adore them as they deserved and repeat them to the holy apostles and disciples, who would then preach them to the faithful.

This is what we mean by the admirable heart of the beloved of God. It is a perfect image of the adorable heart of God and of the Man-God.

Bérulle and the French School, 326–30.

6.10   The Vow of Martyrdom

(St. John Eudes, O.C. 12, 135–37)

Elevation to Jesus to offer oneself to him as a sacrifice and victim which must be immolated to his glory and his pure love.

Oh my most lovable Jesus, I adore you and glorify you endlessly in the most bloody martyrdom you suffered through your Passion and Cross.

I adore you and bless you with all my might in the state of offering and victim in which you are present in the Blessed Sacrament of the altar, where you are continually sacrificed for the glory of your Father and out of love for us.

I honor and venerate you in the most sorrowful martyrdom suffered at the foot of the Cross by your Holy Mother.

I praise you in the martyrdoms of your saints who endured so many atrocious torments for love of you.

I adore and bless all the thoughts, intents and infinite love you have had from all eternity with regard to all the blessed Martyrs there ever were in your holy Church since the beginning and will continue to be until the end of the world.

I adore and venerate, in every way I can, your extreme desire and most ardent thirst to suffer and die in your members until the end of the world, in order to fulfill the mystery of your Holy passion and glorify your Father through suffering and death until the end of time.

In honor of and in homage to all these things, and in union with the boundless love in which you offered yourself to the Father from the very first moment of your incarnation, as a sacrifice and victim, in order to be immolated for his glory and for love of us through the most sorrowful martyrdom of the Cross; in union also with the love of your Holy Mother and all your holy Martyrs, I offer and abandon myself, I vow and consecrate myself to you, my Lord Jesus, in the capacity of sacrifice and victim, that I may suffer in body and soul, according to your pleasure and with the help of your holy grace, all manner of pain and torments, even to shedding my blood and sacrificing my life for you through any death pleasing to you; and this, for your sole glory and for pure love of you.

I solemnly promise, Oh my Lord Jesus, never to revoke, that is to say, never to make a formal act of disavowal of this my oblation, consecration and sacrifice of myself to the glory of your Divine Majesty. And should there arise an occasion on which I should have to choose between dying or renouncing your holy faith, or else doing something of consequence against your divine will, I make a vow and promise to you, as firm and constant as possible, while trusting in your infinite goodness and the help of your grace, to confess, acknowledge, adore and glorify you in the presence of everyone, at the price of my blood, my life and all the martyrdoms and torments imaginable, and to suffer a thousand deaths, with all the tortures of earth and hell, rather than deny you or do anything serious that is contrary to your holy will.

Oh good Jesus, receive and accept this vow of mine and this sacrifice which I make to you of my life and my being in homage to and by the merits of the most divine sacrifice you made of yourself to your Father on the Cross. Look upon me henceforth as an offering and victim dedicated to be wholly immolated to the glory of your holy name. Grant, through your great mercy, that my whole life may be a perpetual sacrifice of love and praise for you. Let me live a life that may perpetually imitate and honor your own life and that of your Blessed Mother and your holy martyrs. May never a day go by without my suffering something for love of you. May I die a death in keeping with your holy death.

Lectionary, 196–98

CHAPTER SEVEN

The Theology of the French School

T he general overview we have taken of the four great masters of the French School has, perhaps, already allowed us to recognize a number of recurring accents and several major emphases in this well-structured spiritual doctrine. We can, indeed, speak of a *school of spirituality* in the strict sense of the term. Before discussing the principal themes of the French School, it is most important to remember that this doctrine was addressed to all Christians. This teaching, so deeply rooted in the Scriptures and in the Fathers of the Church, was meant as much for laywomen and men and for men and women religious as for priests. Sometimes the doctrine of Bérulle and his followers has been reduced to what they had to say about the priesthood. Actually, Bérulle, no less than Olier and John Eudes, sought to bring about renewal of the Christian life in all the faithful. Olier and John Eudes, as we have seen, pursued this goal through the countless missions they preached and by the writings that resulted from that experience. Their message to priests, first of all, concerned the application of the great principles of the Christian life. Olier would insist that "Holy Orders presuppose a Christian who has reached perfection." Furthermore, a Spiritual Directory (*Pietas Seminarii*) for use by the directors and the seminarians at Saint-Sulpice contains not one clerical overtone and can be used as the foundation for Christians in every state of life.

It is clear, then, that if we speak of the theology of the "four great masters," we mean, more precisely, a spiritual doctrine whose purpose was to nourish an authentic Christian life. Their frequent use of the word *Christian*[1] indicates the major thrust of their teaching, even if what has been called their mystical christocentrism forms a most coherent and solid doctrinal totality. While they were not professional theologians, they had all received an excellent theological formation at the Sorbonne. They all read the Bible and the church fathers regularly and seriously. For these reasons, the various elements of their thought fit together extremely well and constitute a synthesis of spiritual theology.

God is God

It is well known that the complete conversion of Maurice Clavel (1920–1979), a French playwright and novelist, was due to his discovery of Bérulle, and his reading of Paul Cochois's book awakened in him a dormant sense of God as absolute Being.[2] The primary message that comes to us from Bérulle and his disciples is that of the grandeur and the holiness of God. Our response to this reality must be an attitude of adoration, the virtue of religion carried to the point of total consecration of oneself. "The first thing necessary is to look at

God and not at oneself; to do nothing through self-consideration or self-seeking, but only through a gaze fixed purely and solely on God."[3] We must remember that, for Bérulle, the words *gaze* and *to look at* have a very special meaning. They do not mean only a simple or single attention, nor even contemplation. To *look at* God means, as Cochois has pointed out, "to give assent to God as one's End and to long wholeheartedly for him." This is an attitude of love and acceptance as much as of veneration. Bérulle's thought is reflected in Elizabeth of the Trinity's definition of *adoration*: "the ecstacy of love." If, however, the fundamental attitude of the creature is loving adoration, it is because "nothing is as great as God and whatever renders homage to God."[4]

Bérulle's disciples were deeply impressed by statements like these, which reacted to a certain kind of humanism that threatened our awareness of the grandeur, the transcendence and the holiness of God. On this point, Denis Amelote wrote:

> He [Bérulle] is the one who has reawakened in our days a virtue which had been dead and buried; he has aroused our century to remember its most ancient duty.... In this day and age, ... we see souls that act more through familiarity than reverence, there are many Christians who love God, but few who revere him.[5]

For Bérulle, the human being is a creature who belongs to God and who exists for God. By our very nature, we exist in a condition of *belonging to* and servitude. Adoration is the means by which we ratify this servitude. "To serve God willingly and to rejoice in this servitude is supreme delight."[6] The soul must forget itself, lose itself, annihilate itself, become "a pure capacity for God," and thus be filled by God. Condren and Olier would speak of sacrifice "in order to acknowledge God and render homage to him" for all the divine perfections.

Bérulle did not think of adoration or self-offering

merely in terms of isolated acts, but also and above all as a *state* of adoration: offering and abandonment of the creature to honor God in the depth of one's being, acceptance of the Creator's possession of the creature's very self. Our perfection lies in giving consent to the divine will:

> and since he has chosen us, prepared us, lifted us up to himself, made us worthy of him, let us not fail to recognize his vocation [his call], let us not resist his grace, let us not be attached to ourselves, to engage in perishable works, but let us accomplish eternal deeds.[7]

Condren, Olier and John Eudes, each in his own way, would insist, at one and the same time, on the grandeur of God and on the importance of adoration and the virtue of religion. Thus, we can understand why they all attached such importance to the dignity and integrity of liturgical prayer. In the Eucharist and the Divine Office, the whole Church gives to the Father the honor due to him, in offering the sacrifice of Jesus, in union with his prayer as son and priest.

The christocentrism of the French School needs to be well understood. By definition, Christianity recognizes Jesus Christ as its center. Each school of spirituality, however, follows its own way of contemplating Christ and emphasizing one or another aspect of his mystery. Each proposes a particular way of following Christ. Bérulle and his followers attached great importance to contemplation of the Incarnate Word. In the divinized humanity of Jesus Christ, they adored the perfect *servant*, the true religious of God, the perfect adorer. Over and above Christ's times of prayer or saving deeds, the union of his humanity with his divinity is seen to constitute a permanent *state*. He is the sole mediator of our worship, through whom and in whom every creature can offer glory to the Father.

Thus, the loving contemplation of a Christian is to be

directed toward the grace-bearing mysteries of the life of Jesus. Devotion to the infancy of Jesus, to his hidden life, to his Passion, Resurrection, Ascension and to the Eucharist is neither marginal nor secondary. They all lead, always, to the same mystery of Jesus "in his two natures, in his divine person, in all his glory."[8] We think here of Bérulle's masterpiece, published in 1623: *Discours de l'Estat et des grandeurs de Jésus.*

Beyond the exterior events that marked Christ's life, Bérulle would have us contemplate "the interior and spiritual activities of the soul of Jesus in his relations with the Father."[9] Olier would speak of "the interior of Jesus," or his "sentiments" and "dispositions." Father Bourgoing would evoke the "threefold gaze" of Jesus: "towards God the Father, to glorify him; towards himself, in view of his self-sacrifice; and towards our souls to sanctify and reconcile us to God."[10]

For Bérulle, adoration always became love, desire, "communion." The Christian life, life in Christ, is, in the end, the life of Jesus in us. The leit-motif of Bérulle's entire spiritual doctrine can be found in the words of Paul: "It is no longer I who live, but Christ lives in me" (Gal. 2.20). The essence of prayer, according to Bérulle and his disciples, is an echo as well as a fulfillment and interiorization of the *Maranatha* of the first Christians. It is a cry for Christ to "come and live in us," as he lived in Mary. Olier would address Jesus in these words:

> You have always given me this desire to be not only your image, but another self for you, as you want this to happen in the hearts of all your faithful. (*Mémoires* 2:268)

This coming of Jesus in us reaches into the very heart of our being to transform our existence totally. This school takes Paul's words literally: "Christ lives in me." "Let your mind be that of Christ" (Phil. 2.3); "may Christ dwell by faith in your hearts" (Eph. 3.17). All spiritual masters, following the church fathers, have commented on these texts. The French School acknowledged them as the center and summit of the entire Christian life. This is not only unity of mind, nor simple conformity to the example of Jesus, but, more deeply, *adherence*, communion with his life, his states and his mysteries, his interior sentiments, attitudes and dispositions. St. John Eudes has written that the "Christian life" is the continuation and the fulfillment of the life of Jesus Christ:

> You see what we mean by the Christian life: it is a continuation and a fulfillment of the life of Jesus. All our actions must be a continuation of the actions of Jesus. We are to be, as it were, Jesus on earth, so as to continue his life and his works, to do and to suffer all that we do and suffer in a holy, divine manner, in the spirit of Jesus. That means, with the holy and divine dispositions and intentions with which Jesus carried out his actions and his sufferings. . . . "[11]

This understanding of the Christian life can be found also in Dom Marmion and in Elizabeth of the Trinity.

Since Mary was the first and the most perfect Christian, "living in Jesus, through Jesus, and for Jesus," prayer is addressed to "Jesus living in Mary." Marian devotion, this school believes, will flow naturally from contemplation of Jesus and will be one aspect of our union with him. Olier, John Eudes, and later, Grignion de Montfort were to develop devotion to Mary in their own manner, but always in fidelity to Bérulle's deeply theological and christological tradition.

Eucharistic communion is the means par excellence for communion with Jesus:

> Indeed, Christ lives in the sacrament only to share all his marvels as nourishment, to extend their vitality and virtue: in his sovereign worship of God, his gentle charity towards others, his profound self-annihilation, his vehement opposition to the world and to sin.[12]

Silent prayer and meditation are to be centered on Jesus: Jesus before our eyes, in our heart, in our hands—that is: adoration, communion and cooperation. Everything was meant to let Jesus come to live and act within us through his Spirit.

The Spirit of Jesus

If the Christian life is, indeed, nothing other than the very life of Jesus in us, it is brought about within us by the Holy Spirit. A Christian, according to Olier, is "one in whom the Spirit of Jesus is present." "Let the Spirit act"; "surrender to the Holy Spirit of Jesus," John Eudes would say, "is the secret of secrets, the devotion of devotions."

In his *Vie de Jésus*, Bérulle multiplies his reflections on the activity of the Holy Spirit in the realization of the Incarnation. This same Spirit forms Jesus in us:

> We are in the hands of the Holy Spirit who rescues us from sin and binds us to Jesus, as the Spirit of Jesus which proceeds from him, belongs to him and has been sent by him.[13]

Again, he would write: "I desire that the Spirit of Jesus Christ be the Spirit of my spirit and the life of my life.[14]

Jean-Jacques Olier, who tells us that he had "asked insistently for the Spirit," affirms that he felt the presence and influence of the Spirit in his life. He speaks unceasingly of this Spirit of Jesus Christ. It is not by chance that the entire first chapter of his *Catechism of an Interior Life* is consecrated to the Holy Spirit. Olier insists "in season and out of season" on the positive, interior attitude of docility to the Holy Spirit, as Paul calls for in his exhortations to the Galatians (chapters 4 and 5) and to the Romans (chapter 8): "Let yourselves be led by the Spirit." Olier's advice can be summed up in a simple phrase: "We must abandon ourselves entirely to the Holy

Spirit and let the Spirit act in us" (*Mémoires* 7:241). His own spiritual and apostolic journey illustrates this docility that he prayed for with such insistence and lived out in such fidelity. St. John Eudes, disciple of Bérulle and de Condren and friend of Olier, expresses the same convictions in his life and teaching.[15]

This great devotion to the Holy Spirit explains why the feast of Pentecost was so important to Bérulle and his followers. In Condren's eyes, it was the principal and most useful of all feasts.[16] As for Olier, he asked the artist, Le Brun, to produce a large painting of the Pentecost scene. This canvas was placed over the main altar in the seminary chapel, reminding everyone that the source of the entire Christian spirit and of every "apostolic spirit" was nothing other than the Spirit of Jesus, received in the prayer of the Church: the prayer of the disciples with Mary.

The Church: the Body of Christ

The work of Father Mersch on the mystical body of Christ[17] has helped us realize the extent to which the French School reaffirmed the value of the mystical vision of the Church, as developed by the church fathers in their reflections on the Captivity Letters. Our contemporary theology of the mystical body owes much to Bérulle and his followers, and we find in the Dogmatic Constitution on the Church of Vatican II many of the themes they enunciated.

We do not have to insist at length on this aspect of their doctrine and their contemplation. We must, however, highlight the striking difference between their understanding and that of other "churchmen" of their day. The large, profoundly mystical vision of the French School was a dramatic departure from the extrinsic, too exclusively juridical, centralized concept of the Church that seems to have prevailed in their era. They were, without a doubt, realistic enough to recognize the blemishes and wrinkles in the Church. They also contemplated the Church as the spouse of Christ and, ultimately, Christ himself. They insisted, as well, on the *construction* of this body. Condren or Amelote asserted, "Everything we do in this world is the building up of this Christ. All the saints labored for this purpose." The Church, then, is nothing in itself and can do nothing except in Jesus.

Jesus continues his life in the Church. Bérulle and his followers insist again and again on two aspects of the mystery of the Church: liturgical prayer and mission. They understand that the liturgical year enables us to relive the states and mysteries of Jesus.[18] The preaching and commitment of missionaries, under the inspiration of the apostolic Spirit of Jesus, are the continuation and the fulfillment of the mission of the Incarnate Word.[19]

The Priests of Jesus

A prevailing opinion concerning Bérullian spirituality is that it is totally centered on the priesthood. This comes from the influence of seminaries and from what most of these individuals had to say about the dignity and the responsibility of priests. It is, indeed, true that the primary objective of the pastoral and spiritual reform they designed and initiated was directed to the "sanctification of the clergy." It is also true that one of the most visible consequences of their activity was the establishment of major seminaries. Thus, they contributed to a particular notion of the priesthood.

All of the masters of the French School were certainly filled with acute concern for the dignity, the holiness and the formation of priests. As Cognet has pointed out, "Bérulle was haunted by concern for priestly perfection." Olier was conscious of having received from Jesus the mandate "to bring contemplation into the priesthood"

(*Mémoires* 7:290). All of them were involved in the foundation of seminaries. They perceived the essential mission of the priest, the urgent need for a strong correlation between the priest's life and ministry, and the call to sanctity implicit in his vocation and mission. This urgency was clearly recognized by all the reformers of this era. They were aware of the lamentable situation of the clergy: the ignorance and negligence of many priests and bishops. There was a need for authentic spiritual renewal, solid formation and a true discernment in regard to vocations. Thus, Olier stated as an objective for those "who come to be formed" in his ideal seminary: to come "to know who they are in the Church of God and to understand the grace of their state."[20]

A closer examination of this point is necessary:

1. Most of the writings of the masters of the French School are addressed to all Christians. Thus, we have seen the *Discourse on the State and the Glories of Jesus*, the *Life and Kingdom of Jesus*, the *Catechism of an Interior Life*, the *Introduction to Christian Life and Virtues*. Bérulle, Olier, and John Eudes worked as much for the laity and religious as for priests, especially if we are to judge by their letters. All were missionaries who labored for the renewal of the whole Church. Their apostolic activity was never specialized, nor limited to a single category of Christians, even though they dedicated a great amount of their time and energy to the service of priests. There were strategic and theological or mystical reasons for this attention. They viewed sanctification of the clergy as the best means of assuring a true evangelization of the people. Also, Christ continues his life and mission in the world in a particular way through priests, whom he inspires and impels by his own Spirit. Nonetheless, all the great masters clearly understood that *ministerial* priesthood was meant to serve the *baptismal* priesthood of all Christians. Free from a spirit of negative clericalism,

they insisted on the priestly dimension of the Christian life. In this, they were faithful to Paul's teaching in Romans 12, and foreshadowed concepts reiterated in the documents of Vatican II.

2. The masters of the French School were not "professional" theologians. Certain historians find that Bérulle's concept of the priesthood is not always coherent,[21] and the same opinion has been expressed regarding John Eudes.[22] Nevertheless, their thought and teachings on the ministry of bishops and priests are, on the whole, most reliable. They are, in fact, founded on the writings of the New Testament and the church fathers. Their ecclesiology and their sense of the apostolic spirit kept them from pietistic individualism. They located priestly ministry within service to the whole Church, but they saw priests as the representatives of Jesus, "true pastors in Christ the pastor." To what extent were they marked by the ideas of Pseudo-Dionysius regarding the mystical hierarchies and his questionable notion of the grace that "flows" from bishops, through priests, to the faithful? Studies are needed in this area, following those already undertaken by Dupuy, Cochois and Chaillot. It is not difficult, however, to go beyond the limits of the French School's thought, founded on the seventeenth century conviction that Dionysius was the disciple of Paul, the first bishop of Paris, and a great mystical theologian. Actually, the writings of "Pseudo-Dionysius" date from the sixth century.[23]

3. The essence of the grace, message and heritage these masters bequeathed to us can be found at the level of a spiritual conviction regarding the mission, dignity and holiness of the priest. Their primary concern is the *spiritual life of priests*, bound to their consecration and their mission in the church.[24]

This heritage and this message are in harmony with certain orientations of Vatican II, the Council that has treated the Church and apostolic ministry more fully than any other. Both emphasize these points:

a. a great desire, inspired by the Spirit, to work for renewal of the church through the spiritual renewal of priests; a concern to promote authentic interiority and to raise up "apostolic men" who are moved by the Spirit more than by material desires or interests;

b. the sense of priestly holiness, which comes from the priest's personal union with Jesus—with his intentions, desires and prayer and, ultimately, with his Spirit. Bérulle would insist: "We ought to act only through the Spirit of JESUS."

c. a deep spiritual, ecclesial, personal and corporate experience. All these men were touched by God, experienced God and shared their experience; they all received from the Spirit a mystical sense of the Church, one rooted in theology but, at the same time, most realistic.

We must also note, in their thought, the idea of the bishop as father of his church and of his priests, and their great devotion to the Eucharist and to Mary. Finally, they were, themselves, true priests of Jesus.

Mary, Mother of Jesus

The major place given to Mary in the doctrine of Bérulle and his followers has already been pointed out. Mary stands at the heart of the Christian mystery because the Word became incarnate in her, because she was perfectly docile to the Holy Spirit, and because she is, for all time, the queen and mother of all men and women.

In his *Vie de Jésus*, Bérulle has left us a wonderful theological and mystical presentation on the Annunciation. Nothing can replace a reading of these pages. Mary

is, in the Church, what the dawn is in the heavens, immediately preceding the sun . . . but she is more than the dawn, because she not only precedes Jesus, but carries him and brings him forth into the world.[25]

Cochois tells us that Bérulle sings the praises of Mary in "pages of exquisite purity":

> Sanctified from the first moment of her existence . . . she
> was born with little attention or clamor. . . . If earth did
> not think of her, the first and most tender gaze of God on
> the earth was directed towards this humble, unknown,
> unrecognized Virgin. It was, at the time, the most exalted
> thought which the Most High bore towards all that had
> been created.[26]
>
> God exists and accomplishes in her more than her own
> being. . . . [27]
>
> She enters into the love and adoration which Jesus offers
> to God, his Father. . . . She loses the use of her own life
> and interiority in the abyss of the new, interior life of her
> Son . . . and she bears the impression and the communi-
> cation of his divine actions.[28]

From this time on, Mary is queen of all humanity with
a "right and a power to give Jesus to souls."[29] The French
School's vow of servitude to Mary rests on this foundation. This vow, as Cochois notes, "is, thus, not a work of
supererogation, but one flowing from the place reserved
for the Mother of the Incarnate Word in the design of
God."[30]

Bérulle's Marian "devotion" was both highly theological and full of tenderness, as it was, again, with his followers. Each one, in his own way, cherished a loving attachment to the mother of Jesus. This devotion found
expression in pilgrimages, prayers, the vow of servitude
or of slavery. We know how Olier transformed Condren's
little prayer into a prayer to "Jesus living in Mary." John
Eudes wrote wonderful pages on the heart of Mary:

> Jesus lives and reigns in Mary so fully that he is the soul
> of her soul, the spirit of her spirit, the heart of her heart;
> we can thus readily affirm that the Heart of Mary is
> Jesus.[31]
>
> For John Eudes, Mary is truly the icon of Jesus.[32]

When we look to Olier, there is one particular characteristic to note. He was very much aware of the Virgin's

presence in his daily life, and he spread devotion to Mary in his parish. More than anything, however, especially at the seminary, he insisted, as did Bourgoing, that Mary was the queen of priests. In his eyes, Mary was the model of the clergy. The feast of the Presentation of the Virgin, on 21 November, was essential in the seminary's liturgy. It was the occasion on which the priests and seminarians renewed their commitments to God and to the Church. This feast would also be celebrated solemnly by other members of the Bérulle School and by the Carmelites in France. In fact, up until Vatican II, the Carmelite nuns in France always renewed their vows on the feast of the Presentation of Mary.[33] Studies on Mary and the priesthood exist,[34] but further research on this topic remains to be done. The Bérulle School's devotion to Mary in reference to Jesus authenticates the theological integrity of this type of devotion. Grignion de Montfort would prove to be one of its most dedicated proponents.

Bérulle and his followers brought a strong sense of pedagogy to the transmission of their spiritual doctrine. Cochois wrote that Bérulle had "but one passion in his life: to make known to souls the unsearchable riches of the Incarnate Word, so that they might have life through them." Like other schools of spirituality, the Bérulle School sought to initiate its disciples to union with Jesus, teaching them to "live totally for God in Jesus Christ," to have Jesus "be formed in them" (cf. Gal. 4.19). They promoted this formation through certain practical means and did not hesitate to create new pedagogical methods. A thorough study of this aspect of their teaching needs to be undertaken. Here, we shall simply give a brief presentation of a few of the exercises they suggest. These can be compared to methods suggested by St. Francis de Sales, whom several of these individuals had met and whom all of them admired.

The Prayer of the Church was, for all of those in the French School, the heart of the adoration, sacrifice and

worship of the Church. It was a major means of formation. They spoke and wrote frequently about the mysteries of Jesus as celebrated in the liturgy. According to
their vision of the Christian life, they insisted on the
solemnities of the Incarnate Word: the Annunciation,
Christmas, the Infancy, Holy Week, Eastertide and Pentecost. The feast of the Presentation of Jesus in the
Temple, 2 February, the feast of the light of Christ "who
enlightens the nations," was the occasion of profound
spiritual experiences for several of them.

They did not hesitate to compose particular offices:
the office of Jesus (Bérulle); of the Heart of Mary and of
the Heart of Jesus (John Eudes); of the interior life of
Jesus, and of Mary (Olier). They solemnized already existing feasts, as Olier did for the Presentation of Mary in
the Temple (21 November). All of this was meant to
form true Christians inspired and impelled by the very
Spirit of Jesus.

Initiation to prayer was a permanent concern for the
masters of the French School. Condren, Olier, John
Eudes, and later, John Baptist de La Salle would propose
methods of prayer and even texts for meditation. Their
followers sought to adopt and popularize these methods,
with moderate success. The main aspects of Sulpician
prayer, for example, would initiate generations of priests
to prayer: Jesus before our eyes, in our heart, in our
hands. The *midday prayers* of John Eudes are not as
much a form of "particular examen" as a time truly to
adore Jesus and to enter into communion with his dispositions. This is exactly what prayer in the Bérulle School
is all about. To foster such prayer, these leaders composed wonderful prayers or *elevations*: to the Trinity, to
Jesus, to Mary.

Worship of the Word and the Eucharist was also emphasized. The Bible was not only the principal source of
their doctrine, but was also their prayer book. They insisted repeatedly on the prayerful reading of Scripture.

Olier, especially, has left us splendid pages on the great respect that was to be had for Scripture in the "house" of Saint-Sulpice. Moreover, every evening in a *Scripture conference*, he commented on a passage of the Bible for the seminarians. In his mind, devotion to the Bible went hand-in-hand with devotion to the Blessed Sacrament. He promoted both, as much in the seminary as in Saint-Sulpice parish.[35]

Spiritual direction was a particular object of attention for the French School, as evidenced in their letters. Bérulle would exclaim, "to govern a soul is to govern a world." Further, a careful reading of the letters of Condren, Olier, or John Eudes allows us to see this same emphasis.

The vows of servitude to Jesus and to Mary have already been discussed, an object of heated controversy. Bérulle, probably, committed a pedagogical blunder in wanting to impose the vow of servitude to Mary on the Carmelite nuns in 1615, even though this vow was already a common practice among the priests of the Oratory at the time. As Cochois has very clearly demonstrated, such commitments follow directly from baptismal consecration, which they ratify and renew. This is another important area that calls for further study in terms of the history of spirituality as well as of spiritual pedagogy. In fact, many saints have recommended such *self-offerings*. We have only to think of the *Suscipe* of St. Ignatius, the *surrender* of St. Therese Couderc (26 June 1864) or the prayer of Teresa of Jesus: "I am yours, I was born for you, what do you ask of me?" When Father Voillaume speaks of a *second call*, he seems to be walking this same path.

All the *devotions* of the French School, in the last analysis, are only means to reach its one, single goal: to help women and men who seek to respond to the Lord's call in their lives. These *pedagogical methods* are designed to achieve this goal: "surrender to the Spirit" of Jesus, "adhere" to his dispositions, "enter into his prayer." This means to renounce and deny oneself and be filled with the Spirit. It means to strive for communion with the inner attitudes of Jesus, to be one with his *looking at* the Father in adoration and praise; with his *looking at* others in love and service; with *looking at* oneself in forgetfulness of self and self-annihilation. In this way, the French School's theology proclaims, the life of the risen Christ will invade the hearts and the lives of Christians who are renewed by the Spirit.

DOCUMENTS FOR CHAPTER 7

7.1 A School of Spirituality

What is a school of spirituality?

A spirituality or a spiritual tradition is a certain, symbolic way of hearing and living the gospel. This "way" is conditioned by a period, a "fertilized soil" the particular influence of a specific milieu. It can be incarnated in a clearly identified group of human beings and can continue, historically, enriched or impoverished.... In this way, a "spiritual tradition" or a "school" of spirituality comes to be.

There are a number of elements that describe a school of spirituality:

1) The most noteworthy characteristic is a given number of emphases or constants regarding one or another aspect of Christian faith or life in the Spirit.

However, as J. de Guibert has remarked, "each of the great spiritual schools constitutes a totality, bringing into unity and balance the essential elements of every healthy spiritual life."

2) *Each spiritual school or tradition is characterized by a certain way of praying and a specific understanding of mission.* The Church that "worships and prayers" and the Church that proclaims the gospel to the world do so in different ways. A collection like "Prayer for All Times" is meant to present the many paths of prayer found in diverse spiritual traditions.

3) Schools of spirituality nearly always have their own pedagogical methods, implicit or explicit. The Rule of St. Benedict, the Exercises of St. Ignatius, Teresa of Jesus' way of perfection, methods of prayer, all express and envision practices to nourish a given spirituality.

4) Each school has it *preferred biblical texts* that call for close attention.

5) Finally, schools of spirituality are rooted in an *intense spiritual experience.* As de Guibert has written:

In the beginning, there was always a unique experience which led to a surprising realization. . . . In general, the experience that gives birth to a new spiritual school is twofold: the experience of the personal, interior life of the founder, and the experience of spiritual formation of the first disciples, both successfully achieved in a new form.

> (Toulouse, *Leçons de théologie spirituelle*, 1946;
> 117).
> R. Deville, *Approches ecclésiologiques des traditions spirituelles*, in "Discernement et traditions spirituelles," Session USMF CPR, 1984, Francheville; 16–17.

7.2 Spiritual Directive for a Seminary

The primary and the ultimate goal of this Institute is to live in a supreme manner for God in Our Lord Jesus Christ, so that the interior life of God's Son penetrates to the most intimate depth of our heart, and that each of us will be able to say with confidence what St. Paul said of himself: "It is no longer I who live, but Christ lives in me" (Gal. 2.20). This will be the only hope and the sole thought that fill us all; the one exercise in which we shall engage is this: to live the life of Christ interiorly and to show it forth in our mortal bodies.

> *Pietas Seminarii*, trans. F. Tollu, éd. Amiot, 1954;
> 163.

7.3 The Religion of Jesus Christ

Our Lord Jesus Christ came into this world to bring love and respect for his Father and to establish his reign and his religion. He never asked anything else of him during his lifetime. In the 33 years that he lived on earth, he laid these foundations. His incessant desire was to open the minds and hearts of the faithful to this religion. He foresaw that they had been destined to be the ones in whom he would instill his own religion in order to honor his Father through them as he honored him in himself.

He requested this grace for men and he merited it for them during his life. Through his death he not only continued this prayer, but also gave clear witness to the respect and love he had for his Father, which are the two realities that constitute the virtue of religion. He experienced his Father to be so pure and holy that he could see nothing that deserved to live or even exist in his presence. This was what he affirmed by the death that he suffered in order to witness to this truth and bring it to light.

He died not only out of reverence but also from love. For he accepted his death most willingly and joyfully because he saw that the Father was both satisfied and pleased by it. He had understood that no worthy reparation had been offered to God for the sins committed against him. He died then to satisfy him completely and to leave nothing for which he was not abundantly satisfied.

In this way he gives an example to Christians who commit themselves to Jesus' own religion, respect and love. He shows them that they must spare nothing to bear witness to genuine sentiments of religion, which will on occasion call for sacrifice. This will make their sacrifice more authentic than simply being content with a mere inner inclination, which can often be deceptive.

By all sorts of loving strategies, our Lord has continued after his death to procure for men this religion toward his Father. He gave them his own Spirit, the Spirit of God dwelling within him, so that he might plant within them the very sentiments of his own soul. In this way Jesus dilates his holy religion so that he and all Christians might become one religious of God.

Reigning in heaven, Jesus lives in the hearts and the pens of the evangelists in order to inculcate everywhere a sense of disdain for creatures and a respect for God alone. He lives in the hearts and mouths of his apostles and his disciples to proclaim everywhere the kingdom of God, thus obtaining an adoration worthy of his holy name and offering him perfectly obedient subjects and worshipers who respect him in spirit and truth. (Jn. 4.23).

The Spirit of God also fulfills his particular role in priests by continuing in them what he accomplished in Jesus Christ. Through their words, writings and example as well as in all other possible ways, the Spirit gives birth to the holy religion of God to whom we owe all adoration and respect while we hold all else in contempt. Everything outside of him is nothing but vanity and mere symbol. For all of created reality is only a flimsy shell of the being that is hidden in him but becomes visible in some way through the appearance of all that is visible. Every reflection will pass away (1 Cor. 7.31) on that day when God will no longer reveal himself through his reflections, but rather will plainly show forth all that he is. Once our spiritual sight is awakened and strengthened by the light of glory, then the world will no longer please us. We look beyond a shadow once the body that has cast it appears. We are no longer interested in a portrait once the actual person arrives. A mask loses its appeal when the face is uncovered. In the same way, all will seem to us mere appearance, mask and nothingness when God will reveal himself fully to our souls.

May God be adored in himself and may everything else perish before him in our spirit; for everything else is as nothing in his presence. In this spirit of religion let us anticipate the abnegation and universal sacrifice of all manner of being which is called to perish on God's behalf as a witness to his grandeur and holiness. May our faith be the light and the torch of our religion so that we may sacrifice every existing thing before God. For if Jesus Christ himself desired to be sacrificed because of the great respect and esteem he had for God and his holiness, how much more ought we to sacrifice everything for God and disdain all things. In this way we will value and see only the One who is true, the One who alone deserves to be esteemed and revered.

In the presence of the true God, no idols are to be adored. Everything must be reduced to ashes. Thus may all creation perish before my God. In his sacrifice our Lord claimed to annihilate everything and to sacrifice all things in himself because he had brought everything together in his person. Therefore, it is right that we condemn and sacrifice all things that are outside of him, since they are less holy for being less closely related to him. It is the true sign of our religion to offer everything in sacrifice to God and thus to testify how vile and despicable all things are in his presence. In this way we value and respect nothing other than him alone.

Finally our Lord comes to us in order to dilate his holy religion toward God and to multiply it in our souls. He remains on earth in the hands of priests as a host of praise so that we might commune in this spirit of host-victim, giving ourselves over to praising him and communing inwardly in the sentiments of his religion. He fills us with himself. He invades every part of us and anoints our soul, filling it with the interior dispositions of his religious spirit. Thus his soul and ours become one. He breathes into our souls a similar spirit of respect, love and praise; a spirit of the interior and exterior sacrifice of all things to the glory of God his Father. This is how he brings about out soul's communion in his religion so that we may be, as we said earlier, true religious of his Father.

Berulle and the French School, 217–19.

7.4 The Mystery of the Incarnation

Christ is ours by reason of His office (*par état*), and not merely because of certain actions; He is ours by birth, and not simply in virtue of His office: "He was born for us" (Isa. 9.6). He is ours forever, and not merely for a time; He is ours for all our needs and for all our uses; He is ours by the same power whereby the Father generates Him in Himself.

Jesus is a divine capacity for souls, and He is the source of the life whereby they live in Him.

There are in Jesus two wonderful capacities. By the one He is rendered capable of divinity, capable of the fullness of the divinity and of equality with God, though with dependence. The second is a capacity for souls; this He possesses in Himself, in His authority, in His power. For, if He has a capacity for the divinity, there is all the more reason way He should have a capacity for creatures. Our Lord receives this second capacity from the fullness of the divinity that is in Him; it makes Him a capacity for souls just as God is a capacity for His creatures: a capacity that contains, preserves, protects, and places souls in a continual and profound dependence upon Jesus and upon God. And it pleased Jesus Christ to institute the sacrament of His body in order to bind our souls to Himself, and to draw them into the plenitude of the divinity that abides in Him, by means of His lovable and adorable capacity to contain them and to give them life and subsistence in Himself. Thus we have a representation of that wondrous chain composed of three links, of which the Fathers speak. The first link binds the only Son to the eternal Father by the bond of consubstantiality and unity of essence. The second binds the Son to our nature by the unity of His sacred Person. The third binds this deified humanity, this Man-God, to the person of each of us, by the efficacious and singular virtue of the Sacrament of His body, which incorporates us in His sacred humanity and causes us to live in Him, to share His life as His members, and to live with Him in His Father. Thus man ascends to this deified flesh and even to God, while God descends to the flesh and even to us.

Jesus is all, and He must be all in us. And we must be nothing, treat ourselves as nothing, be nothing in ourselves, and be only in Him. . . . This is the work that we must begin on earth, and which will be consummated in heaven, where Jesus shall be all in all.

Œuvres de Piété. Paris: 1657; 33:530, 634.

7.5 A Contemporary Prayer

O my beloved Christ crucified for love, I would be a spouse for Thy Heart; I would cover Thee with glory, I would love Thee . . . unto death! But I feel my powerlessness and I ask Thee to clothe me in Thyself, to identify my soul with all the movements of Thy Soul; to submerge me, to invade me, to substitute Thyself for me, so that my life may be nothing but a radiation of Thy life. Come into me as Adorer, as Repairer, and as Savior.

O consuming Fire, Spirit of love, overshadow me, so that there may be produced in me something like an incarnation of the Word; let me be to Him an additional humanity in which He may renew the whole of His Mystery.

And Thou, O Father, lean down toward Thy poor little creature; see in her only the well-Beloved in whom Thou art well pleased.

Elizabeth of the Trinity, O.C.D.; 21 November 1904
(*Trinity Whom I Adore*; 58, 115, 131)

7.6 The Christian Spirit

In order to be a Christian, is it enough to have the dispositions that you have explained to me thus far?

No. Christians must also take part in all the mysteries of Jesus Christ; for our lovable Redeemer performed them in His person precisely in order that they might be the source of the most abundant and most special graces in His Church.

Did each mystery obtain a special grace for the Church?

Yes. Each mystery obtained for the Church sanctifying grace and a variety of dispositions and special graces which God confers upon purified souls when He pleases, but particularly at the times when the mysteries are solemnly commemorated....

What grace is wrought in us by the mystery of the Incarnation?

The grace of annihilation to all self-interest and all self-love.

What is meant by annihilation to all self-interest and self-love?

It means that, as by the sacred mystery of the Incarnation our Lord's sacred humanity was annihilated in its own person, in such wise that it no longer sought itself, no longer had any interest of its own, no longer acted for itself, since for its own personality of the Son of God, who sought only the interests of His Father whom He saw always and in all things—so we too must be annihilated to all our own designs, to all our own interests, and entertain only those of Jesus Christ, who is present within us in order to live in us for His Father. "Just as My Father, in sending Me to earth, cut away every root of self-seeking, when instead of giving Me a human personality, He united Me to a divine Person in order to make Me live for Him; so when you eat Me, you will live wholly for Me and not for yourselves, for I shall live in you. I shall fill your souls with My desires and My life, which will consume and annihilate in you all that is your own, so that it will be I, not you, that live and desire all things in you; and, thus annihilated in yourselves, you will be wholly clothed in Me."

Is this putting on of Christ another grace of the Incarnation?

Yes, for besides the fact that the mystery of the Incarnation, properly speaking, effects in us a complete stripping off and renunciation of ourselves, it likewise clothes us with our Lord, by a total consecration to God; just as on the day of the Incarnation our Lord wholly consecrated Himself and all His members to His Father, thereby sanctifying in advance each individual occasion which He and His members should ever have of serving and glorifying God.

On the most holy day of the Incarnation, did our Lord Jesus Christ offer His life and the lives of all His members to God His Father?

Yes, He offered them, and He still continues to make the same offering. He is still living in the same disposition that He had during His whole life. He never interrupts them, and He is ever offering Himself to God, in Himself and in all His members, in all the occasions that they have to serve, honor, and glorify Him. Our Lord in His divine Person is an altar, upon which all men are offered to God with all their actions and all their sufferings. This is that golden altar (Apoc. 8:3), on which every perfect sacrifice is consummated. The human nature of Jesus Christ and of all the faithful is the victim, His spirit is the fire, and the offering is made to God the Father, who is thus adored in spirit and in truth.

Catéchisme de la vie intérieure, ch. 1, p. 20; 477–79.

7.7 The Spirit of Jesus

Because we are children of God and one with the Son of God, as members of the body belong to its head, it follows necessarily that we must be animated by the same spirit. . . . So, the Holy Spirit was given to us to be the mind of our mind, the heart of our heart, the soul of our soul, and to always be with and within us.

Lectionary, 78.

As a necessary consequence, just as the members are animated by the spirit of the head and live of the same life, so too must we be animated by the spirit of Jesus, live of his life, walk in his ways, be clothed with his sentiments and inclinations, perform all our actions with the same dispositions and intentions with which he acted. In a word, we must continue and fulfill the life, religion and devotion which he had on earth.

Lectionary, 32.

I beg you to note well that the practice of practices, the secret of secrets, the devotion of devotions is to have no attachment to any particular practice, exercise, or devotion. Rather, in all your exercises and actions, you must have great care to submit yourself to the Holy Spirit of Jesus. Give yourself to his Spirit humbly, trustingly, and detached from everything. When the Spirit finds you free from attachment to your own spirit, your own devotion and dispositions, he will be able to act in you in the fullness of his power and liberty, according to his own desires. This Holy Spirit will fill you with the dispositions and sentiments, and devotions he wills, and he will lead you by pathways that are pleasing to him.

Œuvres complètes 1:452

7.8 The Whole Christ

[This text is an excerpt from a manuscript that reproduces conferences by Condren or his disciple, Denis Amelote.]
What does this mean: the Christ of God?

Does not this word, "Christ," which is so frequently found in the Scriptures, always refer to Our Lord, Jesus? Do you understand something else?

I shall answer that the word, "Christ," in the Bible and in the Fathers, has two meanings:

In the first place, it refers to the person of Our Lord Jesus Christ, Son of God and true man.

Secondly, the word, "Christ," has a more extended meeting and signifies the Christ of God. According to St. Paul, this means the whole Christ, entire and fulfilled. In clearer terms, this refers to the assembly of all the elect, united with Our Lord Jesus Christ and constituting together a single person, the whole Christ, perfect Man, as the Apostle says, made up of Jesus Christ and his Church, that is, the faithful.

Thus, this Christ is a body, not like a human body, but in a way beyond our understanding, in which Jesus Christ is the Head and the faithful are the other parts and members. Jesus Christ is the Lord, the life, the heart, in a word, all that gives life to the rest. Even more, he is the Person, he is the cause of the entire Body of Christ. If Christ praises God, we must say that it is Jesus Christ who praises God. If Christ speaks or suffers, it is Jesus Christ who speaks and who suffers. . . . Do you want proof that it is Jesus Christ who speaks in me? St. Paul says, "I live, but it is Jesus Christ who lives in me; it is no longer I." It is he who suffers . . . , crying out from heaven, Saul, Saul, you persecute Christians; why do you persecute me? I am Jesus of Nazareth, whom you persecute.

God's greatest plan has been to make this wonderful Christ, whole and entire. Today, everything we do in this world is the building up of this Christ. All the saints work to this end. The goal of ministry, as St. Paul states (Eph. 4.13, 16) is to build up the body of Christ until all together we form a perfect Man, according to the full measure of Christ's age. . . . Let us grow in him who is the Head, the one from whom the whole Body takes its growth that it may be built up, bound and joined together through its ministry in this Body so structured and fitted together. St. Augustine (*In Ps.* 86) tells us that this building is Christ. . . . This Christ is God's admirable design, kingdom, image: his Son in whom he takes delight . . .

Théologie chrétienne, Archives St-Sulpice, ms. 347, 574 ff.

7.9 Bérulle on the Priesthood

To a Priest of the Oratory
Father,
  The grace of Jesus be with you forever.
  I feel obliged to speak to you a bit at length about the subject of which you wrote me so that, when appropriate, you can instruct those people of note who might wish to understand it. You should know that the church is divided into two parts and both of them are holy, if we consider its institution and origin. One is the people, and the other is the clergy. One receives holiness, and the other brings it about. In the period closer to its birth these two parts brought forth many virgins, confessors and martyrs who blessed the church, filled the earth, populated heaven and diffused everywhere the odor of the sanctity of Jesus.
  This holy body, animated by a holy Spirit and governed by holy laws, has lost its fervor and diminished in holiness through the corruption of the ages. This slackening began in its weakest part, the people. Then, from among the people, some withdrew to preserve in themselves the holiness proper to the whole body. These were the monks who, according to Saint Denis, constitute the highest and most perfect part of the people. They were governed by priests in the early church, receiving from them direction and perfect holiness, to which they aspired in an extraordinary way.
  At that time holiness dwelt in the clergy as in its fortress, and it struck down idols and worldly impieties. At that time the clergy, composed of prelates and priests, radiated only holy things and dealt only with holy things, leaving worldly things to the worldly. At that time the clergy bore nobly the mark of God's authority, holiness and light: three beautiful jewels in the priestly crown, joined together by God's design for his anointed ones, his priests and his church. The first priests were indeed both saints and doctors of the church. God preserved within this same order authority, holiness and doctrine, uniting these three perfections in the priestly order in honor and imitation of the holy Trinity, in which we adore the authority of the Father, the light of the Son and the sanctity of the Holy Spirit, divinely united in the unity of their Essence.

However, time, which corrupts all things, brought about laxity in most of the clergy. These three qualities, authority, holiness and doctrine, which the Spirit had joined together, were separated by the human spirit and the spirit of the world. Authority has remained in prelates, holiness in religious and doctrine in the schools. In this separation God preserved in different segments of his church what he had joined in the clerical state. Such is the plan of God and the institution of his Son, Jesus. Such is the excellence of our state. Such is the power, light and holiness of the priestly condition.

However, alas! We have fallen from it. The evil of the world in which we live has demoted us from this dignity. It has passed into foreign hands, and we can rightly utter these words of lamentation: *Our inheritance has been handed over to strangers* (Lam. 5.2). For no matter how much they are at home in grace and in the unity of the body of Jesus, they are foreign to the ministry; and God, in his original, primary plan did not choose them for it.

It is the prelates and priests who are called to it. It is them that Jesus, in the gospel, refers to as the salt of the earth. It is to them that these three attributes apply. He gives ordinary people faith, hope and love, but he gives also to public persons these three other gifts: holiness, authority and doctrine. This is the core of the inheritance of the tribe of Levi, that is, the clergy, whose name in Greek means "inheritance," in order to show that they have no possession on earth and that the only wealth Jesus Christ has left them is this possession of heaven and this sharing in himself, that is to say, in his holiness, light and authority, adoring and receiving authority from the Father, light from the Son and holiness from the Holy Spirit. But we have reason to lament this loss of which we have been guilty. Also we have reason to praise the goodness of God, who gives us the means to unite once again holiness and doctrine with the authority of the clerical state, without prejudice to those who received it and made such holy use of it in our absence.

It is God's will and plan for us. This is what he has called us to. This is why we are gathered together; in order to reclaim our inheritance, to recover once again our rights, to enjoy our legitimate succession, to have the Son of God as our portion, to share in his Spirit, and through his Spirit to share in his light, holiness and authority, which are communicated to prelates by Jesus Christ and through them to priests.

Bérulle and the French School, 183–85.

7.10 The Heart of the Priest and the Church

The spirit of the priest is completely different from any other Christian's heart. It is the spirit of the entire Church united and contained in the priest alone. The priest is the one who takes on himself the interests and concerns of the Church and stands, bearing them, in the presence of GOD. He is the servant of the Church. He loses himself in the cares and interests of the Church. . . .

The priest must have a general, universal spirit of prayer, of religion, and of penance. The priest must pray for everyone. His heart must be open and large enough to embrace all. In him, The Spirit of GOD must be revealed and manifested as much and, even, more than in the whole Church and in all people in whose name and in whose place the priest prays to, praises, and worships God.

The Priest's heart must be as large as the Church. His duty is to pray for the whole Church taken together and as much as the whole Church would pray. He must pray more fervently, more purely, more humbly, and more trustingly than the whole Church together, in each of its members.

What are you, O soul of the priest? Where can anyone find a length and breadth such as you must have? How few priests there are and how am I to write these words, so miserable, so impure, so far removed as I am from the state to which the holy and divine priesthood calls us?

O apostolic priest, whoever you may be, if your grace is great and widely poured out, how rigorous and severe must be your suffering and your penance!

If your grace and your vocation are apostolic, you must be concerned with everyone. If you are restricted as a pastor, know that you are particularly restricted and bound by duty to the people who are your own. Even St. Paul ranks the dignity and grace of a pastor among the lower services, counting apostolic grace and the grace of the priest who feels called to the love and service of the whole Church as one of the first graces and dignity of the gifts that JESUS CHRIST has distributed in diverse manner to men on earth.

Olier, *Mémoires* 8:27–33.

7.11 Spiritual Direction According to Bérulle

The direction of a soul is like ruling a world—a world with more secrets, more diversity, more perfections and uniqueness than the world we see.... [This world] that we behold with our eyes has less value before God than a single soul, because of its great dignity, state, and importance.... For God has not made the world for the sake of the world, but for the souls in it which are the object of his care and his providence....

...*Ars artium, cura animarum* [The leadership of souls is the art of arts. *Pastoral Care*, Gregory the Great]. This art is a science not of the memory, but of the spirit; not of study, but of prayer; not of conversation, but of action; not of argument, but of humility; not of speculation, but of love—the love of Jesus who gave himself up, in abandonment, self-forgetfulness, and total self-giving for the salvation of souls. This science belongs to the science of the saints, as Scripture says. It is a spiritual science coming from the Father of spirits, the Father of lights. It is a science made for saints, it produces saints and directs them along eternal paths. The light proper to this science is not the light of nature whether human or divine, but the light of life.... This light of life proceeds from him who is life, and it is given only by him. He gives it only to those who adhere to him and to his spirit, a spirit of love and humility. This spirit is far removed from the cold, dry, proud, earthly spirit of those who study not at heaven's school, but at the world's.

This science is learned not so much in books and Academics, but in the book of life at the foot of the Cross, by those who adhere to Jesus, to his ways, to his love.... This science, properly speaking, is a spiritual science, for it belongs to the Spirit of God. It is found among things which are truly spiritual and divine and makes those who possess it spiritual, as an emanation of that great light which, as St. John tells us, is the true light, the light of the Father, the light which enlightens every man coming into the world and transforms into itself and its brightness those who draw near to it. Through the grace of Jesus, this science belongs to Christians, yet is so rarely found among them. It is a science proper to those who are superiors among Christians, yet is rare even among them. This science has the light, not the lampshade; the spirit, but not the earthly side of things. It is given by Jesus, having emanated as it were from Jesus crucified; in him and in his Cross it knows all things and reaches the end of all things: Jesus, the Alpha and the Omega. . . .

Let us, then, aspire to this holy, divine, saving science: it is the daughter of prayer, the disciple of humility, the mother of discretion. It calls for disciples who desire to do more than merely know; who desire to put into practice what they have learned. Its characteristic is this: that one who thinks he is a master is, in fact, a disciple, the first disciple in its school. Such a one learns while teaching others, becomes holy in helping others to be holy. Jesus is the sole, unique master of this science.

> *Mémorial de quelques points servant à la direction des Supérieurs*
> 1:810, 11–12. 818–19.

7.12 To the Marquise de Portes

[The following text can be taken as a model of a letter of direction. It was written by Olier in the summer of 1649.]

My daughter, my most dear daughter, let us walk in paths that are simple, humble and unknown to everyone else. This is how Our Lord establishes his kingdom. His way of acting, my daughter, is not what so many people think today, producing huge books in eloquent language to say that we have to proceed by such-and-such a road. O my daughter, there is not a single soul who does not have her path prepared by God and who ought not fail to adore in the depths of silence, so as to submit in the particular manner willed by God. My daughter, in the name of God, love your Love alone; love the spouse of your heart who has brought you this far by his own pathways.

Be his, my daughter, in the way he desires, and he will not fail to reveal himself fully to you.

I shall confide to you the gospel words that have touched me most in my life. They are the words of Jesus Christ quoted by St. John: *To the one who will love me, I shall manifest myself fully*. My daughter, that is what we aspire to through our sufferings, humiliations, and trials, so that we may be happy in being able to receive the light of Jesus Christ, to live in him, in his virtues, and in his grace.

My dear daughter, do not fill your mind with quarrelsome questions; avoid taking sides on such issues. Such argumentation, as St. Paul states, gives rise to questions which provoke quarrels and turn us away from charity, leading us to a point forbidden by the Church and, even, by God, who would conceal from us things we yearn to know. It is much better to sacrifice all that entirely and without reserve, adoring the unknown mystery of grace that the majesity of God has purposely kept hidden from us, and which holy Church has always kept unresolved. That is preferable to seeking involvement in a decision that risks arriving at a judgment other than God's. To do that would be to oppose the designs of Jesus Christ and his Father, who has reserved to himself for Judgment Day the revelation of the holy mystery of the Most Blessed Trinity, knowledge of the grace by which Christ dwells in us and we in him, as he lives in the Father and the Father in him. St. John records these words of the Son of God: *In illo die intellegetis sicut ego in Patre et Pater in me et ego in vobis.* You will understand on that day only (and not today) that I am living and working in you through grace, as I am in the Father and the Father in me.

My daughter, you cannot believe how profitable it is to keep silent about these things and how silence preserves the soul in liberty, humility, and simplicity. On the other hand, curiosity, idle questions and conversation about what does not concern us and which we have not the grace to consider weigh us down, parch, and puff up our hearts.

You know, my daughter, that Jesus must be all in all for us. He must be in our words, our thoughts, and our actions. If he is not the author of everything, there is nothing but the evil of our flesh and the vanity of our own deeds, pride and self-love that fill us and infect everything. We must not allow anything but the operations of grace in us and we must adhere to him in the greatest intimacy. You will find through experience that when your heart is in the most intimate union and the deepest recollection with God, he will annihilate all such thoughts in you. He will lift you to his love alone, without allowing you to be distracted by examining the nature of the love which possesses you. He so greatly desires and loves a simple, annihilated heart, one lost totally in him and in nothing outside of him: *Porro unum est necessarium.*

My daughter, you must see to this for the greatest good of your soul. Anguish and aridity will afflict it if your heart and mind are taken up by concern for things that are not of God.

My sister, how I long to see you holy in Jesus, our all and our love (and who ought to be this for the whole world)! How I long to see you living in charity and through the activity of the one Spirit! How I hate self-love, the sworn enemy of faith and charity! How I desire to see you living in the faith of that just man of whom St. Paul and the prophet speak! How vain are the thoughts and opinions of men who lack the knowledge of God as strength, support, and rule, Solomon declares. My daughter, faith in everything. It is the blindfold of one's own spirit, preventing useless, vain and uncontrolled activities. My daughter, the spirit of man is good only to be offered in sacrifice. It is good for it to be immolated, crucified, restrained, absorbed in faith and divine wisdom, just as all the desires of the heart and will ought to be fulfilled in the holy charity of Our Lord Jesus Christ. Oh! how peaceful the soul transformed and consummated in Jesus! How joyful, free, independent of every fantasy of human imagining! How such a soul grows in the strong, clear light of Jesus Christ! How she is continually purified, sanctified and abandoned in God! My daughter, outside of Jesus, his faith, his love, take hold of nothing, take delight in nothing. Every day read the holy Scripture of Jesus Christ, with deep respect and openness of your mind and your human reason. Let yourself find nourishment through being filled and penetrated with Christian virtue. Read St. Teresa, Francis de Sales, Gerson—all those blessed books which the universal Church approves, writings in which nothing is questioned or doubted. I desire that everything superfluous be taken from you. I desire that what is vile be separated from what is price-less, just as Our Lord desires. He asks perfect holiness of his chosen souls and he cannot suffer that anything imperfect be united to his spirit of purity.

Olier, *Lettres,* éd. Levesque 1:177. Paris: 1935;
443–46.

Chapter Eight

John Baptist de la Salle

A mong the many heirs to the Bérulle School, there are two who merit special attention: St. John-Baptist de La Salle (1651–1719) and St. Louis-Marie Grignion de Montfort (1673–1716). Indeed, the apostolic commitments and the spiritual doctrine of these two holy men follow the tradition of the founders of the French School. Moreover, both were formed at Saint-Sulpice Seminary and were influenced in a decisive way by their directors, Louis Tronson (1622–1700) and François Leschassier (1641–1725). Furthermore, the influence exercised by John-Baptist de La Salle and Louis-Marie Grignion de Montfort, personally and through their religious families, has contributed in the past and will contribute in the future to furthering our knowledge of French School spirituality and its themes.

An Educator and a Saint

John-Baptist de La Salle, the founder of the Brothers of the Christian Schools, is well known for his pedagogical work, and particularly for the innovations he introduced into education for the lower classes: *simultaneous teaching*, that is, the instruction of a number of pupils at one time; free education; the suppression of Latin as a requirement in beginners' classes, and the prohibition of compulsory manual work. He is equally well known throughout the entire world for the institute he founded, using a structure and principles that were completely new for his era. His companions were laymen, religious and educators, living in community, sharing the life of their students. The source of their apostolic zeal was a spirit of faith, nourished by fervent prayer. However, his personal spiritual experience along with his teachings on prayer and the greatness of the ministry of Christian educators is practically unknown, except by members of his institute or those familiar with the history of spirituality. Even so, La Salle was a truly great spiritual master, closely related to the Bérulle School. He spent only 18 months at Saint-Sulpice as a student, because the death of his father obliged him to assume the guardianship of his six younger brothers and sisters. He was also influenced by other spiritual movements, especially those of Francis de Sales and Teresa of Jesus, whose works he read often and thoroughly. Still, Bérulle's influence was the dominant one, revealed, for example, in an invocation that his Brothers have repeated 20 times a day for the last three centuries: "May Jesus live in our hearts." This prayer is a resounding echo of the prayer that comes to us from Condren and Olier: "O Jesus, living in Mary. . . ." It recalls, as well, the fundamental affirmations of John Eudes in the *Life and Kingdom of Jesus*.

A Life Moved by the Spirit

On 7 April 1719, as he lay dying, John Baptist de La Salle summed up in a single phrase the basic attitude of his life as a Christian: "In all things, I adore God's action in my life." Throughout his life, his goal had been to respond faithfully to the invitations of the Holy Spirit. Day after day, in circumstances that were often unexpected, he tried to provide for the needs of the children of his day, to provide for the formation of his Brothers, with the help of one or another adviser. The will of God, God's "action in his life," he accepted as his light and rule, at each step of the way, despite sufferings, heartbreak, separation, contradiction and every kind of darkness.

At the beginning of his priesthood, La Salle had adopted several rules. The third rule gives us an insight into his personality:

> It is a good rule of conduct to avoid making a distinction between matters proper to one's state and the matter of one's salvation and perfection. One must be convinced that one's salvation and perfection will never be better assured than by accomplishing the duties of one's state of life, provided they are fulfilled in keeping with God's plan. One must strive to keep this always in mind.[1]

John Baptist de La Salle was born in Rheims on 30 April 1651, of a well-to-do family of merchants and magistrates. He was the eldest of 11 children, seven of whom survived. Family life was deeply Christian and somewhat austere, with a touch of rigorism. In fact, one of his brother and several cousins and nephews became Jansenists.

La Salle began his classical studies in Rheims, at the College of *Bons Enfants*. At the age of 11, he received the tonsure and gave himself seriously to the pursuit of the ecclesiastical state. In 1667, he became a canon of the Cathedral of Rheims. He studied philosophy, then theology in Rheims and in Paris. He was marked forever by the year and a half he spent, from the autumn of 1670 to the spring of 1672, at Saint-Sulpice Seminary, and he continued to stay in touch with his professors, Tronson and Leschassier. He loved to speak to his Brothers about "the holy house . . . the seedbed of apostolic laborers . . . which had given him the spirit of God." His spiritual growth, along with his teaching on prayer and apostolic zeal, carried the imprint of this formation.

In 1672, after the death of his father, La Salle returned to Rheims to take on the responsibility of his brothers and sisters. He did so, from all accounts, with an amazing sense of dedication and affection.

On 9 April 1678, La Salle was ordained to the priesthood in Rheims by Archbishop Charles-Maurice Le Tellier. His first priestly ministry seems to have been unexpected, but it gave him the opportunity to continue with other children the task as an educator that he had fulfilled with his own brothers and sisters. From 1679 on, he was to take part in the opening of two, then three schools for boys, in Rheims. His commitment, at first, was financial, but gradually he became more and more involved in the project. With a keen sense of insight, he understood that the first condition needed to assure the stability and the effectiveness of Christian schools was the formation of teachers. This became a consuming priority in his life. On 24 June 1681, the feast of his patron, St. John the Baptist, he invited eight or ten teachers, who already took their meals with him, to live in his house. The following year, on the same date, he left the family home to live in poverty with these companions in a house close by. That same year, 1682, Louis XIV moved definitively to Versailles.

In choosing to share life fully with these men in this fashion, he was not proposing a simple cohabitation of salaried teachers. His ideal was to pursue a life of consecration in community, in service to the Christian education of poor children. Gradually, without undue haste, but deliberately and without delay, he left everything, renouncing his status as canon and his patrimony. Some of his first followers chose to leave the group, but others came and he soon counted a large number of associates.

Thus, he was able to send teachers to schools in Rethel and Château-Porcien in 1682 and to Guise and Laon in 1685. In 1687, he created a seminary for teachers in rural areas, a Teachers' Training College ahead of its time. Next to this center, he opened a novitiate for the young men who chose to join his community. From this time on, his entire life was governed by his preoccupation with forming educators.

In February 1688, La Salle left Rheims with two Brothers to take charge of the charity school for boys in Saint-Sulpice parish. He was to stay in Paris for 12 years, laboring with perseverance, despite a great deal of opposition. For example, his program was viewed unfavorably by some pastors of Saint-Sulpice and by the *master writers*, schoolmasters who earned their living by teaching individually the children of those able to pay.

Nonetheless, the work that was to become the Institute of the Brothers of the Christian Schools gradually took shape. Following the Assembly of Rheims, on Pentecost 1686, a number of important steps were taken. On 21 November 1691, he and two of his earliest associates definitively committed themselves by the vows of association, obedience and stability. In 1692, a novitiate was opened in Vaugirard, at the time a suburb south of Paris. On the feast of Pentecost, 6 June 1694, a retreat opened at Vaugirard, followed on 7 June by La Salle's election as superior of the Institute and the perpetual vows of several Brothers. On the feast of Pentecost in 1716, at the Assembly held in Saint-Yon (Rouen), Brother Barthélémy was elected successor to John Baptist. The first *Common Rules of the Institute* probably date from the Assembly of 1694. From this point on, new schools or acceptance of those already established would multiply in diverse fashion throughout France and as far as Rome. The years between 1699 and 1711 were marked by countless foundations.

Continually, John-Baptist de La Salle encountered difficulties and contradiction. At one point, he thought of resigning, but he returned to Paris in 1714 and settled definitively in Rouen in 1715. Once he was replaced by Brother Barthélémy in 1717, he lived simply and discreetly as chaplain of his community in Saint-Yon. There, he began writing a number of spiritual works, an activity he continued until his death.

One of his Brothers has recently given us a description of La Salle's activity and mission:

> John-Baptist de La Salle was a man of genius for things pertaining to a school, with keen intuition for what was needed in education. In order to provide for these needs, he created the most diversified kinds of instruction: free schools and professional schools, Sunday Academies, boarding schools, and special training schools for difficult or backward pupils. Still, his first mission was the formation of disciples, invited to serve in one of the most demanding of all apostolates.[2]

What idea—or ideal—of the life and mission of his Brothers inspired La Salle in the realization of these projects?

The Ministry of the Christian Educator

John-Baptist de La Salle organized his schools and his Institute in a most precise way. He gave his Brothers instructions on the *Conduit des écoles chrétiennes* and *Règles de la bienséance et de la civilité chrétienne*. Above all, he bequeathed to them spiritual texts of great value.

His writings are marked by an impressive clarity and precision. All, like the *Recueil de différents petits traités à l'usage des Frères des écoles chrétiennes* are meant to nourish and renew two fundamental attitudes: the spirit of faith and apostolic zeal. La Salle placed the essence of his Brothers' spiritual life at the heart of their ecclesial service as Christian educators.

It seems, however, that one of the main ideas of La Salle was that the ministry of the Christian educator should continue the very ministry of the apostles. He repeated this conviction unceasingly to his Brothers, whom he wanted to remain as laymen. We find his thought expressed in many ways: "Those who instruct youth are *co-workers with Jesus Christ* for the salvation of souls." . . . "Jesus Christ says to you what he said to his apostles." . . . "You are successors to the apostles in their work of catechizing and teaching the poor." . . . "Thank God for the grace that is yours in your work of sharing in the ministry of the holy apostles, the principal bishops and pastors of the Church. '*Honor your ministry*' (Rom. 11.13) by being, as Paul says, '*worthy ministers of the gospel*' (2 Cor. 3.6). Such quotations could be multiplied. A careful reading of La Salle's spiritual masterpiece, *Meditations for the Time of Retreat*, is highly recommended. In this work, the founder expresses his fundamental conviction: the Brothers have been called to live out and exercise the apostolic ministry, to continue the mission of the apostles. Countless quotations from Paul, especially from the Second Epistle to the Corinthians, where the apostle reflects at length on the meaning of his ministry, give us an indication of what can be called the apostolic identification of La Salle's Brothers.

John-Baptist de La Salle was formed at Saint-Sulpice, which was to be, according to the desire of Olier, an apostolic house. La Salle had prayed daily before Le Brun's painting of the descent of the Holy Spirit on the apostles. His devotion to the Holy Spirit and to the feast of Pentecost can be explained, then, partly by the inseparably spiritual and apostolic dimension of his formation. Olier himself described this characteristic:

> The seminary of Saint-Sulpice . . . is consecrated and dedicated to Jesus Christ our Lord, not only to honor him

as High Priest and the great Apostle of his Father, but also to venerate him living in the college of the Apostles; there, prayer is offered daily that the apostolic Spirit be poured out on its community and on the whole Church, so as to renew in her the love of Jesus Christ and his worship of the Father.[3]

La Salle's genius consisted in understanding and repeating ceaselessly to his Brothers that their "labor" was bound to their "state" and was totally apostolic. Thus, they were to live under the influence and "the action" of the Holy Spirit. This Spirit was, as Bérulle and his followers had asserted, nothing other than the Spirit of Jesus, a Spirit both filial and apostolic.

Jesus Living in Us!

The mystical christocentrism of the Bérulle School found expression in countless prayers: the Oratorian Office of Jesus; the little prayer of Father de Condren, developed by Olier into, "O Jesus, living in Mary . . . "; the *Ave Cor* of John Eudes. John Baptist de La Salle not only proposed daily prayers "in honor of and in union with" one or another mystery of Jesus. He also gave his Brothers a short prayer they were to repeat several times a day, one that was sung and is still sung by his disciples. We may be surprised at the lyrical accents with which this austere ascetic contemplated and adored Jesus. He prayed, as Olier had, that Jesus "come and live in our hearts," so that his entire existence, most profound interior attitudes and daily behavior might be transformed by the Lord. This short prayer was a cry of love and desire. It must be understood as the dynamic summary of an entire body of teachings on prayer and texts for meditation left by the founder to his Brothers.

La Salle was introduced to mental prayer, first of all, at Saint-Sulpice; later, he was assisted by spiritual guides, such as Nicolas Roland and Nicolas Barré. He consecrated long hours to prayer every day. Prayer was the crucible where his spiritual and apostolic life came together, where he felt a deep experience of God, of the Cross of Jesus, and of the mystery of the Church. This experience is reflected in the 208 meditations he left to his Brothers and in the wonderful *Explanation of a Method of Prayer* that he developed. This method had already been presented in an earlier work and was to be untiringly repeated to his disciples in Rheims, Vaugirard and Saint-Yon.

It is not possible, within the limits of these pages, to enter into the details of La Salle's teaching on prayer. However, a few of its major characteristics can be considered here:

1. Great emphasis is placed on the presence of God. La Salle did not consider this point as a simple preparation for prayer; it was, in itself, already prayer. One would almost think that "the prayer of simple attention" or "of simple contemplation"—which certainly reflects his personal experience—was nothing but a very simple, extended act of the presence of God. La Salle often visited the monastery of the Carmelite Fathers on the rue de Vaugirard; he had very probably met Brother Lawrence of the Resurrection who lived there until 1691. This unassuming layman was visited by many Christians who sought to live the gospel to its depth, but in an uncomplicated way. Brother Lawrence simply taught them the practice of the presence of God.

2. The stages of every spiritual life can be found in the various forms of prayer presented by La Salle: conversation through repeated reflections; through a single reflection extended in time; through simple attention. Several methods are proposed for application to a mystery, consideration of a virtue or a text.

3. The *meditations* of the founder have a clearly practical orientation. Each consideration is followed by one

or two related questions or exhortations: "Have you not, at times, or are you not now in this unhappy state? If so, lament the fact before God and pray earnestly that he draw you out of it as soon as possible; the remedy for this malady must be applied promptly." The realism of John Baptist de La Salle is just as evident, when he invites us to reflect on the demands of community life. He frequently returns to this theme, particularly in a rightly celebrated meditation on "The duty of persons living in community to endure the faults of their Brothers." His psychological sense of reality is, above all, a spiritual realism enlightened by faith. An excellent example of this can be found in what he writes about the presence of Jesus in the midst of the Brothers:

> Is it not a great joy for us, when we come together with our Brothers, for prayer or for some other exercise, to know with certainty that we are in the company of Jesus, present in the midst of the Brothers? He is in their midst to give them his Spirit, to direct them by this Spirit in all their actions and in everything they do. He is in their midst to unite them as one.... Jesus Christ is in the midst of the Brothers in all their exercises, so that, just as all their actions tend towards Jesus Christ as toward their center, they may be one in him by the union they have with Jesus, acting in them and by them.[4]

The life, the work and the message of a man like John-Baptist de La Salle can be explained, to a great extent, by his personal convictions as well as by his spiritual experiences. Here, we have given a mere overview of his own faith journey and the influences that shaped his life. Moreover, La Salle was not an innovator in every domain. His special gift was, doubtless, knowing how to adopt, masterfully, some of the great apostolic and spiritual orientations of the seventeenth century, and to adapt them perfectly to the needs of his day. He was not a follower of the Bérulle School exclusively, but its influence on his spiritual doctrine makes him a true representative of this tradition. In the last analysis, nothing can replace direct contact with his writings or with his Brothers. We can say of La Salle what Luis de Léon wrote about Teresa of Jesus: "I never met *la Madre* during her mortal life, but I think I know her to some extent through her writings and through her daughters."

DOCUMENTS FOR CHAPTER 8

8.1 Chronology of John Baptist de La Salle's Life

1651 — 30 April: Birth at Rheims
1660 — Studies at the college of *Bons Enfants*, in Rheims
1662 — Tonsure
1667 — Canon of the Cathedral in Rheims
1670 — Entrance into Saint-Sulpice Seminary, Paris
1672 — April: death of his father; return to Rheims to assume responsibility for his sisters and brothers
1678 — 9 April: Ordination to priesthood, in Rheims
1679 — Meeting with Adrien Nyel. Direction of a school
1680 — Invites school teachers to eat with him
1681 — Invites school teachers to live with him
1682 — Goes to live with the teachers
1683 — Renounces his post as canon and distributes his goods to famine victims
1686 — Assembly of Brothers
1687 — First "seminary" for rural teachers
1688 — De La Salle goes to Paris with two brothers
1691 — Vow of association and union with two brothers
1692 — Opening of the novitiate at Vaugirard
1694 — Assembly of Brothers; approval of common rules; first vows
1703 — Beginning of the suit by the "master writers"

1711–1713	—	Travels in Provence. Condemnation. Exiled in Grenoble
1714	—	Return to Paris
1715	—	Definitive departure for Rouen
1717	—	Brother Barthélémy elected first superior general
1719	—	Good Friday, 7 April, death, in Paris

8.2 An Apostolic Ministry

Consider that you are working in your ministry for the building of the church through your teaching of the children whom God has entrusted to your care. These children are becoming a part of the structure whose foundation was laid by the holy Apostles. For this reason you must fulfill your ministry as the Apostles fulfilled theirs. As told in the Acts of the Apostles, day after day, both in the temple and at home, they never stopped teaching and proclaiming the good news of Jesus Christ. It followed that day by day the Lord increased the number of faithful and the spirit of union among those who were being saved.

You are successors to the Apostles in their task of catechizing and teaching the poor. It you want to make your ministry as useful to the church as it can be, you must teach catechism every day, helping your disciples learn the basic truths of our religion. In this way you will be following the example of the apostles and of Jesus Christ himself, who devoted himself daily to this ministry. Like them, also, you must afterwards leave your work and devote yourself to reading and mental prayer, in order to learn at their source the truths and the holy maxims which you wish to teach, and draw upon yourself the grace of God that you need to fulfill this ministry according to the spirit and the intention of the church, which entrusts it to you.

Meditations for the Time of Retreat, Trans. Brother Augustine Loes; Intro. and ed., Brother Miguel Campos. Winona, Wisconsin: St. Mary's College Press, 1975; 70–71.

8.3 Ambassadors of Christ

Since you are ambassadors and ministers of Jesus Christ in the work that you do, you must act as representing Jesus Christ himself. He wants your disciples to see him in you and receive your teaching as if he were teaching them. They must be convinced that the truth of Jesus Christ comes from your mouth, that it is only in his name that you teach, that he has given you authority over them.

They are a letter which Christ dictates to you, which you write each day in their hearts, not with ink, but by the Spirit of the living God. For the Spirit acts in you and by you through the power of Jesus Christ. He helps you overcome all the obstacles to their salvation, enlightening them in the person of Jesus Christ and helping them avoid all that could be displeasing to him.

In order to fulfill your responsibility with as much perfection and care as God requires of you, frequently give yourself to the Spirit of our Lord to act only under his influence and not through any self-seeking. This Holy Spirit, then, will fill your students with Himself, and they will be able to possess fully the Christian spirit.

Meditations, 54.

8.4 Apostolic Prayer

You must, then, devote yourself very thoroughly to prayer in order to succeed in your ministry. You must constantly represent the needs of your disciples to Jesus Christ, explaining to him the difficulties you experience in guiding them. Jesus Christ, seeing that you regard him as the one who can do everything and yourself as an instrument to be moved only by him, will not fail to grant you what you ask. (. . .)

In carrying out your service to children, you will not fulfill your ministry adequately if you conform only to the external actions of Jesus Christ in his guidance and in his conversion of souls. You must also enter into his way of thinking and adopt his goals. He came on earth, as he himself said, that all might have life and have it to the full. This is why he said in another place that his words are spirit and life. By this he meant that his words procure the true life, which is the life of the soul— for those who hear them and, with gladness over what they have heard, act on them with love.

This must be your goal when you teach your disciples, that they live a Christian life and that your words become spirit and life for them. Your words will accomplish this, first, because they will be produced by the Spirit of God living in you, and second, because they will procure for your disciples the Christian spirit. In possessing this spirit, which is the very Spirit of Jesus Christ, they will live that true life which is so valuable because it leads surely to eternal life. (. . .)

Meditations, 56–58.

8.5 A Method of Prayer

We make an act of union, by uniting ourselves interiorly with the spirit of our Lord in the mystery and with the interior dispositions He had therein, begging of Him a share in this spirit and in these dispositions, and earnestly beseeching Him to grant us grace to enter into the spirit of the mystery, and practice the virtues taught us therein. (. . .)

We ought to beseech our Lord to unite us in mind and heart to His interior dispositions in the mystery of the Nativity.

We may make the act of union as follows:

> I unite myself to Thee, divine Jesus, Infant God, animated by an ardent desire to share in the spirit and dispositions of Thy holy Infancy, and in the graces Thou didst merit for me in the mystery of Thy Nativity. I most humbly beg Thee, O most amiable Infant Jesus, to give me a dwelling in Thy divine Heart; to unite my spirit to Thine and allow me to share Thy holy dispositions in the stable of Bethlehem, when laid on hay and straw in the crib, or reposing in the arms of Thy holy Mother. I pray earnestly, that Thou mayest grant me the grace to be humble, docile, submissive and obedient as Thou wert towards Thy heavenly Father, Thy holy Mother and Thy foster-father, the great St. Joseph. May I, by Thy grace, have these dispositions in my relations with those who

have a right to command me; may I be even disposed to submit, after Thy example, to all classes of men.

Grant, I beseech Thee, O Lord, that I may share fully in Thy holy affection for poverty, mortification and sufferings; that I may love and practice them through motives of faith, in union with Thy spirit and dispositions, and by the movement and assistance of Thy grace operating in me, with which I promise to cooperate as far as I possibly can.

Assist me, O my good Savior, in a special manner by Thy grace, for I am weak. Make me a new creature in Thee, so that I may no longer think or act as a child of sinful man, but as a child of God, regenerated, and adopted by the Eternal Father, through Thee.

As the seal is to the wax, so do Thou, O Lord, imprint Thyself upon my soul, and remain there, really and efficaciously. May I no longer live in myself and by myself, but in Thee and by Thee, so that Thou mayest act and live in me. Give me, O Lord, Thy childlike spirit, in virtue of which I may pray with confidence and in union with Thee, saying: Abba: Father.

Meditations, 93–95.

8.6 Community Life

It is not possible for many persons to live together without being a source of mutual suffering. One will have a capricious temper, another will be combative; one will have disagreeable manners, another will be haughty; one will be too obliging, another will speak his mind too freely; others again will be too reserved, or dissimulating or critical. It is rare that such varied dispositions, such different mentalities, do not lead to difficulties among Brothers, and if grace did not come to the rescue, it would be almost impossible for them to be mutually forbearing, and to avoid offending seriously against charity.

Another reason why you should support the defects of your Brothers is because God has made it an obligation. When He placed you in community, He imposed on you a burden which is heavy to bear. And what is this burden if not the defects of your Brothers. Yet, no matter how heavy this may be, St. Paul insists that we must bear it. "Bear the burden of one another's failings," he says, "then you will be fulfilling the law of Christ." Have you grasped this lesson? Have you understood it perfectly? Then practice it. God Himself gives you the example, for He has suffered untold outrages from you, and daily continues so to suffer.

Meditations, 194–95.

8.7 One in the Heart of Jesus

[This meditation on the seventeenth chapter of John was proposed by the founder for the Eve of the Ascension: "What we ought to ask of God in prayer." The third point only of this meditation is given here, on the union that existed among the Apostles. This fraternal union rooted in the union of the three divine Persons, was the object of Jesus' prayer. It must be what the brothers pray for, also. The final lines summarize the entire thought.]

The third petition which Jesus makes to the Eternal Father for His Apostles in the prayer recorded in the gospel of to-day is that they should be closely united among themselves. This union should be so close and firm as to resemble that which exists between the three Divine Persons, not exactly, however, for these are united in essence, but by participation. And this union of heart and mind which Jesus desires to see among His Apostles is to produce the same effect as the essential union between the Father, the Son and the Holy Ghost, that is to say, they are all to share the same sentiments, to have the same will, the same affections, the same rules and the same practices. This is what St. Paul recommends to the faithful in his Epistles, and this likewise is what was remarked in the Apostles and the first disciples of Our Lord, as St. Luke records in the Acts, saying, "there was one heart and soul in all the company of believers."

Since you are privileged to be called by God to live a community life, there is nothing you should pray for with greater insistence than union of heart and mind with your Brothers. Only by means of such harmony will you be able to maintain that peace which constitutes the whole happiness of your life. Ask therefore the Lord of all hearts to make yours one with those of your Brothers, in that of Jesus.

JESUS CHRIST having come upon earth to establish the new Law and to accomplish the mystery of our redemption, there was nothing to retain Him in this world once He had fulfilled His double function of Legislator and Redeemer. Only a species of violence kept Him here below, for the abode of His glorious Body was in heaven, and His place at the right hand of the Father. The relations which He still held with men obliged Him to veil His brilliancy in the apparitions with which He favored them.

You who are separated from the world, should be entirely disengaged from all human inclinations, which draw one towards the earth. You should aspire only for heaven, and constantly raise your heart and mind thither. You are made only for heaven, you should labor only for heaven, and you will find perfect rest only in heaven.

On this day Jesus Christ leaves earth to enter heaven. There He has established His abode for ever. On this day His sacred Humanity is adored by the angels and by all the saints who enter with Him into eternal beatitude.

Adore with all the elect this Sacred Humanity to Whom "all authority in heaven and on earth has been given." Unite with them in acknowledging this Sacred Humanity, and in paying It all possible respect. Look upon It as being, as St. Paul says, that wherein "the whole treasury of wisdom and knowledge is stored up." From this divine source Our Lord takes all those graces which He bestows upon men, who, by their good works, deserve to participate in His merits.

When will you be able to exclaim with St. Stephen that you see the heavens opening and Jesus Christ preparing to shower His graces upon you? Beg of Jesus the grace to be able henceforth to occupy yourself only with things of heaven.

Meditations; 128–92.

CHAPTER NINE

Louis-Marie Grignion de Montfort

W ho has not heard of the *Treatise on True Devotion to the Blessed Virgin* or *The Secret of Mary*? Still, while Grignion de Montfort may be best known as the apostle of Mary, his mission reaches far beyond the essential Marian dimension of his experience and his message. Grignion de Montfort was, above all, a missionary, a passionate witness to the gospel, enamored of eternal Wisdom, working among the poor. The life-sized Way of the Cross at Port-Château is an integral part of his message, just as his vow of slavery to Jesus through Mary.

In many ways, Grignion de Montfort's thought and teaching make him one of the best witnesses to the spirituality of the French School. Bremond does not hesitate to call him the "last master of the Bérulle School."[1] Indeed, particularly on the subject of eternal Wisdom—to

189

which he added his own unique accents—he stands in the tradition of Bérulle and his disciples. And through his profound contemplation of the Wisdom of God—which is, indeed, the person of the Incarnate Word—Grignion de Montfort adds his own color and insight to enrich this teaching.

His life was filled with activity of every kind. It is not possible here to discuss it in all its details, any more than we can claim to present his teaching in all its fullness. It is important, however, to recall a few stages in his growth and development.

Louis-Marie Grignion de Montfort was born on 31 January 1673 at Montfort-la-Cane, known today as Montfort-sur-Meu, located about 12 miles west of Rennes. Louis-Marie was the eldest in a large family that had been reasonably well-to-do until suffering a reversal of fortune. In 1675, his parents moved to Bois-Marquer, in the rural district of Iffendic, quite close to the town of Montfort. Louis-Marie's biographers, following the witness given by Alain Robert, one of his maternal uncles and the associate pastor at Saint-Sauveur in Rennes, highlight his exceptional piety and sense of responsibility as a very young child.

In 1684, Louis-Marie was sent to Rennes, to the Jesuit College of St. Thomas à Becket. This was a very successful school with nearly 3,000 day students. They came from every social class, since there were no expenses to be paid. The program went from first year up to the beginning of theology, including the study of Latin and Greek.

In the early years, Louis-Marie lived with his uncle, Alain Robert. He studied for eight years with the Jesuits: classical humanities, philosophy, and even some theology. Apparently, he won various awards at the end of the year, and he spent part of his recreation periods making religious miniatures and small paintings. He did not associate much with the other students and, by today's standards, would surely seem to have been too serious.

Those who knew him tell us that even in those years, he showed signs of a special devotion to the Virgin Mary.

In 1686, his parents moved to Rennes. Louis-Marie did not always enjoy a happy relationship with his father, who was an extremely quick-tempered man. His mother, it appears, understood and loved her eldest son in a way his father seemed unable to do.

During his years as a student, Louis-Marie Grignion de Montfort often visited a priest at the Cathedral of Rennes, Julien Bellier. This priest would bring together young men who were considering priesthood and send them to visit the sick in hospitals. Grignion de Montfort gave himself wholeheartedly to this service and, on his own initiative, sometimes collected money to help the poor. One of his companions at college, his friend at Saint-Sulpice and, eventually, his biographer, Jean-Baptiste Blain, has preserved a number of details regarding this period of his life. Blain would also write one of the first biographies of John-Baptist de La Salle, another contemporary, in 1733.

Saint-Sulpice and Paris

In November 1692, Grignion de Montfort set out on the road to Paris in order to prepare for priesthood at Saint-Sulpice, sponsored by a benefactor, Madame de Montigny, a lady from Rennes who was living in the neighborhood of Saint-Germain-des-Prés. He visited, in succession, three of the four communities that had been formed in the vicinity of the church of Saint-Sulpice. He lived a life of poverty and self-denial, dedicating several hours every day to prayer. His fellow students often made fun of him for the almost frenzied energy with which he pursued his studies.

The houses of Saint-Sulpice were known for their spiritual fervor as schools of asceticism and strict order. Nothing was repressed as much as what deviated from the "ordinary." Grignion de Montfort, however, although demonstrating an attitude of holiness and piety, also showed signs of original behavior. Historians have noted that he practiced exaggerated penances, and sometimes gave away his possessions and clothing to the poor he met on the street.

Both at the Sorbonne and at the seminary itself, young Grignion de Montfort seems to have followed a solid course of study. As librarian, too, he was in a position to read widely: the church fathers, theologians, ancient and spiritual authors of the day—especially the writings of Bérulle and the works of the Archdeacon of Evreux, Henri-Marie Boudon (1624–1702). He established the catalog of the seminary library, which is preserved today in the Mazarine library in Paris. He also transcribed a number of texts on the Blessed Virgin into a huge note-book that he later carried with him on his missions. Intellectual activities, times of prayer and apostolic service filled his days. He taught catechism in the neighborhood of Saint-Germain, engaged in service of the poor, and participated in other activities.

Grignion de Montfort's life at Saint-Sulpice between 1692 and 1700, the year of his ordination, was filled with more details than we can discuss here. However, it is important to note the influences that marked him most during his time in the seminary.

He was shaped forever by the teachings of his directors, his own readings, and the seminary's emphasis on prayer and the spiritual life. The theocentrism of Bérulle, highlighted at Saint-Sulpice, found an echo in Boudon's *"Dieu seul"* ("God Alone"), which Grignion de Montfort was to make his own. His teaching and prayer continually examine the states and mysteries of Jesus, the Incarnate Word. One of the themes dear to all the followers of Bérulle is the outstanding place of Mary in Christian faith and life, with the "life of Jesus in Mary" being the object of contemplation and prayer. Grignion de Montfort recited daily at Saint-Sulpice the prayer he later included in the evening prayer he recommended to his own disciples: "O Jesus, living in Mary..." (cf. *Complete Works*, 516). He also insisted on the praying of the rosary. In his estimation, the rosary was a prayer both to Mary and to Jesus, son of Mary. It was a prayer to honor Jesus in the mysteries and states of his life, and to draw down upon us the graces of these same mysteries.

We cannot fail to mention the dominant influence of Grignion de Montfort's spiritual directors, particularly François Leschassier (1641–1725). Their relationship continued after Louis-Marie's ordination; Leschassier was an ongoing inspiration and support in the priest's apostolic and spiritual life. Louis Tronson (1622–1700), the superior living in Issy at the time, was the one who revised Grignion de Montfort's "slaves of Mary," to "slaves of Jesus in Mary."

Later, Grignion de Montfort wrote admirable pages on devotion to "the great mystery of the Incarnation," highlighting in his own way the bond between Jesus and Mary. He insisted on "the ineffable dependency on Mary willed by God the Son... a dependency which is manifested particularly in that mystery in which Jesus Christ is captive as a slave in the womb of the divine Mary and is dependent on her for everything." [2]

Last, but not least, the apostolic and missionary spirit that filled young Louis-Marie in Brittany and inspired him to undertake various catechetical activities and works of charity in Paris could only have developed and deepened in the seminary. We have seen that Jean-Jacques Olier willed to make his seminary an apostolic house where prayers were offered daily that the "Apostolic Spirit" be given "to its community and to the whole Church."[3] Since he was not able to go to Canada or to Tonkin, Olier had chosen the first Sulpicians for New France. In spite of the apparently stilted style of his successors, Olier's missionary spirit was still alive, and it is not surprising to learn that Grignion de Montfort volunteered to go to Canada.

He also took on the aspects of Bérulle's and Olier's

teachings in a very personal way. The primacy of God, contemplation of Jesus in his mysteries, particularly the mysteries of the Incarnation and the Cross, union with Mary and the apostolic Spirit were all integrated into his life. His devotion to Mary was especially evident. For this reason, he was entrusted with the care of the Blessed Virgin's chapel in the apse of Saint-Sulpice church, where he celebrated his first Mass. In 1699, he and another seminarian were chosen to make the traditional pilgrimage to Notre Dame de Chartres. From that time on, Mary was to be permanently at the heart of his life and his missionary ministry.

Early Ministry

Filled with enthusiasm, Grignion de Montfort began his priestly ministry in Nantes, in the Community of St. Clement. His experience, if not a failure, was at least a great disappointment. We have a magnificent letter from this period, addressed on 6 December 1700 to Father Leschassier (see document 6 in this chapter). In it, the young priest presents what will eventually constitute his entire ministry and mission. This text is a true apostolic program that reveals Grignion de Montfort's heart.

Through the intervention of Madame de Montespan, the benefactress of his sister, whom he had met at the Abbey of Fontevrault, he was next sent to Poitiers. There, he devoted himself to serving the sick in the General Hospital, where he became chaplain. There, also, thanks to several patients and, above all, to Marie-Louise Trichet, he founded the very first community of the Daughters of Wisdom. This occurred on 2 February 1703, when Marie-Louise put on the gray uniform of the hospital residents, signifying her commitment to live among them, dedicated to working and serving the poor. The *poor* were the beggars, the infirm, pregnant and un-wed women, and other outcasts of society, all assigned to the hospital by King Louis XIV. After a brief stay in Paris, Grignion de Montfort returned to Poitiers at the request of the poor. Throughout his entire life, he would have a special love for these people. In a letter to his mother on 28 August 1704, he told her that he had renounced all things and had taken "Wisdom and the Cross as his spouse." The wisdom of the Incarnate Word finds fulfill-ment in the foolishness of the gospel, in the Cross. The *Wisdom-Cross of Poitiers* still today bears austere, mov-ing testimony to this truth. Henceforth, the theme of wisdom was to stand at the center of Grignion de Mont-fort's prayer and teaching.

The Love of Eternal Wisdom

It was, perhaps, during a stay in Paris during 1703 and 1704 that Grignion de Montfort wrote his first book: *The Love of Eternal Wisdom*, a work less well known than his *Treatise on True Devotion*. According to Huré, S.M.M., a specialist in Montfort studies, it "reveals Montfort's spirituality in its totality . . . and it gives us a more exact and comprehensive idea of true devotion to Mary."[4] It is possible that this work was written for the seminarians of Poullart des Places who, at the time, was founding the Holy Spirit Seminary in Paris. This work, certainly, was the fruit of Grignion de Montfort's reflec-tions and extensive readings; even more, it demonstrates his deep and fervent prayer.

Bérulle had delighted in speaking about divine wis-dom, but neither he nor the other great masters of the French School had insights as keen or expressions as elo-quent as Grignion de Montfort's in treating this aspect of the mystery of the Incarnate Word. His meditation on the Books of Wisdom truly inspired and overwhelmed him. The Wisdom of God is revealed in Jesus, but Grig-nion de Montfort insists on two essential aspects of this revelation. In the first place, he sees the tenderness of

God, that is, "Wisdom's friendship for man . . . this beauty which so desires the friendship of human beings . . . which needs man in order to be happy." Secondly, this Wisdom, which is the Incarnate Word, invites us to follow his steps in submission to and dependency on Mary, with love for the Cross. *The Love of Eternal Wisdom* must be read before any other work by Grignion de Montfort, if we want to understand his thought.

The Apostolic Missionary

During the following years, Grignion de Montfort traversed the dioceses in the west of France, preaching missions and retreats. In 1706, he made a pilgrimage to Loretto and to Rome. He confided his aspirations to proclaim the gospel in distant lands to Pope Clement XI who confirmed his vocation as a missionary *in France*:

> You have a large enough field in France for the exercise of your zeal. Do not go anywhere else, and labor always in perfect submission to the bishops.[5]

At this time, the pope bestowed on him the title of "apostolic missionary."

For 16 years, Grignion de Montfort exercised a ministry that led him to travel thousands of miles, often on foot. He preached nearly 200 missions or retreats, especially in the dioceses of Saint-Malo, Saint-Brieuc, Rennes, Nantes, Poitiers, Luçon and La Rochelle. In 1710, the affair of the Calvary at Port-Château occurred, with the bishop of Nantes forbidding the blessing and ordering that the life-sized way of the Cross be totally demolished. On several occasions, Grignion de Montfort spent time in Paris, and then returned to Rouen between July and October 1714. In Rouen, he met Jean-Baptiste Blain, his former fellow student and friend from Rennes and Saint-Sulpice. Not satisfied with having brought together the first group of Daughters of Wisdom with Marie-Louise Trichet (Marie-Louise de Jésus), he formed another group composed of several brothers and priests. Louis-Marie Grignion de Montfort died on 28 April 1716, while preaching a mission at Saint-Laurent-sur-Sèvre. He was only 43 years old. He had followed the dream confided, in the first months of his priesthood, to his spiritual director, Leschassier, in the letter to which we have already referred (see document 6).

The Apostle of Mary

An essential aspect of the spiritual experience and the message of Grignion de Montfort can be found in his *Treatise on True Devotion to the Blessed Virgin* as well as in the *Secret of Mary*, which is in a way a précis of the longer work. He may not have titled the *Treatise* himself. The manuscript was published for the first time in 1843, without a title, but also without the first pages of the work. The author himself defined it as a "Preparation for the Reign of Jesus Christ." He saw it as the outcome of his missionary labors: "I took up my pen to write . . . what I had taught with success for many years, in public and, particularly, during my missions." During each mission, he prepared his listeners to renew within themselves the spirit of Christianity. Before administering absolution and communion to them, he required that they renew their baptismal commitments, their "covenantal contract with God." The formula he proposed contained the following words: "I give myself entirely to JESUS CHRIST through the hands of MARY, to carry my cross after him all the days of my life." This was Grignion de Montfort's version of the *Life and Kingdom* of John Eudes. This renewal took place within an imposing religious service marked by appropriate solemnity. Here, as in his famous mission hymns, Grignion de Montfort appears as the master of a pedagogy perfectly adapted to the simple people he addressed.

The principal aspect of his pedagogy was, of course, his emphasis on devotion to Mary and the proposal of holy slavery. The *Treatise*, which had been carefully composed toward the end of his missionary activity, is based on the patristic tradition and on the teaching of the great spiritual leaders of the French School. The vocabulary itself echoes Bérulle and Olier, in witness to this tradition:

> This devotion, essentially, consists in a state of soul. . . . Who will remain in it permanently? Only the one to whom the Spirit of Jesus Christ reveals the secret.[6]

The ultimate goal of all we do is the reign of Jesus in the world and in souls, but for Grignion de Montfort the way to the goal is Mary: "It is through the most holy Virgin Mary that Jesus Christ came into the world. It is also through her that he must reign in the world." Following the best theologians, including Olier, Grignion de Montfort insists repeatedly on the role of the Holy Spirit and on the bond that exists between the Spirit of God and the Virgin Mary:

> Together with the Holy Spirit, Mary produced the greatest thing that ever was or ever will be: A God-Man. She will, consequently produce the marvels which will be seen in the latter times. The formation and education of the great saints who will come at the end of time are reserved to her, for only this singular and wondrous Virgin can produce in union with the Holy Spirit, singular and wondrous things.
>   When the Holy Spirit, her spouse, finds Mary in a soul, he hastens there and enters fully into it. He gives himself generously to that soul, according to the place it has given to his spouse. One of the main reasons why the Holy Spirit does not now work striking wonders in souls is that he fails to find in them a sufficiently close union with his faithful and inseparable spouse.[7]

In season and out of season, Grignion never failed to recall the absolute primacy of Jesus in the faith and life of the Christian:

Jesus our Savior, true God and true man, must be the ultimate end of all our other devotions. Otherwise, they would be false and misleading. Jesus Christ is the *Alpha* and the *Omega*, the beginning and end of everything. "We labor," says St. Paul, "only to make all men perfect in Jesus Christ."

For in him alone dwells the entire fullness of divinity and the complete fullness of grace, virtue and perfection. . . . If then, we are establishing sound devotion to our Blessed Lady, it is only in order to establish devotion to Our Lord Jesus Christ more perfectly, by providing a smooth but certain way of reaching Jesus Christ. If devotion to Our Lady distracted us from Our Lord, we would have to reject it as an illusion of the devil. But this is far from being the case. As I have already shown and will show again, later on, this devotion is necessary simply and solely because it is a way of reaching Jesus perfectly, loving him tenderly, and serving him faithfully.[8]

At a practical level, Grignion de Montfort's secret of slavery to Jesus in Mary takes up and, to a degree, unites the vows of servitude to Mary and to Jesus practiced and counseled by Bérulle and Olier. However, he goes into greater detail than they regarding the advantages of this practice and the concrete ways of assuring its authenticity and its fruit. *The Secret of Mary* popularizes this form of consecration to Mary for the public at large, but the *Treatise* is still the classic work on Marian devotion.

Among all the spiritual leaders of his era and perhaps, one might say, of all time, Grignion de Montfort is probably the one who developed the deepest theology of devotion to Mary in the Christian life for simple, humble people. John Paul II, a faithful reader of the *Treatise of True Devotion*, has said: "Grignion de Montfort even shows the working of the mysteries which quicken our faith and make it grow and render it fruitful."[9]

Grignion de Montfort's Special Grace

Grignion de Montfort is often represented as a high-strung, nervous ascetic, brandishing the cross and threatening sinners with hell-fire. Actually, he was a priest filled with tenderness and compassion, known as "good Father de Montfort" by the simple people who knew him. He himself acknowledged that God had given him "the grace to touch hearts."

Here, we are at the source of the widespread missionary and mystical influence experienced by this man: he felt an overflowing love for Jesus, for Mary, for the poor. Three of his Canticles, entitled *The Lovers of Jesus*, echo this reality in his life:

> Jesus is my love,
> Jesus is my treasure,
> Both night and day,
> I repeat unceasingly:
> Love.
> Both night and day,
> Jesus is my love.

The last two lines are repeated as a refrain for 40 verses. The slavery proposed by Grignion de Montfort is a pathway of liberty and love, leading to total union with God, in Jesus, through Mary.

Like Bérulle and Olier, Grignion had a gentler side to his personality. His teaching on the demanding austerity of the Cross and annihilation was balanced by light and sweetness, we might say, by the love and the maternal presence of Mary. He desired to see an increase in the number "of loving slaves who, with great love, would give and surrender themselves to serve as slaves, for the sole honor of belonging to her."

In Louis-Marie Grignion de Montfort's existence, ministry and widespread influence, we find a striking unity. It corresponds to the "ineffable bond formed by three who love one another: Jesus, Mary and Louis, in a heart which has become the temple of the Spirit, through the ineffable dimension of a shared experience."[10]

Documents for Chapter 9

9.1 Montfort's Life Journey

1673	–	31 January: Birth, in Montfort-la-Cane
1675–1684		Childhood in Iffendic
1684–1692		Studies with the Jesuits in Rennes
1692–1700		At Saint-Sulpice, in Paris. Member of the communities of M. de la Barmondière and M. Boucher, in the Minor Seminary.
1700	–	Ordination to priesthood. First Mass in the Blessed Virgin's chapel in St-Sulpice Church.
1701–1703		At Saint-Clément, in Nantes, and in the General Hospital, in Poitiers.
1703	–	2 February: Clothing of Marie-Louise Trichet. Autumn: stay in Paris.
1704	–	Return to Poitiers.
1706	–	Trip to Loretto and Rome. Audience with Clement XI.
1706–1716		Missions in the West of France. 13 September 1710: Forbidden to bless the Port-Château Way of the Cross.
1712	–	Writing of the *Treatise on True Devotion to the Blessed Virgin*
1716	–	28 April: Death in Saint-Laurent-sur-Sèvre, during a mission.

9.2 Night Prayer

Savior Jesus, we offer you our sleep in honor of, and in union with your sleep, your death and burial; and our awakening tomorrow in honor of and in union with your holy resurrection. We adore your holy dispositions in these actions, and we beg of you the grace to obtain the same.

Amen.

> *God Alone: The Collected Writings of St. Louis Mary de Montfort.*
> Bayshore, NY: Montfort Publications, 1987; 516–17.

9.3 Methods of Praying the Rosary

FIRST METHOD

I unite with all the saints in heaven and with all the just on earth; I unite with you, my Jesus, to praise your holy Mother worthily and to praise you in her and by her. I renounce all the distractions that may come to me while I am saying this Rosary. O Blessed Virgin Mary, we offer you this creed to honor the faith you had upon earth and to ask you to permit us to share in that same faith. O Lord, we offer you this Our Father to adore you in your oneness and to acknowledge you as the first cause and the last end of all things. Most Holy Trinity, we offer you these three Hail Marys to thank you for all the graces which you have given to Mary and which you have given to us through her intercession.

Our Father, three Hail Marys, Glory be to the Father. . . .

We offer you, Lord Jesus, this First Decade in honor of your Incarnation. Through this mystery and the intercession of your holy Mother we ask for humility of heart.

Our Father, ten Hail Marys, Glory be to the Father. May the grace of the mystery of the Incarnation come into me and make me truly humble.

(...)

SECOND, SHORTER METHOD

Of Celebrating the life, death and heavenly glory of Jesus and Mary in the Holy Rosary and a method of restraining our imagination and lessening distractions.

To do this a word is added to each Hail Mary of the decade reminding us of the mystery we are celebrating. This addition follows the name of Jesus in the middle of the Hail Mary: and blessed is the fruit of thy womb,

Decade   1st   "Jesus becoming man"
            2nd   "Jesus Sanctifying"
            3rd   "Jesus born in poverty"
            4th   "Jesus sacrificed" (. . .)

At the end of the first five mysteries we say:

> May the grace of the joyful mysteries come into our souls and make us really holy.

At the end of the second:

> May the grace of the sorrowful mysteries come into our souls and make us truly patient.

At the end of the third:

> May the grace of the glorious mysteries come into our souls and make us eternally happy. Amen.

God Alone, 234, 237, 238.

9.4 Jesus Living and Reigning in Mary

Since the principal mystery celebrated and honored in this devotion is the mystery of the Incarnation where we find Jesus only in Mary, having become incarnate in her womb, it is more appropriate for us to say, "slavery of Jesus in Mary," of Jesus dwelling and reigning in Mary, according to the beautiful prayer, recited by so many great souls, "O Jesus, living in Mary."

These expressions show more clearly the intimate union existing between Jesus and Mary. So closely are they united that one is wholly in the other. Jesus is all in Mary and Mary is all in Jesus. Or rather, it is no longer she who lives, but Jesus alone who lives in her. It would be easier to separate light from the sun than Mary from Jesus. So united are they that our Lord may be called, "Jesus of Mary," and his Mother "Mary of Jesus."

Time does not permit me to linger here and elaborate on the

perfections and wonders of the mystery of Jesus living and reigning in Mary, or the Incarnation of the Word. I shall confine myself to the following brief remarks. The Incarnation is the first mystery of Jesus Christ; it is the most hidden; and it is the most exalted and the least known.

It was in this mystery that Jesus, in the womb of Mary and with her cooperation, chose all the elect. For this reason the saints called her womb the throne-room of God's mysteries.

It was in this mystery that Jesus anticipated all subsequent mysteries of his life by his willing acceptance of them. Consequently, this mystery is a summary of all his mysteries since it contains the intention and the grace of them all.

Lastly, this mystery is the seat of the mercy, the liberality, and the glory of God. It is the seat of his *mercy* for us, since we can approach and speak to Jesus through Mary. We need her intervention to see or speak to him. Here, ever responsive to the prayer of his Mother, Jesus unfailingly grants grace and mercy to all poor sinners.

God Alone, 368.

9.5 Grignion at Chartres

Having arrived at Chartres, he hastened to throw himself at the feet of the statue of the Blessed Virgin that is venerated in the crypt chapel. . . . His heart was at peace. . . . Time seemed to pass quickly. He took delight in staying there, and left, regretfully. It seemed long before he could return. The next day, . . . he received Holy Communion . . . and prayed for six or eight hours, uninterruptedly, that is, from morning until noon. He prayed kneeling, unmoved, and motionless. (Following) lunch, he returned to pray, in the same posture, with the same fervor, as long as he had in the morning, that is, until nightfall, when he was told he had to retire.

Blain, *Abrégé de la vie*, 184–85; éd. de Rome, 1973; 101.

9.6 Letter to his Director

To Reverend Fr. Leschassier,
Superior of the Seminary of St. Sulpice,
Paris.

6th of December, 1700

Dear Reverend Father,
    May the perfect love of God reign in our hearts!
    I cannot tell you how much pleasure your short letter gave
me. It shows the bond of charity which unites you and my
unworthy self, a bond God has established and wishes to
maintain. It is with this in mind that I am writing to tell you
briefly about my state of mind at the moment. I have not
found here what I had hoped for and what led me to leave such
a holy place as St. Sulpice, almost against my better judgment.
    My intention was, as yours was too, to prepare for mission
work and especially for teaching catechism to the poor, since
this is what attracts me most. But I am not doing that at all
and I do not think that I shall ever do it here, for there are very
few people in the house and no one has any experience except
Fr. Lévêque. He is unable to undertake missions now because
of his age and even if his great zeal impelled him to undertake
them, Fr. Desjonchères would not allow it as he told me himself. There is not even half the organization and observance
here as there was at St. Sulpice and it seems that as things are,
there could never be any improvement. It seems to me that
there are four types of people here, whose aims and intentions
are quite different:

1) There are five people in the community proper of
   whom two are incapable of any active work.
2) There are the parish priests, curates, ordinary priests
   and laymen who come occasionally for retreats.
3) There are a few priests and canons who reside here
   just for a quiet life.
4) There are some priests and a greater number of young
   students who go out for theology and philosophy
   courses—most of them are dressed in lay clothes or
   without full clerical dress.

All these different people have their own rule which they have made up by taking what suits them from the common rule. I must admit that it is not Fr. Lévêque's fault that the rule is not kept. He does what he can and not what he would like to do, especially with regard to certain members of the community who dislike his simple, saintly ways.

With conditions as they are, I find myself, as time goes on, torn by two apparently contradictory feelings. On one hand, I feel a secret attraction for a hidden life in which I can efface myself and combat my natural tendency to show off. On the other hand, I feel a tremendous urge to make our Lord and his holy Mother loved, to go in a humble and simple way to teach catechism to the poor in country places and to arouse in sinners a devotion to our Blessed Lady. This was the work done by a good priest who died a holy death here recently. He used to go about from parish to parish teaching the people catechism and relying only on what Providence provided for him. I know very well, my dear Father, that I am not worthy to do such honorable work, but when I see the needs of the Church I cannot help pleading continually for a small and poor band of good priests to do this work under the banner and protection of the Blessed Virgin. Though I find it difficult, I try to suppress these desires, good and persistent though they may be. I strive to forget them and self-effacingly place myself in the hands of divine Providence and submit entirely to your advice which will always have the force of law for me.

I still harbor the desire I had in Paris to join Fr. Leuduger, a student of Fr. de St. Brieuc. He is a great missionary and a man of wide experience. Another of my wishes would be to go to Rennes and, with a good priest I know there, work in seclusion at the general hospital, performing charitable services for the poor. But I put aside all these ideas, and always in submission to God's good pleasure I await your advice on whether I should stay here, in spite of having no inclination to do so, or go elsewhere. In the peace of Christ and his holy Mother I am completely at your command.

I take the liberty of asking you to greet Fr. Brenier for me. If you think it useful, I will tell him what I have told you.

Grignion, priest and unworthy slave of Jesus in Mary.

God Alone, 5–7.

9.7 To the Superior General of Saint-Sulpice

(March 1704)

> Through the death and Passion of Jesus.
> Sir,
> We, four hundred poor people, humbly beg
> you, for the greatest love and
> glory of God, to send our venerated pastor
> back to us, M. Grignion, who loves
> the poor so much.

T. Rey-Mermet, *Louis-Marie Grignion de Montfort.*
Paris, 1984; 56.

9.8 The "Wisdom" Cross of Poitiers

When Fr. de Montfort was chaplain at the poorhouse at Poitiers from 1701–1703, he formed a group of young girls who gathered together regularly in a house which he called "La Sagesse" (Wisdom). Soon afterwards Marie Louise Trichet and Catherine Brunet, who were to become the first Daughters of Wisdom, joined them.

Montfort composed for them a program of the spiritual life based upon the words of Jesus Christ, Incarnate Wisdom: "We must renounce self and carry our cross after Jesus Christ, under Mary's guidance."

He wrote this program in a very simple way on a cross, which has been preserved by the community of the Daughters of Wisdom in Rome.

> Deny
> Oneself
> Carry
> One's Cross
> To Follow
> Jesus Christ

If You Are Ashamed Of The Cross
Of Jesus Christ, He Will Be
Ashamed Of You Before His Father.

Love
The Cross
Desire:
Crosses
Contempt
Pain
Abuse
Insults
Disgrace
Persecution
Humiliations
Calumnies
Illness
Injuries.

May Jesus Prevail
May His Cross Prevail

Divine Love
Humility
Submission
Patience
Obedience:
Complete
Prompt
Joyful
Blind
Persevering

God Alone, 437.

9.9 Love of Eternal Wisdom

TO LOVE AND SEEK DIVINE WISDOM WE NEED TO KNOW
HIM.
[Our need to acquire knowledge of divine Wisdom]

Can we love someone we do not even know? Can we love
deeply someone we only know vaguely? Why is Jesus, the
adorable, eternal and incarnate Wisdom loved so little if not
because he is either too little known or not known at all?

EARNEST DESIRE OF DIVINE WISDOM TO GIVE HIMSELF TO MEN.

The bond of friendship between Eternal Wisdom and man is so close as to be beyond our understanding. Wisdom is for man and man is for Wisdom. "He is an infinite treasure for man," and not for angels or any other creatures.

Wisdom's friendship for man arises from man's place in creation, from his being an abridgement of Eternal Wisdom's marvels, his small yet ever so great world, his living image and representative on earth. Since Wisdom, out of an excess of love, gave himself the same nature by becoming man and delivered himself up to death to save man, he loves man as a brother, a friend, a disciple, a pupil, the price of his own blood and co-heir of his kingdom. For man to withhold his heart from Wisdom or to wrench it away from him would constitute an outrage.

[Eternal Wisdom's letter of love]

This eternal beauty, ever supremely loving, is so intent on winning man's friendship that for this very purpose he has written a book in which he describes his own excellence and his desire for man's friendship. This book reads like a letter written by a lover to win the affections of his loved one, for in it he expresses such ardent desires for the heart of man, such tender longings for man's friendship, such loving invitations and promises, that you would say he could not possibly be the sovereign Lord of heaven and earth and at the same time need the friendship of man to be happy.

In his pursuit of man, he hastens along the highways, or scales the loftiest mountain peaks, or waits at the city gates, or goes into the public squares and among the gatherings of people, proclaiming at the top of his voice, "You children of men, it is you I have been calling so persistently; it is you I am addressing; it is you I desire and seek; it is you I am claiming. Listen, draw close to me, for I want to make you happy."

God Alone, 51, 67.

9.10 Perfect Consecration to Jesus Christ

As all perfection consists in our being conformed, united and consecrated to Jesus it naturally follows that the most perfect of all devotions is that which conforms, unites, and consecrates us most completely to Jesus. Now of all God's creatures Mary is the most conformed to Jesus. It therefore follows that, of all devotions, devotion to her makes for the most effective consecration and conformity to him. The more one is consecrated to Mary, the more one is consecrated to Jesus.

That is why perfect consecration to Jesus is but a perfect and complete consecration of oneself to the Blessed Virgin, which is the devotion I teach; or in other words, it is the perfect renewal of the vows and promises of holy baptism.

This devotion consists in giving oneself entirely to Mary in order to belong entirely to Jesus through her. It requires us to give:

1) Our body with its senses and members;
2) Our soul with its faculties;
3) Our present material possessions and all we shall acquire in the future.
4) Our interior and spiritual possessions, that is, our merits, virtues and good actions of the past, the present and the future.

God Alone, 327.

9.11 The Devout Slave of Jesus in Mary

"Que mon âme chante et publie" No. 77

1 Let this my song declare
    (Thus honoring her Son)
  Our Lady's boundless care
    Toward her poor serving-one.

2 O that my voice might say
    Thunder-loud east to west
  Far happiest are they

On earth who serve her best.

3   Predestined ones, prepare
       Your ears. I tell things true,
    Marvels sublime and rare
       Of her who mothered you.

4   Mary is my great wealth;
       With Christ she is my all,
    My tenderness, my health,
       My honor's treasure-hall.

5   She is the covenant-ark
       Of purity's defense;
    My refuge from the dark,
       My robe of innocence.

6   She is the chaste retreat
       Where I can always pray
    In Jesus' presence sweet
       And not be turned away.

7   She is the citadel
       Where I am safe from harm;
    Amidst the deluge-swell
       She takes me by the arm.

8   Depending on her care
       The better to depend
    On Jesus, I stake there
       This life and its last end.

9   When from the Tempter's stings
       I struggle up toward God,
    It is on Mary's wings
       I mount, no more a clod.

10 My just Redeemer's ire
       By Mary's plea is eased.
    "Behold," I cry, "your Mother!"
       At once He is appeased.

11 This Mistress, when I call,
       Comes to my aid with power.
    If, being weak, I fall
       She helps me in that hour.

12 At times when like a plague

Some daily sin assails,
"O Mary, help!" I beg,
And grace once more prevails.

13 She answers when I cry
    For strength God's will to do:
"Have courage, son, for I,
    Shall not abandon you."

14 When as a nursing child
    I seek her breast's pure milk,
This Virgin chaste and mild
    Feeds me celestial milk.

15 Here is a mystery:
    By Mary's motherhood
I carry her in me;
    Her goodness is my good.

16 She fructifies my soul
    By her fecundity;
She makes me meek and whole
    By her humility.

17 She is the limpid pool
    Wherein my sores show plain,
Wherein, refreshed, I cool
    My passions and their pain.

18 Through Jesus I must go
    To see His Father's face;
Through Mary's help, just so,
    I seek to gain that grace.

19 I do all things through her.
    This is the surest way
To do God's will, the spur
    And key to sanctity.

20 Christians, arise! Outrun
    My laggard constancy.
Love Mary, love her Son
    Now and eternally.

CHAPTER TEN

The Role of Women in the French School

O ur study of the French School has already introduced us to a number of women who influenced
one or another of the great masters: Madame Acarie,
Agnès de Langeac and Marie des Vallées, among others. It
is only appropriate, now, to consider more directly the
role played by countless women in the Christian renewal
of the seventeenth century, especially in the tradition
that comes from Bérulle.

Writing of this period, one historian has referred to the
feminization of the church in France during the seventeenth century.[1] There was a striking increase, at the beginning of the century, in the number of women consecrated to God in the religious life as such or in new
forms—for example, those known as *secular daughters*,
consecrated laywomen. This phenomenon was due, in

part, to a change in the situation of women in this era, but also to renewal of the Christian life.

Consideration of a few outstanding women will allow us to complete the tableau sketched in earlier chapters. It will also highlight one area of interest and value of the French School for our own time. While it is necessary to avoid artificial comparisons, we cannot help but notice similarities, in this area as in others, between our day and the seventeenth century in France. The Bérulle School has still more than one lesson for us!

Women in the French School

The inferior position of women in France in the seventeenth century has been pointed out by historians and sociologists without exception. Actually, however, women exercised a major influence and had an important role in society in that period. One author states:

> ... what a delight it was to be a woman in France: one enjoyed a thousand liberties and a thousand pleasures. . . . The memoirs of travelers in that period all echo the same sentiments. Outside of France, the life of women seemed sad and social life was dull, because of the absence of women. And, when a French woman traveled abroad, she dazzled everyone with her grace and ease of conversation. At the same time, she knew how to call for respect from others, being unwilling to let anyone think that she would in any way abuse the external liberty she enjoyed.[2]

The situation of women in the Church, particularly in the Catholic church, was both inferior and able to assert significant influence. Marriage was not always held in high regard: one was subject to a husband, tied down by one pregnancy after another, living in constant dependency. It was common to speak of the "harsh yoke of marriage. . . . I would almost advise no one to take it on."[3] Duvergier de Hauranne claimed that "marriage was never as holy or as unhappy as in Christianity."[4] Widowhood was often presented as a state that promoted holiness. The devotions of women, however, were frequently scorned and criticized. Still, Du Bosc would write, "Those who imagine that the piety of women is only a matter of a sentimental temperament or a weak mind hold an opinion with which we do not agree."[5]

In this rich social, psychological and religious context, so full of contrasts and dynamic energies, a good number of Christian women would emerge, blaze their own trail and initiate lasting accomplishments. At times, both the Church and the world, which were so closely associated, would acknowledge this. Between Madame Acarie (1556–1618), the great spiritual leader responsible for bringing Carmel to France, and Madame Guyon (1648–1717), a rich constellation of great spiritual women appeared. In their relationships with countless laymen, men religious, and other churchmen, they would help to make the seventeenth century in France a time of intense apostolic activity, marked by works of charity and education.

An Overview

In order to appreciate more fully the situation, the role and the influence exercised by women in the world of religion in seventeenth century France, it is important to recall Paul Cochois's distinction. In the strict sense of the term, the French School refers to "the disciples of Bérulle who took up the major themes characteristic of his doctrine." In a large sense, the French School corresponds to "the great christological movement made possible by Bérulle's influence."

On close examination, relatively few women can be attached to the Bérulle School in this strict sense. Madeleine de Saint-Joseph would surely be the best example of one of them. We might also include Madame Acarie, although she, rather, shaped Bérulle to a certain degree, before becoming more or less his disciple. There were also, as we have seen, many difficulties and misunderstandings between them.

However, a good number of women, both lay and religious, were truly sources of inspiration for the followers of Bérulle. Olier was helped by Agnès of Langeac, a contemplative Dominican; Marie Rousseau, a Parisian widow; and Marie de Valence. John Eudes was greatly assisted and enlightened by Marie des Vallées, a mystic from Normandy, although she was the source of many problems for his contemporaries. Other women, also, influenced the spiritual masters of the day. Henri Bremond insists on their role as innovators of movements or activities: "in most of the great religious undertakings of the seventeenth century, we discover a woman's inspiration."[6]

There is still another area where women must be acknowledged, that of the *devouts*. They lived and were active in the company of Bérulle's disciples or followed other spiritual movements somewhat colored by teachings of the Bérulle School, either at the beginning of the century or throughout the course of this era. It is sometimes difficult to make clear distinctions among various mystical-apostolic movements that intertwine or seem to belong to more than one tradition.

Nonetheless, a singular phenomenon must be emphasized. Along with countless laywomen like Madame d'Herculais or Madame Hélyot, and "authentic" women religious like the Carmelites, the Visitandines and the Ursulines, several other groups developed in a most astonishing manner in seventeenth century France. There were the *secular daughters* who lived in community, without cloister or solemn vows, without "veil or wimple." They were women who lived their consecration at the heart of intense activity, in apostolic works of charity, in hospitals and schools. Various studies have been published recently on this phenomenon, for example, by Elisabeth Charpy, Lorraine Caza, C.N.D., and Elizabeth Rapley. It is important for us to realize that many of these women were deeply marked by the teachings of Bérulle and his disciples. In the larger sense of the term, at least, they belong to the French School.

From among the many Christian women in seventeenth century France who represent the tradition of the Bérulle School, several will be considered in greater detail in the following pages. They represent a variety of spiritual and apostolic lifestyles of the era:

- Madame Acarie: an innovator;
- Madeline de Saint-Joseph: a Carmelite of the Bérulle School;
- Marie de l'Incarnation Guyart: an apostolic Ursuline;
- Louise de Marillac and Marguerite Bourgeoys: *secular daughters*, both of whom were associated with the foundation of important congregations.

These few examples cannot exhaust the wealth of women's presence in this era, even if the Bérulle School alone is to be considered. There were many others: Sisters of the Holy Family known as the *Miramionnes*; the *Teachers of Charity*; women like Françoise Duval, associated with the foundation of four groups of educators; and Anne-Marie Martel.

Madame Acarie

Like Jeanne de Chantal (1572–1641), Madame Acarie is a good example of what a Christian woman, living in the seventeenth century as a wife, a widow, and a religious, could bring to the Church of her day. In a very particular way, her relationship with Bérulle and with Carmel, as it came into France, invites us to know her better as a woman who represents the French School of spirituality.

Unfortunately, Madame Acarie wrote little, so it is through the witness of her life that we know her. Barbe Avrillot was born in Paris on 1 February 1556. She belonged to a well-to-do family and enjoyed a good education, studying with the Poor Clares of Longchamp. On 24

August 1582, she married Pierre Acarie, a master account-ant. He was a devout man with a trying personality, who had pledged allegiance to the League of Catholics united against the Huguenots. Madame Acarie raised their six children amidst her constant worries about the political positions taken by her husband. He was exiled and de-spoiled of a portion of his possessions in 1594, because of his membership in the League. In 1599, Madame Acarie obtained his liberation.

Long before then, as early as 1588, Madame Acarie had experienced mystical graces, spiritual insight and intu-ition, accompanied both by ecstasy and suffering. With the encouragement of the Capuchin, Benoît de Canfeld, she assembled a group of spiritual persons, both clergy and laity. In addition to Benoît de Canfeld, there was an-other Capuchin, Archange de Pembrocke; the Jesuits, Pierre Coton and Etienne Binet; and André Duval, doctor at the Sorbonne, professor of Bérulle, friend of Vincent de Paul and Olier, biographer of Madame Acarie. Others in the group were Jacques Gallement, her cousin, the pastor of Aumale; Michel de Marillac and Francis de Sales, when he was in Paris. Richard Beaucousin, the Carthu-sian, directed the group and suggested what they ought to read: the Rheno-Flemish mystics, and, beginning in 1601, the writings of Teresa of Jesus.

This spiritual group was also a heart of apostolic ser-vice, and a center of preparation for renewal of the Chris-tian life among the laity and in religious orders. Madame Acarie herself contributed either to the reform or the foundation of monasteries for women: Montmartre and Soissons, for the Benedictines; and, in 1610, with her cousin, Madame de Saint-Beuve, for the Ursulines, in Paris.

However, Madame Acarie's greatest claim to glory was her contribution to efforts to bring to France the Carmelite nuns of the reform of St. Teresa. She herself gathered together and formed the first candidates for

Carmel. She obtained all the necessary permissions from
the king in 1602; from Pope Clement VIII in 1603; and
from the Spanish Carmelite friars. In 1604, despite many
difficulties, six Spanish Carmelite nuns were brought to
Paris by Pierre de Bérulle. Madame Acarie also worked to
found several other Carmels. After the death of her husband in 1613, she herself entered the Carmel at Amiens.
Later, she joined the monastery at Pontoise, where three
of her daughters had preceded her. She died on 18 April
1618 and was beatified on 5 June 1791.

Aside from a few letters and a small booklet, Madame
Acarie—in Carmel, Marie de l'Incarnation—left no spiritual writings. She is still to be counted among the great
spiritual leaders of seventeenth century France. Henri
Bremond dedicated nearly 70 pages to her in volume two
of his literary history, under the title "mystical invasion." His praise of her is unqualified, and he compares
her to Francis de Sales: he, the great mystical doctor of
the age; she, "the great innovator and perfect model."[7]

If it is true to say that Bérulle was the dominant character of the age, it is also true to say that Madame Acarie
prepared the way for the French School. Her devotion to
the person of Christ, nourished by the doctrine of St.
Teresa, had only to be taken up and developed theologically by Bérulle, Condren, Olier and John Eudes.

Madeleine de Saint-Joseph

Mother Madeleine, the first French prioress of the first
monastery of Discalced Carmelite nuns in France, exercised a most significant influence. She is actually quite
unknown and deserves more attention than she has ever
received, because of her role and her spiritual doctrine,
marked by the teachings of both Teresa and Bérulle. She
spent almost her entire life either as directress of novices or prioress of the Great Monastery, the first Carmel
founded in Paris in 1604. She was responsible for the

formation of most of the prioresses of the more than 40 new foundations that were made in the space of several years. It was through Madeleine de Saint-Joseph that Bérulle's doctrines of adoration, of mystical christo-centrism through "adherence" to the states and mysteries of Jesus, and of particular devotion to the Mother of God were spread through the Carmelite monasteries in France.

> In his book on Bérulle, Cochois has included the following text:
> In 1635, she asked Father Gibieuf to write a book on the glories of Mary and, in it, to explain to the Carmelite nuns "that among all other creatures and all other religious, they were most particularly bound to love Our Lord Jesus Christ and the holy humanity he had taken from the pure and holy Virgin; that they were to have . . . a continual application (adherence) to his most holy life, his qualities and his Mysteries, and since they had the grace to be daughters of (his) Mother . . . , they ought to imitate her in the love and honor she gave him." Furthermore, they had the duty "to enter into union with her Son through her, and to be presented to him through her holy hands; for the Virgin has claimed this Order (Carmel) only to offer it to him and in a more worthy manner; she wants nothing for herself, but only for Him." From 1614 on, Bérulle used this argument to present his special *devotion* to the Mother of God to the Carmelite nuns. When Madeleine de Saint-Joseph would repeat, after him, that Carmel is the *Order of the Virgin*, she was using the word, *order*, in the Dionysian sense of Choir or mystical *hierarchy*. Here, we discover the primary idea of the vows of servitude. At the moment of her death, Madeleine de Saint-Joseph was to see Pierre de Bérulle praying for her and showing her JESUS and his Mother, for the last time.[9]

There have been times when the Carmels of Bérulle have been opposed to the Carmels of Teresa, in France. This distinction needs to be eliminated. It is clear that

the beginnings of Carmel in France bore the characteristics of Bérulle's doctrine. This influence only confirmed the christocentrism of Teresa of Jesus and gave
the Carmelites in France a taste for piety and devotion
based on solid doctrine. Paul Cochois has pointed out
that "it is not a coincidence that an Elizabeth of the
Trinity lived in a monastery (Dijon) where Bérulle had
always been honored." This young Carmelite described
adoration in words that would have made Madeleine de
Saint-Joseph proud of her daughter: "It is a word from
heaven, it is the ecstasy of love!"

Cochois also identifies devotion to the infancy of Jesus
as part of Bérulle's legacy to Carmel in France. This devotion, which was so dear to him, was spread throughout
France, due to the Carmel of Beaune. The spirit of childhood, that essential gospel value, has been admirably
demonstrated by another French Carmelite closer to our
own day, Thérèse of Lisieux (1873–1897).

If the Spanish Carmelites, Anne of Jesus and Anne of
St. Bartholomew, brought the spirit of Teresa of Jesus
with them to France, Madeleine of St. Joseph, daughter
both of Teresa and of Cardinal de Bérulle, exercised a
major role as the innovator of mysticism in Carmel in
seventeenth century France and later.

Marie de l'Incarnation Guyart

This Ursuline from Tours and Quebec does not belong
to the Bérulle School in the strict sense of the term.
However, she does deserve special mention here, because
she represents well one of the mystical-apostolic movements of her century. She also stands fully at the heart of
the spiritual and missionary renewal of the era marked
by the dominance of the French School. Furthermore, her
intuitions and even her vocabulary place her in the
Bérullian tradition.

Marie de l'Incarnation Guyart (1599–1672) was a great

mystic, whom Bossuet, following Father Jérôme Lallemant, would call "the Teresa of the New World." At the
same time, she was filled with a powerful missionary
spirit. The witness of her life, her letters, and her auto-
biographical accounts (*Relations*) are a living legacy that
faithfully reflects seventeenth century France.

As an Ursuline, Marie de l'Incarnation led a cloistered
life, within which she received a missionary vocation
from God, "through the emanation of the apostolic spirit
which is the very Spirit of Jesus Christ." This Spirit led
her to Canada, the mission land toward which all eyes in
France turned at the time. There, she was known as an
outstanding educator and is rightly considered one of the
"mothers of the Church in Canada," along with Marguerite Bourgeoys, Jeanne Mance, Catherine of St. Augustine and several other women.

Several major themes in Marie's spiritual and apostolic
life correspond to the teachings of the Bérulle School: a
pronounced christocentrism; love for Scripture, which
she quoted constantly; an apostolic spirit, identified as
the Spirit of Jesus. This last characteristic reminds us of
Bérulle and his missionary zeal, of John Eudes and the
emphasis he placed on apostolic zeal, and, above all, of
Olier.

Father Guy-Marie Oury has called Marie's autobio-
graphical *Relations* "the most perfect masterpiece of our
French mystical literature." The work, published in
1654, was written between June and October 1653, and
between May and August 1654. Along with her *Letters*,
this work is an excellent introduction to the spirit and
grace of a woman in seventeenth century France.

Louise de Marillac

Louise de Marillac (1591–1660) was the cofoundress,
with Vincent de Paul, of the Society of the Daughters of
Charity. She is not too well known, due on the one hand

to the prestige of St. Vincent de Paul, her spiritual father and friend, and on the other, to the discretion of the Daughters of Charity. A full presentation of the details of the astonishingly rich and active life of this woman lies beyond the limits of our study. Her extraordinary spiritual journey has been well presented in a work by Sister Elizabeth Charpy. However, it is appropriate to note that, like St. Vincent de Paul, she was influenced in a different, but no less authentic way by Bérulle's thought. She had always had a great devotion to the will of God, through her reading of Canfeld and Francis de Sales, and through association with Jeanne de Chantal. She was at home with words and ideas that belong strictly to the Bérulle School: "honor" God and "Jesus in his mysteries," the "holy Humanity of Jesus" and other similar expressions. She had a great devotion to the feast of the Annunciation, the Incarnation of the Word; to the infancy of Christ, to the Eucharist, and to the grace of Baptism. Like Condren and Olier, she considered the feast of Pentecost as one of the greatest of all feasts.

It is in reading her personal spiritual texts and letters that we see the extent to which Louise was marked by the tradition of the Bérulle School, even though she was influenced by many other spiritual movements as well. She deserves to be much better known. As one of the *secular daughters* who lived without cloister or solemn vows, she is a model of that of form consecration known in the church today as the Societies of Apostolic Life.

Marguerite Bourgeoys

Marguerite Bourgeoys (1620–1700) is known for having created in Montreal a new form of religious life that had met with many difficulties in France. She herself endured periods of trial and opposition in her efforts to win recognition for her concept of a life of consecration that was authentically religious: "the life of a wayfarer, in dialogue with the neighbor." The first and primary model of this form of life was Mary, the Mother of Jesus.

The entire spiritual and apostolic itinerary of this native of Champagne, born in Troyes in 1620, is of great interest. Two of the characteristics that mark her thought are of particular importance and are to be noted:

> 1. Her *keen sense of intuition regarding a new form of consecrated life*. Among the *women disciples* who followed Jesus, she recognized Mary Magdalene, the mother and model of cloistered religious; Martha, imitated by those in hospital services; and Mary, the Mother of Jesus, who continued her wayfaring life with the *secular daughters*.
>
> 2. *The inspiration of Bérulle and Olier in her spiritual thought*. On this point, the studies carried out by Sister Lorraine Caza are very enlightening. It is true that it is almost impossible to identify explicit quotations from the masters of the Bérulle School in Marguerite's writings. However, a careful analysis of her expressions and the influence of French Sulpicians on her thought lead us to affirm that the writings of Olier, for example, constitute the deepest roots of the Congregation of Notre Dame of Montreal, founded by Marguerite Bourgeoys.

One further point can be made. The apostolic spirit and devotion to Mary in her "life as a wayfarer, in conversation with the neighbor" are themes essential to the inspiration of Marguerite, as they had been for Bérulle and his followers.

A Final Word

This very brief overview has identified only a few representative Christian women in seventeenth century France. Many others might have been considered: religious, like Catherine de Bor (Mother Mechtilde of the

Blessed Sacrament), foundress of the Benedictines of the Blessed Sacrament; secular daughters or consecrated lay-women, like Jeanne de Mâtel, who remained in her own way of life, but who founded the Religious of the Incarnate Word.

Too much can never be said about the astonishing role and the extraordinary influence of certain women in the Church in seventeenth century France, and many studies could be devoted to this topic. Indepth research ought also to be pursued on the place of Mary Magdalene and, especially, of Mary, the Mother of Jesus, in the spiritual and apostolic movement we have been following. The mysteries of the Incarnation, the Visitation and Pentecost were subjects of constant meditation during the seventeenth century. The Virgin Mary, during that era, was the great inspiration for the devotion and the commitment of every woman.

DOCUMENTS FOR CHAPTER 10

10.1 Women in the French School

One cannot study the French School for long without being struck by the important, even critical role that women played throughout. The phenomenon of Cardinal Bérulle is very bound up with the Christocentric spirituality of the great St. Teresa of Avila, with the mystical aspirations of Madame Acarie and her circle, with St. Catherine of Genoa's thought, with the work of the French Carmelite nuns in Paris, and especially with the Venerable Madeleine de Saint-Joseph, the first French prioress of Paris' Great Carmel. So, too, biographers of Olier stress the crucial role of women in his evolving spirituality. One thinks of Marie Rousseau's important role in helping Olier through his dark night and in his seminary reform work. One thinks, too, of the Mère de Bressand, Mère Agnès, and especially of Marguerite de Saint-Sacrement. All played important roles in Olier's life. John Eudes was also deeply impressed by Marguerite's holiness, particularly her devotion to Jesus' infancy. And who can forget the important bonds he had with Marie des Vallées?

As feminist theological criticism is beginning to teach us, much of the contribution of women to theology and spirituality in general is only now beginning to receive the attention it has always deserved.

Alerting ourselves to the role of women in the history of the French School seems an appropriate place to say something about the theology of women present there too. So far as I know, no studies exist on this issue, and we must reply upon educated guesses stimulated by the newly emerging feminist criticism of theology. If we borrow a clue from Rosemary Ruether and speak of three basic "types" of understanding of women—patriarchal, androgynous and liberationist/the-refusal-to-stereotype—then we might suggest that the French School seems predominantly influenced by the androgynous viewpoint.

By androgyny we mean the tendency to associate certain characteristics with either males and females. Both characteristics may be present in males and females in varying degrees, but the crucial facet of androgyny is to name a certain set of characteristics properly male or female. This is the source of the so-called masculine and feminine archetypes. Olier employs them frequently, it appears. God is like a mother who nourishes her son, and in imitation of this the church's prelates are like mothers who engender and nourish their babes. Spiritual directors are like fathers in their force, courage and ability to correct; like mothers in their tenderness, patience and compassion. They "enter into the two great qualities of Our Lord . . . [who] is truly father and mother." Is this androgyny behind Bérulle's great elevation on Mary Magdalene, in which her founding of a school of love is contrasted with the Beloved Disciple's founding of a school of knowledge of the Lord? She has more fervor and love; he, more discernment and light.

One senses that much of the Marian theology and piety characteristic of the French School particularly lends itself to an androgynous viewpoint. Mary is, after all, the great example of servitude to the Lord through her maternity and virginity. "The great desire of the Mother of God is to see her son perfectly loved," says Mère Madeleine. This Marian piety lends itself to a stress upon the mothering, nourishing aspects of woman. And yet Mary's servitude is her elevation, just as Jesus' servitude is his elevation. And, in line with this, Bérulle speaks of Mary Magdalene as the first to witness the Risen Jesus; indeed, as one who did not flee from the cross, but who was strong. "The first bull and patent" the Risen Jesus issued was to Mary Magdalene "making her an apostle, but one of life, of glory, and of love; and an apostle to the apostles." Do these texts indicate that the French School was perhaps on the way to breaking out of the limiting, androgynous viewpoint? Androgyny seems too limiting a framework for this kind of experience and spirituality.

Could we perhaps sum up by saying that despite an occasional patriarchal text, misogynist in viewpoint, the French School leans more in the direction of androgyny, yet with indications of a move toward a more liberationist perspective? Much more research needs to be done, but for a first and tentative approach, this conclusion seems legitimate.

> *Bérulle and the French School*, Introduction, 22, 25–26.

10.2 Madame Acarie

The contemporaries of Madame Acarie found in her a living type of that sublime life towards which so many souls of the time felt themselves vaguely called. Her ecstasies were but signs, as a light hung out for travelers seeking their way at night. Their attention was caught at first by such extraordinary phenomena, but they soon learned from her truths far simpler and of quite different import. Her message consisted of a sentence from the Gospel, the full sense of which only mystics realize, "The kingdom of God is within you." "One must," she said, "penetrate to the depths of the soul, and see if God is, or will be there." She meant most certainly that more intimate Presence of God which is the whole of the mystic life. (. . .)

I ask pardon for repeating the keyword simplicity so often. There is none more appropriate to the beginnings of the religious movement which we are trying to describe. François de Sales was the great exponent of Mysticism reduced to its essential and wholesome simplicity, but Madame Acarie was at once his inspirer and the perfected model. Both alike were quick to make decisions and break down established customs, both alike were wise, but they differed in their modes of teaching, as in their gifts and position in the Church, yet they taught the same doctrine.

Bremond. A *Literary History of Religious Thought in France*, 3:193–94.

10.3 Madeleine de Saint-Joseph

My good Mother,

May the love of Jesus Christ fill your soul.

I have been thinking about what you asked me for a long time, but since I received your letter I have applied myself more to the question and I continue to have the same thought that I had: to prefer the act of adoration to that of thanksgiving, because it is more extensive and it exposes us less to the danger of too much self-preoccupation even under the pretext of thanking God for the blessings he has given us, especially when they are unique to us. Moreover, the respect toward the majesty of God that adoration creates in us moderates the excesses of sensibility many good souls experience easily in their devotional exercises.

What is most important to understand is that not only is adoration imperfect without love, but that it does not even deserve to be called adoration, nor is it welcomed by God as such, if love is not its soul and its life, if we can speak thus. Otherwise it is only a pretense of adoration and the kind of cult practiced by [some] Jews about which God complained a long time ago when he said through one of his prophets that this people honored him with their lips, but that their hearts were far from him (Is. 29.13). Now just as adoration cannot be perfect without love, so that the creature is fully possessed by its Creator, it is likewise true that love cannot be perfect unless it is accompanied by adoration. These are the two obligations that must be necessarily linked together in order to offer God what we owe him and what he asks of us.

We must further notice clearly that, as the Son of God gives us in his own person the example of all the virtues that he teaches with his sacred lips, he does it most particularly in this matter, which deals with our first duty toward God. We see from the words of St. Paul, which we have already mentioned, that from the moment he took on our nature, he humbled himself before God his Father. He recognized his supreme authority over him; he submitted to his will. He offered himself to him as a perpetual victim. When he said that his law was in the center of his heart, that shows the burning love with which he fulfilled his duty. Thus it is only in as much as we conform to this divine model and unite ourselves to his holy dispositions that we can accomplish perfectly the first and greatest commandment of the law, which contains all the others. Since it is not in our power to give God the final and most important proof of our love, which is to sacrifice ourselves to him physically, not being permitted to take our lives (and God does not ask it of us), Jesus Christ, our head, on his part makes up for what is lacking in us. He remains continually on our altars and deigns to come into our souls and even our bodies through holy communion, so that becoming one with him, we can, through this union, offer him to his Father and offer ourselves as well as a holy and acceptable sacrifice in the eyes of his majesty.

Bérulle and the French School, 200, 202–03.

10.4 Marie de l'Incarnation

Then at the age of 34 or 35, I entered into that state which, as it were, had been shown me and of which I had remained in expectation. This was an outpouring of apostolic spirit (which is nothing else than the Spirit of Jesus Christ) which took possession of my soul so that it could no longer live except in him and by him. I was thus wholly dedicated to zeal for his glory so that he would be known, loved, and adored by all peoples whom he had redeemed by his Precious Blood.

My body was in our monastery but my spirit, united to that of Jesus, could not remain shut up there. This apostolic spirit carried me in thought to the Indies, to Japan, to America, to the East and to the West, to parts of Canada, to the country of the Hurons—in short, to every part of the inhabited world where there were human souls who belonged by right to Jesus Christ. With inner certainty I saw the demons gaining victory over these poor souls, whom they snatched from the domain of Jesus Christ, our divine Master and Sovereign Lord, who had redeemed them by his Precious Blood.

As I watched this happen so surely, I became jealous, unable to endure the sight. I yearned for these poor souls; I gathered them to my heart; I presented them to the Eternal Father, telling him that it was time he exercised his justice in favor of my Spouse, to whom he had promised all nations for his inheritance. I reminded him that his Divine Son, through the shedding of his blood, had satisfied for all the sins of men who had previously been condemned to eternal death; yet there were still souls who did not live or belong to him. It was these souls whom I carried in my heart and whom I presented to the Eternal Father, begging that they all be given to Jesus Christ, to whom they rightfully belonged.

In spirit I roamed through the vast stretches of the Indies, of Japan and China, and kept company with those laboring to spread the Gospel there. I felt closely united to these workers because I felt that I was one with them in spirit. While it is true that in body I was bound by my rule of enclosure, nevertheless, my spirit did not cease its travels, nor did my heart cease its loving solicitations to the Eternal Father for the salvation of the many millions of souls whom I constantly offered him. The spirit of grace which acted in me moved me to such boldness and familiarity with the Eternal Father that it was impossible for me to do otherwise. "O Father, why do you delay? It is a long time since my Beloved shed his blood. I beg you in the interests of my Spouse," I would say to him, "be faithful to your word, O Father, for you have promised him all nations."

By a light infused into my soul, I saw more clearly than by any human light the meaning of this passage of Holy Scripture which speaks of the sovereign power which the Eternal Father has given the adorable Word Incarnate over all men, and this bright light which revealed so many wonders now kindled in my soul a love which consumed me and increased my longing that this Sacred Word would reign as absolute master—to the exclusion of all the demons—in the souls of all rational creatures. I felt that justice was on my side. The Spirit which possessed me made this clear and compelled me to say to the

Eternal Father: "It is only just that my divine Spouse be master. I am wise enough to teach all nations about him. Give me a voice strong enough to be heard to the ends of the earth to proclaim that my divine Spouse is worthy to reign and to be loved by all hearts."

In my eagerness and yearning toward the Eternal Father, I gave tongue, without any effort on my part, to passages from the Apocalypse which speak of this divine King of nations. I never sought out these passages, but they were urged on me and produced by the Spirit which possessed me.

> "The Relation of 1654" in *Marie of the Incarnation: Selected Writings*, ed. Irene Mahoney, O.S.U. New York/Mahwah: Paulist, 1989; 112–14.

10.5 St. Louise de Marillac

[This text comes from the last months of Louise's life (1660). It resembles the last "Relation" of Teresa of Jesus (1581), as a striking witness to the saint's spiritual maturity. Several themes from Bérulle can be readily identified in this selection.]

On the Feast of Saint Genevieve, in 1660, as I was receiving Holy Communion, I felt, upon seeing the Sacred Host, an extraordinary thirst which had its origin in the belief that Jesus wanted to give Himself to me in the simplicity of His divine infancy. When I was receiving Him and for a long time afterward, my mind was filled by an interior communication which led me to understand that Jesus was bringing not only Himself to me but also all the merits of His mysteries. This communication lasted all day. It was not a forced, interior preoccupation. It was rather a presence or a recurrent recollection, as sometimes happens when something is troubling me.

I felt that I was being warned that, since Jesus had given Himself entirely to me, laden with the merits of all these mysteries, I must make use of this occasion to participate in His submission to humiliations.

One means to attain this end is to be found in the fact that, without any cause in me, I appear to others as having received some graces from God. This both humbles me and gives me courage.

No desires, no resolutions. The grace of my God will accomplish in me whatever He wills.

10.6 *Marguerite Bourgeoys*

The Three States of the Daughters Assembled in Montreal

[As a result of a variety of circumstances, a number of women came together to live for a time in the same house, under the guidance and protection of the Priests of St. Sulpice. They included: a recluse (Jeanne Le Ber, Mary Magdalene), the Hospitallers (of Jeanne Mance [1606–1673], a laywoman close to Olier), and the Sisters of the Congregation of Notre Dame. For Marguerite this became a meaningful sign.]

In 1695, the Hospitallers of Montreal, deprived of their residence by a fire, went to live with the Congregation, from 24 February to 21 November. That same year, the Congregation's chapel was built and a woman from Montreal, Jeanne Le Ber, led the life of a recluse there. She had drawn up the plan, modeled on the house of Loretto, and received permission to live with the Congregation, in a cell that opened on the altar of the chapel. Jeanne belonged to a family that had played an important role in the origins of Montreal. Her decision surely touched many people deeply and a great number of people must have accompanied her from her father's house to the sisters' chapel, on the evening of 5 August 1695. Marguerite Bourgouys recorded this event:

> I rejoiced greatly the day Miss Le Ber entered our house to lead a solitary life. This took place on Friday, 5 August 1695, about five o'clock in the evening. She was brought to us by Monsieur Dollier, the diocesan vicar and superior of the seminary. He exhorted her to persevere in the life she was to lead. In the chapel outside the main body of the house, she was to sing the Litany of the Blessed Virgin, as St. Mary Magdalene did in her grotto. She was not to leave this place or speak to anyone. Her food is brought to her through an exterior door and given to her through a small opening in it. In her cell, there is also a small grill through which she can see the Blessed Sacrament and receive Holy Communion. (*EMB*; 199f.).

Then, in 1695, there lived under the same roof Jeanne Le Ber (Mary Magdalene), the Hospitallers (Martha), and the daughters of the Congregation (Mary, the mother of Jesus).

> When Monsieur Le Ber's daughter came to our house, where the Hospitallers had been living since their fire, I had the great joy of seeing daughters representing the three states of life, gathered together in the Blessed Virgin's house. (*EMB*, 207)

> Lorraine Caza, CND. *La vie voyagère et conversante avec le prochain: Marguerite Bourgeoys.* Montreal/ Paris, 1982; 46–47.
> (N.B. the letters *EMB* refer to the writings of Marguerite Bourgeoys.)

CHAPTER ELEVEN

The French School Today

A s we come to the end of this overview of the French School, a critical question emerges. Aside from a purely historical interest, which is essential, can these spiritual leaders of the past contribute anything to us today? If so, what are the conditions of this transmission? Can women and men in our century find anything of interest in reading and studying the doctrine of the French School? To what degree can Bérulle and his followers nourish and foster the present renewal of prayer, of the apostolic spirit, of a sense of the Church and its ministries, across the great cultural distance that separates us from them?

A Living Tradition

A first observation seems clear: like every other spiritual tradition, the spirituality of the Bérulle School is still very much alive in a number of priestly or religious families: Oratorians, Sulpicians, Eudists, Brothers of the Christian Schools, Daughters of Wisdom, Montfort priests and brothers. The list could be extended, because of the great number of religious congregations of men or women who claim to take their inspiration from the French School. Among these are Libermann's Spiritans, Mazenod's Oblates of Mary Immaculate, and the countless congregations of women founded in the seventeenth century or later. Thus, the tradition that comes to us from Bérulle is like other traditions: Benedictine, Dominican, Franciscan, Ignatian, Carmelite, Salesian. They are all represented by clerical or religious communities spread throughout every part of the world.

Following the Second Vatican Council, the religious families influenced by the Bérulle School undertook and realized a tremendous work of *aggiornamento*, which was accompanied at all times by a "return to the origins." The study and renewal of the *charism* of the founders, requested by the conciliar documents, were faithfully implemented. The fruit of all these efforts cannot yet be measured quantitatively, because of the present vocation crisis in many countries. However, renewal in spirituality, apostolic service and community life is obvious. This renewal, adaptation and return to the origins have found expression in new and carefully wrought texts of Constitutions or Rules of Life. They reveal the primary inspiration that impelled men and women founders in the "beginning," even as it takes a new form today.

The return to the origins is not reserved to religious or priests. Following the tradition of the spiritual leaders of the seventeenth century, various groups of laypersons have taken up the study of texts by Bérulle, John Eudes and Grignion de Montfort, discovering in them light and inspiration for daily living. While these groups can be found in several countries, they are particularly numerous and well organized in Europe and Canada, at the present time.

In addition to the values reaffirmed by the families directly or indirectly influenced by the French School, there are important contributions from this tradition that have been "incorporated" into the common patrimony of all Christians.

The first of these is a spiritual life founded on the major realities of faith as found in St. John and St. Paul. We recognize the great orientations of the Bérulle School in *Christ, the Life of the Soul* by Dom Marmion (1858–1923), as well as in the message of Elizabeth of the Trinity (1880–1906).

A second contribution is an interiorized liturgical life. Here again, *Christ in his Mysteries* by Dom Marmion can be read once more in the light of Bérulle, Olier and John Eudes. Conciliar texts presenting the Christian liturgy as a continuation and an actualization of the praise and intercession of Jesus call to mind more than one page written by the leaders of the Bérulle School.

A third contribution is the sense of the Church as Mystery: the Body of Christ, Temple of the Spirit, and People of God, realized in a hierarchical society.

Another contribution is the call of all Christians—laity, religious and priests—to holiness, through personal union with Jesus, at the heart of the church and in apostolic witness.

Finally, the greatness and the responsibility of bishops and priests are to be noted. They are called to the perfection of their ministry and of their state of life through communion with the prayer and charity of Christ. Here, again, the conciliar documents on the church and on episcopal and priestly ministry seem to be penetrated by the ideas of Bérulle, Olier and John Eudes.

It is important to point out that certain elements in this spiritual tradition have been spread widely in the church through priests formed in Sulpician and Eudist seminaries, between the seventeenth century and our own day. This influence has extended to nearly every corner of the world: to North and South America as well as to the Far East, especially to Vietnam and Japan. In these seminaries, the great themes that come from the Bérulle School are still alive. They are reflected in both pedagogical practices and in a total spiritual formation, inspired by the writings of St. John and St. Paul, as Olier and John Eudes read, meditated and lived them, following Bérulle.[1]

The Message of the French School

We have to admit that a reading of the masters of the French School is difficult and presupposes a certain number of conditions. Still, knowledge of their doctrine seems to be of great benefit to us today, no matter what our situation or vocation in the church. What we need is not a kind of "archeological reading, but one that enters into dialogue with our current situation," as Sauvage wrote regarding the *Meditations* of John Baptiste de La Salle.[2]

One of the primary aspects of their message is *the witness of their own existence*. This is often neglected, even though it is reflected in their writings. We might apply here the words that Francis de Sales wrote to Bishop Frémyot, the young archbishop of Bourges, who had asked for advice concerning his preaching. Francis encouraged him to speak about the saints: "There is no greater difference between the written text of the gospel and the life of the saints than there is between a sheet of music and that music when it is sung."[3]

The words of Pius XI, who called Therese of Lisieux a "Word of God for our times," might also be applied to the leaders of the Bérulle School. As Bergson has affirmed, their very existence, their spiritual journey and their apostolic development constitute a summons for us to heed. But t*heir doctrine* itself and many of their writings can provide spiritual nourishment for us now. We can also apply to them what Congar wrote concerning the church fathers.

> The Fathers are not men who belong to an age that is
> now over and gone. It is not their chronological position
> in the history of the Church which describes and attri-
> butes to them the character of paternity by which they
> are identified. It is much more their spiritual qualifications.[4]

Again, we find a good expression of what we want to
say about Bérulle and his followers in the words of Father
Besnard regarding St. John of the Cross:

> Is it possible for us to find in St. John of the Cross the el-
> ements of understanding and, thus, also some practical
> guidelines for the destiny of faith which is our common
> experience today? . . . I would like to demonstrate that we
> can find some of the light we seek in St. John of the
> Cross. I do not say he has answers for us. I do claim that
> his doctrine, which is the fruit of a deeply radical and
> most pure experience, can offer several reliable guide-
> lines, thanks to which we can better foresee our way
> through the uncertain land we have to explore.[5]

The "reliable guidelines" of the Bérulle School have
already been presented. Here, it will be helpful to review
them and to point out their relationship to some aspects
of contemporary Christian renewal. Paul Cochois has repeatedly insisted that "the French School stands at the
heart of our needs or of our struggles."[6]

The sense of God, that *religion* of loving adoration that
characterizes the Bérulle School, invites us at one and
the same time to an authentic, interiorized recollection
in the presence of the Trinity, and to a fully aware and
active participation in liturgical prayer. In an age like our
own, which is experiencing a true renewal in prayer, the
reading of one or another text from Bérulle, Olier or John
Eudes is a way of nurturing a prayer that is truly theological and ecclesial.

A personal relationship with Jesus, especially as understood and lived out by these mystics, can enable us to
move beyond an *extrinsic* concept of the Christian life.

They perceived this relationship as one of communion with the sentiments, states and mysteries of Jesus, centered in the Eucharist as the source of this profoundly *spiritual* communion. In their thought, Jesus is not only a master to listen to and follow; he is not only a king to be served, or even only a friend. He is all of that, but he is also the dynamic principle of our being: he lives, prays and loves in us. As Therese of Lisieux wrote, "When I love my sisters, it is JESUS alone who loves them in me." Our age is marked by a renewal of interest in christological studies. What has been written about Bérulle in this domain applies also to what has been written by his disciples.

The *Holy Spirit* is the Spirit of the risen Jesus, according to the masters of the French School. This is the Spirit poured out in Christians at Pentecost, the Spirit we receive in Baptism. This Spirit continues to "labor" in us, so as to make us like Jesus, filling us with his prayer, his love, his patience, his humility. Everything that Paul wrote in the epistles to the Galatians and the Romans regarding the Christian life, vivified by the Spirit, was taken up and "orchestrated" by the French School. Olier spoke for everyone when he wrote, "the Christian is one in whom the Spirit of Jesus Christ dwells."[7]

The charismatic renewal in all its forms invites us to deepen this theology of the Holy Spirit. For example, Olier's highly intense experience of the Spirit enabled him to speak often and clearly on this subject. His witness is a valuable one to which we ought to attend.

In a particular way, the insistence of Bérulle and his followers on *the apostolic spirit* is important for us today. Their idea of this spirit, "which is nothing other than the Spirit of JESUS CHRIST," as Olier and Marie de l'Incarnation wrote,[8] can help us to understand better their concept of *the Church in its mystery and its mission*, and their convictions regarding *apostolic men* and the *Priests of Jesus*. Bérulle and his followers were not only men of prayer, true mystics, but they were all missionaries, also. They have given us the foundational elements of a theology and a spirituality of the Church and of mission. They perceived Jesus as the first one sent by the Father. He is at the source of every mission and, according to Condren, "since he is at the origin of the gospel mission, he has willed to be as well its law and its rule of perfection."[9]

The zeal of today's apostles and their apostolic spirit are nothing other than the very Spirit of Jesus with whom we are in communion. Missionaries not only imitate Jesus; they are, at one and the same time, bearers of Jesus Christ and they are borne by his Spirit. They are, in Olier's words, "like sacraments which bear Christ, so that in them and through them he might proclaim the glory of his Father."[10] Priests are inseparably both the religious of God and successors of the Apostles. Inspired and impelled by the Spirit of Jesus, they bear him everywhere they go.

The Acts of the Apostles present their twofold mission as "consecrated to prayer and service of the Word." This idea corresponds to the apostolic awareness of Paul, "the servant of Jesus Christ among the Gentiles, consecrated to the ministry of the gospel of God, so that the pagans might become an offering, sanctified by the Holy Spirit and agreeable to God" (Rom. 15.16). This Pauline theology of the apostolic ministry as both mystical and evangelizing, because it is vivified by the Spirit of Jesus, can be found developed, at times in a cumbersome style, by the masters of the French School. In any case, the connection between their spirit of religion and this apostolic spirit is essential. They could not separate an authentic spiritual and mystical life from a total, unconditional apostolic commitment. Both of these dimensions originate in the one Spirit of Jesus, the Son, sent by the Father.

This theology of the Spirit of Jesus, of the Church,

and of apostolic mission seems perfectly adapted to our era. Despite crises and difficulties, we are aware of an authentic charismatic renewal and a concern to develop new forms of ministries in service to the gospel and works of charity.

Devotion to Mary, as understood by the masters of the French School, would bring about a balance in certain, at times, excessive manifestations in honor of the mother of Jesus and, indirectly, could facilitate ecumenical dialogue. Their devotion was profoundly theological and mystical. Mary was never separated from Jesus; it was the reflection of the holiness of her Son, "living in her," that was the object of their contemplation. Their affection for the mother of Jesus was solidly rooted in the biblical and patristic traditions, even though it was often filled with tenderness, not unlike the devotion of St. Bernard. Here again, the current renewal of Marian devotion, especially in shrines and centers of pilgrimage, can only be enhanced and profit from association with the thought of Bérulle, Olier, John Eudes and Grignion de Montfort.

A Few Guidelines

Any attempt to know and understand the masters of the French School will meet with a number of great difficulties. The first of these is the result of a cultural distance that separates their era from our own. What Gendrot said of his founder could be said of any of the leaders of the Bérulle School: If "Montfort really belonged to his time, he cannot belong to ours in every possible way."[11]

It is impossible to transmit their message such as they proposed it, without following a certain number of guidelines. Frequently, their vocabulary has to be "decoded." Above all, the central questions of the seventeenth century were very different from the ones we ask today. For

244 The French School of Spirituality

example, our times are deeply marked—at least in Europe—by indifference and relativism, while the seventeenth century was an age of faith, despite the existence of some atheists and libertines.

Thus, it is important to know at least the major trends that marked the situation of the Church and society in their day, and to try to understand their mentality, as much as possible. Over and above a knowledge of the human, social and Christian conditions in which these spiritual leaders lived, several other criteria must be met if our reading of their documents is to be fruitful.

1. *It is important to read the texts themselves.* No matter how useful introductions and commentaries may be, nothing replaces direct contact with the texts. It is true that not all their documents have been published in a practical format. Some writings have even been corrupted. The recent publication of Olier's texts used by Tronson for the composition of the *Treatise on Holy Orders* has brought to light a number of changes imposed on the founder's thought. Despite such difficulties, we must acknowledge that we actually possess an excellent choice of texts that allow us to encounter the thoughts of these writers directly.

2. *Attention must be given to certain words* whose meaning has been modified or impoverished in the last three centuries. In order to be clearly understood, some expressions need to be contextualized or translated: *elevation, regard* (gaze, looking at), *adherence, spirit of religion, apostolic spirit, annihilation, victim-host.* Such terms are like musical notes whose full range of tonality can be easily lost. Some publishers suggest that a glossary or a "lexicon" would prove to be most useful as a companion to selected texts.[12]

3. In every school of spirituality, in a most particular way, *prayer formulas* call for careful attention. Just as, according to St. Thomas, "the Psalms contain the entire Bible in the form of praise" (S.T. IIIa, qu. 83, art. 4), so

too, prayer formulas and methods of prayer manifest most clearly the full range of thought and experience of the leaders of the French School. Lao-Tse tells us, "If you want to know a man, watch him pray."

4. *Scriptural quotations*, particularly those from the New Testament, also deserve special attention. Each spiritual tradition has its *preferred texts*. We come to know Bérulle and his disciples well through their quotation of countless passages from John and Paul. In return, these spiritual masters help us to understand more fully certain aspects of the biblical message.

If we strive to locate and read the biblical quotations in light of the way Bérulle and his followers read them, we may understand them better and hear the word of God more clearly. As Gaucher wrote regarding Therese of Lisieux, we can read the Bible "over her shoulder." This shared reading enables us to understand the Scriptures with a fresh perspective. For example, Grignion de Montfort can help us to read the Wisdom Books with greater insight through his *Love of Eternal Wisdom*.

5. The most important condition of all for reading the authors of the French School is to *continue on the path that one has begun*. Montaigne tells us that, "in order to know someone, it is necessary to follow his steps for a long time, with great intellectual curiosity." Knowledge of the history of Christianity and unremitting, painstaking familiarity with these great witnesses to the gospel demand fidelity and serious, rigorous application. This is the price of an abundant, joy-filled harvest.

The best way to bring this chapter and this book to a close is to quote the words of one of the most knowledgeable experts in the history of spirituality. This friend, taken too soon from our midst, was one who encouraged the writing of this study from its beginning.

> There can be no doubt that the period we are actually living through is one of those which obliges us to seek a new fidelity to our origins. In every domain, we find our-

selves at a moment in time when Christian expressions inherited from a recent past are no longer life-giving, and must be reconsidered. This is true of theological discourse as much as of ecclesial organization. It is still more true of that existential acceptance of the Word of God that we call spirituality.[13]

DOCUMENTS FOR CHAPTER 11

11.1 The Charism of Founders

The very charism of the Founders (*Evan. Nunt.*, 11) appears as *"an experience of the Spirit,"* transmitted to their disciples to be lived, safeguarded, deepened and constantly developed by them, in harmony with the Body of Christ continually in the process of growth. "It is for this reason that the distinctive character of various religious institutes is preserved and fostered by the Church" (LG, 44; cf. CD, 33; 35:1; 35:2; etc.). This *distinctive* character also involves a particular style of sanctification and, of apostolate, which creates its particular tradition, with the result that one can readily perceive its objective elements.

In this hour of cultural evolution and ecclesial renewal, therefore, it is necessary to preserve the identity of each institute so securely, that the danger of an ill-defined situation be avoided, lest religious, failing to give due consideration to the particular mode of action proper to their character, become part of the life of the Church in a vague and ambiguous way.

Religieux et religieuses dans la mission de l'Eglise.
Paris, 1984; 14.
Text from *Mutuae relationes* 11.

11.2 A Contemporary Rule of Life

> Under the mastery of the Spirit,
> we seek continually
>   to live in conformity to Christ,
> in communion with his "states and mysteries"
>   expressed in the liturgy
>   and made more particularly present
>   in the Eucharist,
> communicating above all with the essential attitude
>   of his Heart totally filled
>   with love for his Father and his brothers.
>
>> *Constitutions* of the Sisters of the Good Savior,
>> founded in the seventeenth century in the
>> tradition of the French School.

> We shall always be impelled
> by the Spirit of the Incarnate Word,
> and above all by his Spirit as Son of the Father
> and by his love for his brothers and sisters.
>
>> (*Livre de vie* of the Ursulines of Jesus, founded in
>> the nineteenth century by Louis-Marie Baudouin, a
>> priest-follower of Bérulle.)

11.3 *The Prayer of Jesus in the Church*

Olier	Liturgy of the Hours
Acts for the divine office:	General presentation:
May the Church, O my Lord Jesus, expand what you have contained in yourself. May it express beyond itself this divine spirit of religion which you have for your Father in the secret of your heart, in heaven, and on our altars. . . .	I. THE PRAYER OF CHRIST *Christ the Intercessor with the Father*
	When he came to give men and women a share in God's life, the Word proceeding from the Father as the splendor of his glory,

Thus, my God, may all the praise, all the canticles, psalms, and hymns which we are to sing in your honor be only the expression of the interior dispositions of Jesus Christ. May my mouth speak to you only what the soul of my Savior in its own depths speaks to you

Thus, I adhere in this way to your Spirit,
O my Lord Jesus, you, who are the very life of our religion. I desire to offer to your Father all the praise and duty due to him.
You alone understand all this.
You alone offer him such worship
in your own inner temple.

La journée chrétienne, éd. Amiot. Paris: Le Rameau, 1954; 123.

John Eudes
When a Christian prays, he continues and fulfills the prayer Jesus offered on earth.
Life and Kingdom of Jesus, 2,2.

"Christ Jesus, the high priest of the new and eternal Covenant, took our human nature and introduced into the world of our exile that hymn of praise which is sung in the heavenly places throughout all ages." From then on the praise of God wells up from the heart of Christ in human words of adoration, propitiation and intercession, presented to the Father by the head of the new humanity, the mediator between God and mankind, in the name of all and for the good of all.

II. THE PRAYER OF THE CHURCH
The Church Continues the Prayer of Christ

... He unites to himself the whole community of mankind in such a way that there is an intimate bond between the prayer of Christ and the prayer of the whole human race. In Christ and in Christ alone the religious activity of mankind receives its redemptive value and attains its goal.

There is a special,
and very close, bond between
Christ and those whom he
makes members of his body,
the Church, through the
sacrament of rebirth.
Thus, from the head all the
riches that belong to the
Son flow.

... The excellence of
Christian prayer lies in
this, that it shares in the
very love of the only-
begotten Son for the Father
and in that prayer which
the Son put into words in
his earthly life and which
still continues unceasingly
in the name of the whole
human race and for its
salvation, throughout the
universal Church and in all
its members.

11.4 Shepherds in the One Shepherd

[The French School has left us countless texts on the ministry and spiritual life of priests. Their relationship to the documents of Vatican II are easily recognizable, as the following examples show.]

French School

Vatican II

A priest is Jesus Christ,
living and walking on
earth. He holds the place
of Jesus Christ, represents
his person, acts in his name,
is invested with his authority:

Because it is joined with
the episcopal order the office
of priests shares in the
authority by which Christ
himself builds up and
sanctifies and rules his

"As the Father has sent me," Our Lord says, "I also send you."

John Eudes. *Mémorial de la* vie écclésiastique, 5, 10, 2.

The priest is the one who continues the life of Jesus Christ as leader (= head). . . . Thus, the priest in the Church is a living Jesus Christ and a Jesus Christ, head of his Church.

Olier. *l'Etat ecclésiastique* (Mss.), included in the *Traité des Saints Ordres*, éd. critique; 183.

That is why our life and our way of acting ought to be a living, perfect image, or rather, a continuation of Jesus Christ's life and way of acting.

John Eudes, *loc. cit.*

Body. Hence the priesthood of priests, while presupposing the sacraments of initiation, is nevertheless conferred by its own particular sacrament. Through that sacrament priests by the anointing of the Holy Spirit are signed with a special character and so are configured to Christ the priest in such a way that they are able to act in the person of Christ the head.

Presbyterorum ordinis, 2.

Christ . . . is working through his ministers

. . .

Presbyterorum ordinis, 14.

Priests . . . [exercise] their functions . . . in the Spirit of Christ.

Presbyterorum ordinis, 13.

And by this close union with Christ they share in the charity of God . . . encouraged by the love of the Good Shepherd.

Presbyterorum ordinis, 13.

11.5 An Enduring Spirit

[The following text describes Nicolas Roland (1642–1678), one of the great spiritual leaders in seventeenth century France.]

It would be pointless and mere curiosity to want to resurrect someone long gone by a presentation of the details of his life and his achievement. What we hope to do is reflect on the possible enduring quality of his spirit three centuries after his death. During that time, there has been an evaluation leading to a decisive change in society and the Church, where new problems are found with new conditions of life and new ways of thinking. This reflection is not unlike that undertaken by religious orders and, even, of Christianity itself, through a *return to the sources.* How can we bridge distance in time, differing situations and mentalities, to assure a necessary continuity with the spirit of our origins? How can we preserve an unchanging, precious heritage amid the ceaseless ruptures and accelerated violent separations of history? How can we be faithful to this heritage as we pursue renewal, discern outdated contingencies, and identify the imperishable essential reality of things?

Nicolas Roland, E. Rideau. Paris: 1976; 9–10.

11.6 The Saints Speak to Us

As we encounter the message of one or another of these men and women—saints—who discover the fullness of Christ's love, we are overcome with emotion. A kind of cry then rises out of the depths of our conscience. Why this emotion? Why this cry? The reason is, surely, because in such moments, the deepest meaning of human existence appears before us with contagious power: we perceive life's truth in its fullness. One who has been wandering along the path suddenly is faced with evidence that this way truly does lead to light.

There is also something else. Knowledge that one has not taken the wrong path gives the pilgrim assurance on the way. Still, such a one experiences an even greater shock. It is not only that he knows he can continue moving, fearlessly, toward the goal. He discovers that his best self shares this saint's vision. The saints speak words which his lips have never uttered. They recount spiritual experiences which he has never known. Yet, somehow, these words and experiences are not foreign to him. The cry which breaks out of his heart is the expression of a wondering surprise at the sight of faces on which he recognizes—even from afar, infinitely afar—some of his own features.

Excerpt from P. Carré's preface to
*Les grandes intuitions de sainte Thérèse de
l'Enfant Jésus*, Ph. Vercouestre. Paris: 1984, 7–8.

11.7 Contemporary Significance of the French School

The French School connects with a number of contemporary spiritual themes. There are also aspects of its doctrine and practice that seem offensive to contemporary American sensitivities. It is unfortunate that some negative anthropological language, a hierarchical worldview, and at times a lavish style of writing present a major obstacle to many contemporary readers in the English-speaking world. For there are many valid insights that could enrich our efforts at a theologically balanced spirituality. For instance: Among them are:

1. The heightened sense of the transcendence of God has receded from the contemporary collective consciousness as we have reemphasized, for good reasons, the beauty and holiness of the human as spiritual path. However, since the full truth lies in the paradoxical mystery of God as both transcendent and immanent, this spirituality models for us one way of maintaining both aspects of this divine mystery. For the sense of the awe and mystery of God is continually held in balance with a powerful intuition of the mystery of the incarnate Word.

2. The essential connection between the life of prayer and ministry is another strong belief of the French School. The revitalization of the spiritual life was the cornerstone of their efforts to reform the Church of their day. There is a strong emphasis on the communal spiritual life, experienced through the Church, seen as Mystical Body, and the sacraments. At the same time, the French School has always had a profound respect for the unique work of the Holy Spirit in the individual person. This respect has been the life force and dynamism behind the long and rich history of commitment to spiritual direction. As we experience today a widespread renewal of

interest in this *ars artium* and in directed retreats, there are important insights to be gathered from the French School.

For example, Olier offers us an essential practical teaching about spiritual growth. He points out that progress is best nurtured by admitting our own powerlessness (*anéantissement*) and turning our lives over to the Holy Spirit. Our own efforts are doomed to fail unless they flow from the Spirit of Christ. Furthermore, emphasizing our own agenda for spiritual growth can be a most subtle trap that makes us even more self-centered than before. Therefore we are called to commune in the interior life of Jesus Christ as a way to spiritual fulfillment and let God do the work (*Mémoires* 1:44; see also how Olier embodies this strategy in his approach to prayer, Thompson and Glendon, 228–32).

Of course, we need to cooperate with grace, but the point is that it is primarily *grace*. There seem to be many inner psychic similarities between this strategy of the French School and that of Alcoholics Anonymous and other twelve-step programs, in which recovery begins when people admit their radical powerlessness and turn their lives over to a higher power. They both seem to draw on a similar perennial wisdom.

3. Several communities flowing from this tradition have been able to renew their constitutions credibly for today by drawing on the central themes of the French School and the writings of their founders. These documents model well a dialogue between an older spirituality and our contemporary sensitivity, need, and vocation.

The French School offers a powerful spiritual synthesis, blending profound mysticism with zeal and energy for reform. Rarely has such a deep sense of the communion with God in the Spirit of Jesus Christ been expressed and written not only for priests and religious but for the laity as well. It is a spirituality of profound transformation and exquisite adoration. It is lyrical, poetic, and passionate in its love for Jesus Christ and, through his Spirit, in its devotion to the Father.

"French School of Spirituality," Lowell M. Glendon, S.S. in *The New Dictionary of Catholic Spirituality*, ed. Michael Downey. Collegeville, MN: The Liturgical Press, 1993.

11.8 Living Friends

Holiness has never been lived out in the Church without nourishment from earlier successes. . . .

As we grow in life in the Spirit, the spiritual master whose works we are reading becomes a friend. In other words, his assistance cannot be conceptualized, but familiarity with him will gradually transform me, as if by osmosis. Thus, there are persons to whom we owe nothing in particular, that is, no specific service, yet we owe them everything. That is because we have spent so much time with them that something has passed from them to us, without our being aware of it. . . .

This is a very unique kind of friendship, since it is with a person from another era. Here is someone seeking the goal I seek, but in a different manner. He is from another period of time, and is, thus, different from me. If I am to enter into the communion of friendship with this spiritual master, I must begin by being willing to enter this strange land. I must move out of myself, I must "decentralize" myself. This is, indeed, the most important contribution a spiritual master can give me. He forces me to move away from myself as the center of all things and to center myself in Christ. He initiates me into another life, life in Christ.

> J-Cl. Guy. *Note sur la lecture spirituelle* in "Bulletin de Saint-Sulpice," 9, 1983; 211–15; here, 212.

APPENDIX A

New Testament Texts in the Writings of the French School

The entire Gospel of John was a subject of constant meditation for Bérulle, Olier and John Eudes. The latter, for example, delighted in joining texts from the Fourth Gospel pertaining to life: "I am the life. . . . I have come that you may have life. . . . I live and you shall live. . . . I am in the Father, and you are in me and I am in you" (Jn 14.6, 10.10, 14.19–20). In the same way, Jesus asked, "Remain in me . . . and I in you" (Jn 15).

We know that Libermann (1802–1852) composed an important commentary on the Gospel of John. This work stands in the direct tradition of the Bérulle School, because Libermann had studied and reflected at length on the writings of Olier and St. John Eudes.

Paul is frequently quoted by the leaders of the French School, particularly in two series of text:

1. *Living for God*
Rom. 6.11: "Consider yourselves as dead to sin and alive to God in Christ Jesus."
Rom. 12.1: "Offer yourselves as a living sacrifice, holy and pleasing to God: this is your spiritual worship.
Rom 14.7–8: "None of us lives to himself and none dies to

himself; if we live, we live to the Lord, and if we die, we die to the Lord. ... "

2 Cor 5.14–15: "The love of Christ impels us because we have come to the conclusion that, one died for all, ... in order that they who are alive may live no longer for themselves, but for him who died for them and rose again."

2. *in Jesus Christ*

Eph. 1.10: "God willed to recapitulate all things in Christ."

Eph. 1.23: "Jesus fills all with all."

Eph. 5.30: "We are his members and his body."

Rom. 8.29: "God has predestined us to become conformed to the image of his Son."

Gal. 2.20: "It is now no longer I that live, but Christ lives in me."

Gal. 4.19: "My little children with whom I am in labor, until Christ is formed in you!"

Eph. 3.17: "May Christ dwell by faith in your hearts."

Phil. 1.21: "For to me, to live is Christ."

Phil. 2.5: "Have these dispositions in you which were also in Christ Jesus."

Phil. 3.10–11: "May I know him and the power of his resurrection and the fellowship of his sufferings: become like to him in death in the hope that somehow I may attain to the resurrection from the dead."

Col. 1.24: "I fill up in my flesh what is lacking in the sufferings of Christ for his body, which is the Church."

Col. 3.1–4: "Therefore, if you have risen with Christ, seek the things that are above, where Christ is seated at the right hand of God. Mind the things that are above, not the things that are on earth. For you have died and your life is hidden with Christ in God. When Christ, your life, shall appear, then you, too, will appear with him in glory."

N.B.

1. The writers of the French School cite many other texts from John, Paul, the Synoptic Gospels and other New Testament books. Condren and Olier quote passages, especially from the letter to the Hebrews, in reference to the priesthood and sacrifice of Jesus.

2. Contemporary exegetes specify the meaning that can be

found in one or another text, with a scientific interpretation that is often similar to the insights of Bérulle and his disciples. In reference to Philippians 2.5 ("Have these dispositions in you which were also in Christ Jesus."), the T.O.B. (Ecumenical Translation of the Bible in French) notes: "The dispositions of Christ to which Paul refers remain present and efficacious."

3. Regarding Philippians 3.10: "To know Christ . . . to be in Christ, is to be introduced into past events which remain actively present." Bérulle had written of the "mysteries of Jesus": "They are past . . . but they remain present and perpetual. . . . They are past in terms of their realization, but they are present in their power which will never pass away, and in the everlasting love with which they were accomplished" (*Œuvres de Piété*, 77, éd., Rotuveau, 54).

The shorter edition of the Jerusalem Bible contains the following note on Galatians 2.20: "The living actions of the Christian become somehow the actions of Christ."

3. Among the members of the Bérulle School, Olier, and later, Marie de l'Incarnation, often speak of the special graces and "lights" they received from God for our understanding of the Scriptures.

APPENDIX B

THE DARK SIDE OF THE FRENCH SCHOOL

One of the most frequent criticisms against the French School concerns the excessive pessimism expressed by its leaders regarding human nature. Condren and Olier, more than the others, insist on the sinful condition and the nothingness of the human being as a creature. They seem to stand in opposition to the biblical affirmations of the "goodness" of creation as a theme found also in certain documents of the Second Vatican Council. It is, moreover, possible to find in Bérulle and John Eudes texts that are, apparently, at least as forceful and as negative regarding the limited, sinful condition of humanity.

The authors of the French School have written commentaries on gospel passages that highlight renunciation and the necessity of carrying one's cross in order to follow Jesus. Even more, they provide a theological justification for this attitude: in Jesus, Incarnate Word, human nature "has been despoiled of its own substance or human person, to be established in the divine Person of the Word; also, in the grace that flows from this adorable Incarnation as from a living source, Jesus experiences a kind of annihilation" (Bérulle, *Œuvres de Piété 133*, éd. Migne, Col. 1166). We are far removed from Christian humanism, here.

Bérulle's disciples treat this subject at length, insisting especially on the weakness and nothingness of human nature . . .

"this cesspool of iniquity." In his *Christian Catechism* (1656), Condren consecrates a great number of chapters to sin, the great wickedness of the flesh, and love of the Cross, while chapters devoted to newness of life are much fewer.

As we read one or another of such pages, we feel most uncomfortable. It is surprising, then, to find a contemporary American Benedictine writing the following words:

> His [Bérulle's] teaching is so optimistic, so exhilarating and full of hope that it comes to us fearful, sometimes discouraged people of today as truly good news. (*The American Benedictine Review* 27: 1 March 1976; 126–39, here, 128).

If we are going to understand the writers of the Bérulle School better, we have to take a number of elements into account. Without seeking to defend them, since they do reflect the limitations of their era, we must acknowledge that they deserve to be read attentively. Their ideas of human nature and of Christian renunciation are a challenge for us, or at least, an invitation to read the New Testament texts more clearly and to reread our own experience from another point of view.

1. In the first place, it is necessary to distinguish the problem of their *concept of human nature* from their *insistence on annihilation, and death to self* as a condition of life, even if the two realities are related. Bérulle, Olier and John Eudes have made categorical affirmations on the subject of the death-life dialectic: it is necessary to die, but *what is essential, is life.*

> We must ask God for this state and this spirit of death, since it is necessary to give place to the life of Jesus, which cannot be established unless we are dead to ourselves. Devotion to the death of Jesus is the greatest means of obtaining this grace, for his death is the source of this spirit of death and this grace is meritorious and operative.... After estrangement from ourselves, as from the greatest obstacle to the life of Jesus within us, we must apply to ourselves the sources of the life of this same Jesus, because it is from them that we must expect the effects of this life.... Here, then, are the effects towards which we ought to tend with all our strength: first of all, the death of ourselves within ourselves; secondly, the life of Jesus in us, for this death both tends only

towards this life and can be brought about and established perfectly only through this same life; thirdly, Jesus Christ our Savior, living in us in this manner, desires to appropriate everything that is ours, body and soul. Taking everything to himself in this way, he will not suffer anything of us to live except in his spirit, aside from what we must suffer, through patience and without any wilful attachment, of Adam's miserable life in our own, both of which God wills to destroy (Bérulle, vol. 144, éd. Migne, Col. 1183–184).

Olier reminds us that, following Jesus, we must

die and immolate ourselves for God . . . annihilating self entirely for the one we love . . . which means total, universal death . . . dying not to one thing only, but to all things. . . .

He then continues:

Love of the cross and the death of self do not make up the Christian religion. They are only its principles and foundation. They are nothing more than removal of those things that prevent us from entering into true religion . . . so much so that the basis of religion is contained in these words: "Sequere me," "Follow me." And even St. Jerome states that it is not detachment from all things that constitutes Christian and religious perfection, for the philosophers did as much. The perfection of the Christian religion consists in following our Lord in his interior life and in his holy, divine ways (*Mémoires* 4:12–122).

Elsewhere he writes:

According to St. Paul, in order to be a living victim, we must not only have the external appearance of death; we must have within us an interior life, like the sacred host on the altar (. . . in which) there is the divine, holy, religious life of God (*Divers Ecrits* 1:19).

We know, moreover, to what degree Olier concentrated on the mystery of the Resurrection of Jesus, even if Tronson somewhat minimized this aspect in his edition of Olier's writings that appeared as the *Traité des Saints Ordres*.

2. Still, insistence on the *radical weakness of human nature* and the fundamentally sinful condition of human beings can seem excessive to us. It is true that these authors often

emphasize the distance that separates us from God more than the "image and likeness" affirmed in the biblical accounts of Creation. We have to read *all* their texts to modify this impression. Olier became almost Franciscan "on hearing the birds sing" or when gazing on fire.

a) If we are going to understand the pessimistic mentality of the French School, we must remember that the period was dominated by Augustinianism and, very often, by a rigoristic spirit. The excesses at Port-Royal are a demonstration of this. We must also recognize that the contempt of the world found at Port-Royal and in Jansenism stood in direct opposition to the involvement "in the world" of the Bérulle School, clergy or laity. Gaston de Renty's position demonstrates this clearly.

b) Condren and Olier frequently read St. Augustine and constantly reflected on the texts of St. Paul (Romans) and St. John (the "world," the opposing forces of light and darkness). Their pessimism was also and, perhaps especially, rooted in an experience that was both human and spiritual. In Olier's case, that experience had been extremely terrifying. He had known the tragedy of the human condition and the specifically dramatic states of the Christian life in their keenest, most intense form. This was due, in part, to his very sensitive temperament and to the exterior and interior trials that "reduced him to nothing" at the time of his crisis in 1639–1641. He emerged from the trial free, happy and filled with apostolic zeal, but he would never forget his passage through that dark night.

3. Still more, it is important never to forget that the masters of the French School were *true mystics*. We are far removed from their radical experience of God and of our nothingness. It is also important to listen to the witness they give us. Thus, John of the Cross speaks to us of "the greatest and highest state to which we can attain in this life. It does not consist in refreshment, nor in delight, nor in spiritual feelings, but in a living death, both interior and exterior (*Ascent of Mount Carmel* 2:7,8).

One of the best commentators on John's writings did not hesitate to state: if we want

> to understand the journey lived out by John of the Cross, we must seek to discover it by transforming Jesus Christ crucified into our own being. We are not speaking of the

Cross that merely prepares us for ascetical suffering, but the Cross which is the sign of absolute annihilation (J. Baruzi, Sa*int Jean de la Croix et le problème de l'expérience mystique.* Paris: F. Alcan, 1924; 565–66).

4. Finally, it may be that the essential message of the French School is this: it is in Jesus alone that humanity is, at one and the same time, reconciled and recreated. *The goal of all things is total communion with Jesus,* but the path to this goal can be nothing other than total self-annihilation. The way of the Cross of Jesus is a path we are obliged to travel for "without him, we can do *nothing.*"

APPENDIX C

CHRONOLOGICAL TABLE OF FOUR PRIESTLY FAMILIES OF
THE SEVENTEENTH CENTURY

*(Excerpt from the Bulletin de Saint-Sulpice 6, 1980;
264–73)*

	ORATORIANS	VINCENTIANS
1575	Birth of Pierre de Bérulle. Foundation of the Oratory in Rome by Philip Neri.	
1581		Birth of Vincent de Paul in Pouy, Landes.
1586	Attempt at an Oratory in Provence.	
1597		Theological studies in Toulouse.
1600		Ordination to the priesthood.
1601		
1607		Letter on captivity in Barbary.
1608		
1609		Relationship with Bérulle.
1611	November 11: Bérulle and five priests came together at the Hôtel du Petit – Bourbon, in Paris, to live in Community and work for the sanctification of the clergy.	Temporary residence at the Oratory.

	SULPICIANS	EUDISTS
1575		
1581		
1586		
1597		
1600		
1601		Birth of John Eudes in a "working" family in Ri, near Argentan.
1607		
1608	Birth of Jean-Jacques Olier, in Paris	
1609		
1611		

	ORATORIANS	VINCENTIANS
1612		Named to the pastorate in Clinchy. Intervention of Bérulle.
1613	Papal Bull of Paul V for the institution of the Oratory.	Acceptance of the position as tutor for the Gondi family, following Bérulle's advice.
1614	The Oratory spreads to the provinces: Dieppe, Langres, Luçon, Aix, Saumur; in parishes, colleges, seminaries.	
1615		
1617		First "mission," beginning of the "Congregation of the Mission" on the property of Madame de Gondi.
1618		Meeting with Francis de Sales, whom he will succeed as ecclesiastical superior of the Visitation.
1623		Mission on the galleys in Bordeaux. (M. de Gondi, General of the Royal Galleys of France, was to become an Oratorian priest.)

	SULPICIANS	EUDISTS
1612		
1613		
1614		
1615		Studies at Jesuit College in Caen.
1617		
1618		Birth of John Eudes in a "working" family in Ri, near Argentan.
1623		John Eudes enter the Oratory in Paris and is received by Bérulle.

	ORATORIANS	VINCENTIANS
1624	Foundation of St-Magloire Seminary, in Paris.	
1625		Contract for foundation of the Congregation of the mission. Death of Madame de Gondi.
1626		Approval of the Congregation of the Mission by the Archbishop of Paris.
1627		
1629	Death of Cardinal de Bérulle. The Oratory numbers 400 priests and 60 houses. Charles de Condren becomes superior.	
1631		Beginning of the Exercises for Ordination Candidates.
1633		Beginning of the "Tuesday Conferences" for priests.
1634		

	SULPICIANS	EUDISTS
1624		
1625		Ordination to the priesthood.
1626		
1627		John Eudes goes to work for plague victims in Argentan, then he joins the Oratory community in Caen.
1629		
1631		After the plague in Caen, John Eudes begins missionary life.
1633	Ordination of Jean-Jacques Olier to the priesthood.	
1634	Olier takes Father de Condren as spiritual director. He takes part in missions until 1641.	

	ORATORIANS	VINCENTIANS
1635		First foundation outside Paris (Toul).
1639	New foundations, including the college of Juilly.	
1640		Help brought to Lorraine.
1641	Death of Father de Condren. Father Bourgoing becomes superior.	
1642		Beginning of expansion in Europe (Rome).
1643		Monsieur Vincent becomes a member of the Council of Conscience.

	SULPICIANS	EUDISTS
1635		John Eudes writes his first book, *The life and Kingdom of Jesus in Christian Souls.*
1639		
1640	In December, Father de Condren gives directives for the establishment of seminaries.	John Eudes becomes superior of the Oratory in Caen.
1641	Failure of a seminary in Chartres. *Beginning of the seminary in Vaugirard, on 29 December.*	Meeting of Marie des Valées, the "saint of Coutances." John Eudes founds Our Lady of Refuge, in Caen, for penitent women. It was to become the Order of Our Lady of Charity.
1642	In August, Olier becomes pastor at Saint-Sulpice and brings the seminay to the parish.	
1643		Following an interview with Richelieu and several councillors, John Eudes leaves the Oratory on 19 March, to found a seminary in Caen. On 25 March, in view of this goal, he founds the Congregation of Jesus and Mary, with five companions.

	ORATORIANS	VINCENTIANS
1644	Bérulle's works published. Foundation of several seminaries (15 by the end of the seventeenth century) and a number of colleges.	Monsieur Vincent is named Chaplain General of the Royal Galleys.
1645		
1646		Foundation of a mission in Algiers.
1648		Mission to Madagascar
1650		
1651		Establishment of the Congregation in Poland.
1652		

SULPICIANS	EUDISTS
1644	
1645 The Abbot of St-Germain-des-Prés recognizes the seminary community.	
1646	During a mission in Autun, John Eudes celebrates the liturgical feast of the Holy Heart of Mary, for the first time.
1648	
1650	John Eudes founds the seminary at Coutances.
1651 Olier presents a project for their seminaries to the bishops of France.	Mission preaching in Normandy. Preaching at Saint-Sulpice, in Paris.
1652 Because of illness, Olier resigns from the pastorate of Saint-Sulpice. The "priests of the seminary of St-Sulpice" take charge of seminaries in Nantes, Viviers, Le Puy and Clermont (1652–1657).	

	ORATORIANS	VINCENTIANS
1653		
1657		
1658		Vincent de Paul is present at Olier's death and assists in the election of his successor. Distribution and explanation of the Rules of the Congregation.
1659		
1660		Death of Vincent de Paul. The Congregation numbers 23 institutions in France, including 15 seminaries, along with six institutions abroad. The members number about 220.
1664		

	SULPICIANS	EUDISTS
1653		Foundation of the seminary and the college in Lisieux.
1657	Four Sulpicians are sent to Montreal in Canada. Death of Jean-Jacques Olier. Monsieur de Bretonvilliers becomes superior, until 1676.	Foundation of the seminary in Rouen.
1658		
1659	First Constitutions of the Society.	Preaching in Paris: *Quinze-Vingts*, the asylum for the blind in Paris. St-Germain des Prés.
1660		
1664	Approval of the Society by the Papal Legate.	

	ORATORIANS	VINCENTIANS
1667		
1670		Approbation of the Congregation by Pope Clement X. During the seventeenth and eighteenth centuries, 33 institutions were founded in Italy. The Polish province developed rapidly, but the division of the country led to dispersion of members and disappearance of the province.
1672		
1673		
1676		
1680		

	SULPICIANS	EUDISTS
1667		Foundation of the seminary in Evreux.
1670		Foundation of the seminary in Rennes.
1672		On 20 October, John Eudes celebrated the first liturgical feast of the Heart of Jesus. Preaching at the Royal Court at Versailles.
1673		John Eudes preaches at St-Germain-en-Laye. Disgrace until 1679. His congregation is threatened.
1676	Monsieur Tronton becomes superior until 1700.	
1680		Death of John Eudes, on 19 August. At the time, there were 40 Eudists serving in the missions and in six seminaries.

Notes

Notes——Chapter 2

1. A. Dodin, *St Vincent de Paul et la charité*, Paris: Seuil, Maîtres spirituels, 1960; 5.
2. Lacordaire,
3. This theme recurs in many of Ortega y Gasset's writings. The "I" was the "ego" with its projects and programs; the "circumstance" was everything else: soul, body, historical moment, things, culture. . . . Cf., e.g., *What is Philosophy?* trans. Mildred Adams. New York: W.W. Norton, 1960, chapter 11; also *Meditaciones del Quijote* (1914).
4. R. Sauzet, in *Histoires des catholiques en France*, Privat, Coll. Pluriel, 1980; 94–95.
5. Cf. "*France*," M. de Certeau and J. Orcibal, in *Dictionnaire de Spiritualité*, V, Col. 896–916. This article gives a detailed account of sixteenth century Catholic reformation (Col. 896–910) which prepared the way for seventeenth century renewal (Col. 910–16).
6. L. Cognet, in *La spiritualité moderne, L'essor 1600–1660. Histoire de la spiritualité chrétienne*, 3, 2ᵉ partie. Paris: Aubier, 1966; 234–35.
7. Cf. B. Peyrous, "*Missions paroissiales*," in *Catholicisme*, IX, Col. 401–31. This is, actually, the best synthesis of the subject. For the seventeenth century, cf. Col. 404–12.
8. Peyrous, Col. 404–05.
9. P. Broutin, *La réforme pastorale en France au XVIIᵉ siècle*, 2 vol. Paris: Desclée, 1956. This is still an essential reference work.
10. F. Lebrun, *Le XVIIᵉ siècle*. Paris: A. Colin, Coll. U, 1967; 122.
11. Y. Chiron, *Gaston de Renty*. Montsûrs, ed. Résiac,

1985. This little work is based on the scholarly edition of Gaston de Renty's *Correspondence*, by R. Triboulet. Paris: DDB, 1978. From 1641 to 1649, M. de Renty was directed by Father Saint-Jure, de Renty's biographer.

12. Cf., "Enfance de Jésus," I, Noye, in *Dictionnaire de Spiritualité IV*, Col. 652–82; esp., Col. 665–77: Essor de la dévotion au 17ᵉ siècle.

13. Olier, *Lettres*, éd. Levesque, Paris: de Gigord, 1935; I, Lettre 12, 24 June 1636; 21–24.

14. H. Bremond, *Histoire littéraire du sentiment religieux*. Paris; Bloud et Gay, 1921; I, 95.

15. This phrase of H. Bremond has been cited by Fr. Frédien-Charles, *L'oraison d'après saint Jean-Baptiste de la Salle*. Paris: Ligel, 1955; XIV.

16. B. Peyrous, "Agnès de Langeac et les courants spirituels de son temps," in *Mère Agnès de Langeac et son temps* [*Agnes of Langeac and the Spiritual Movements of her Times*," in *Agnes of Langeac and Her Times*]. LePuy: Dominicans of Mère Agnès, 1986; 44.

17. A. Dodin, *François de Sales-Vincent de Paul—les deux Amis*. Paris: éd. OEIL, 1984.

Notes——Chapter 3

1. Cited by P. Cochois, *Bérulle et l'École française*. Paris: Seuil, 1963; 3.

2. The studies and publications of Dagens, of Orcibal, of Duval and of Cochois, among others, have contributed significantly to this renewed interest.

3. Archives of the Oratory, I bis, 12, 5.

4. In the language of the time, "énergumènes" designated those persons we call possessed.

5. Treatise III, 850.

6. P. Cochois, 17.

7. Cf. *Life*, chapter 22; *Interior Castle* 6, chapter 7.

8. P. Cochois, 34–41; 102–10. Cf. also, H. Peltier, *Histoire du Carmel*. Paris: Seuil, 1958, 170–93.

9. *Glories of Jesus* 8:6.

10. *Glories of Jesus* 4:5.

11. Cognet's thought on Bérulle is expressed in Louis Cognet, "Post-Reformation Spirituality," in *The Twentieth Century Encyclopedia of Catholicism*, trans. P. Hep-

burne Scott. New York: Hawthorn Books, 1959, 66–77.
12. Bérulle, *Œuvres complètes*, 921.
13. Migne, Fragment IV, Col. 1618.
14. Cf. Bérulle, *Œuvres*, 107.

Notes——Chapter 4

1. *Dictionnaire de spiritualité* 2, Col. 1374, art., "Condren," Molien.
2 P. Auvray and A. Jouffrey, *Lettres du Père Charles de Condren*. Paris: Cerf, 1943.
3. Bremond, *A Literary History of Religious Thought in France* 3:250.
4. Amelote, *Life* 2:403.
5. Bremond, 3:251.
6. Amelote, *Vie* 1:41.
7. Amelote, *Vie* 1:41–46.
8. À comparative study can be found in Auvray and Jouffrey, 547–67.
9. *L'idée du sacerdoce et du Sacrifice de Jésus-Christ.*
10. *L'idée du sacerdoce et du Sacrifice de Jésus-Christ.* Cf. Bremond 3:319.
11. Auvray and Jouffrey, Letter 56, 178–82.
12. Auvray and Jouffrey, Letter 166.

Notes——Chapter 5

1. *Se laisser à l'Esprit* (cf. 121, n. 2).
2. *Bulletin trimestriel des Anciens Élèves de Saint-Sulpice*, no. 228, May 1957.
3. M. Dupuy, *Se laisser à l'Esprit*, The spiritual journey of Jean-Jacques Olier. Paris: Cerf., 1982. This work was awarded a prize by the French Academy.
4. Bremond 3:392.
5. *Mère Agnès Langeac et son temps*, Acts of the Colloquium of Le Puy: The Dominicans of Mother Agnès, 1986; 243, esp. 75–90: C. Bouchard, *"Mère Agnès, mère spirituelle des Séminaires de France."*
6. *Mémoires* 2:143.
7. Compagnies des Associés Amis de Montréal, *De La*

Flèche à Montréal. The extraordinary undertaking of M. de la Dauversière. Chambray-lès-Tours: C.L.D., 1985.

8. G.-M. Oury, *Jeanne Mance et le rêve de M. de la Dauversière.* Chambray-lès-Tours: C.L.D., 1983.
9. *Divers écrits* 1:71.
10. I. Noye, in Dupuy, 175.
11. *Divers écrits* 1:67.
12. *Projet pour l'établissement d'un séminaire dans un diocèse.* (1651); réed, in *La Tradition sacerdotale.* Le Puy: Mappus, 1959; 213–32.
13. *Constitutions* 1982, art. 1.

Notes——Chapter 6

1. Eudes, *Memoriale Beneficiorum Dei,* in *Letters and Shorter Works,* trans. Ruth Hauser. New York, P.J. Kennedy & Sons, 1948; 281.
2. C. Berthelot du Chesnay, *Les missions de saint Jean Eudes* [The Missions of St. John Eudes]: *A Contribution to the History of the Missions in France in the Seventeenth Century.* Paris: Procure des Eudistes, 1967.
3. Bremond, *A Literary History of Religious Thought in France.*
4. Henri Joly, *Life of St. John Eudes,* trans. Rev. Joseph Leonard, C.M. New York: Benziger Brothers, 1932; 140.
5. Igino Giordani, *St. Vincent de Paul, Servant of the Poor* (trans. Thomas J. Robin). The Bruce Publishing Company, 1961; 115.
6. *Constitutions,* The Congregation of Jesus and Mary.
7. O.C. (*Complete Works*) 1:447.

Notes——Chapter 7

1. Olier published several works: *Journée chrétienne, Christian Catechism of an Interior Life, Introduction à la vie et aux vertus chrétiennes;* the masterpiece of John Eudes was *Life and Kingdom of Jesus in Christian Souls*—a work that, in itself, proposes an entire way of life.
2. H. Caffarel, *Clavel, adorateur,* in "*La Croix,*" 18 May 1979.

3. Bérulle, *Œuvres de piété, XI*, ed. Migne, 1245.
4. Bérulle, Letter 44, October 1608.
5. D. Amelote, *Vie du P. Charles de Condren*. Paris, 1643; 80–81.
6. Bérulle, *Œuvres de piété, CXXII*, ed. Migne, 1150.
7. Bérulle, *Œuvres de piété, CXI*, ed. Migne, 1129. The preceding lines were inspired by an article by I. Noye, for the *Dizionario degli Instituti di perfezione, "Spiritualita."* Rome: Ed. Paolini.
8. Bérulle, *Œuvres de piété, LXXXVII*, ed. Migne, 1070.
9. Bérulle, *Vie de Jésus*, ch. 29, ed. Migne, 500.
10. F. Bourgoing, Preface to the Works of Bérulle, Migne, 103.
11. John Eudes, *Life and Kingdom of Jesus*, 2:2.
12. Olier, *Pietas*, no.4, éd Amiot, 1954; 165.
13. Bérulle, *Œuvres de piété*, Migne, 1181.
14. Bérulle, *Grandeur de Jésus*, 181.
15. E. Roldan, *L'Esprit Saint chez saint Jean Eudes*, Cahiers eudistes 1977, no. 3, 13–42.
16. Letter 154, eds. Auvray and Jouffrey, 457–60.
17. E. Mersch, *The Whole Christ*, 555.
18. J. Dagens, *Bérulle*. Paris: Desclée de Brouwer, 1952; 373–75.
19. R. Deville, *École française et mission*, in "Mission et traditions spirituelles," a session for the Conference of Major Superiors. Paris: 1985; 77.
20. *Projet pour l'établissement d'un séminaire*, 231.
21. M. Dupuy, *Bérulle et le Sacerdoce*. Paris: Lethielleux, 1969; 103, 245.
22. P. Milcent, *S. Jean Eudes*, 423–33, esp. 428.
23. P. Cochois, *Bérulle*, 131–33.
24. P. Pourrat, *Le sacerdoce, doctrine de l'École française*. Paris: Bloud et Gay, 1931.
25. Cf. Migne, 430.
26. *Life*, 430.
27. *Life*, 431.
28. *Life*, 501.
29. *Correspondence*, ed. Dagens, 2:345.
30. P. Cochois, 108.
31. *Complete Works VII*.
32. R. de Pas, *Marie, icône de Jésus* (texts of St. John Eudes). Paris: Procure des Eudistes, 1980.
33. Cf. the prayer of Elizabeth of the Trinity which she

wrote on the evening of 21 November 1904: "I surrender myself to you.... "

34. R. Laurentin, *Marie, l'Église et le Sacerdoce*. Paris: Nouvelles éditions latines, 1952. A number of pages in vol. one treat this subject.

35. G. Chaillot, "*La pédagogie spirituelle de M. Olier d'après ses Mémoires*," in *Bulletin de Saint-Sulpice* 2, 1976; 27–67.

Notes——Chapter 8

1. Quoted in M. Sauvage and M. Campos, *Jean-Baptiste de La Salle*. Paris: Beauchesne, 1977; 32, n. 22.
2. Frère Maurice-Auguste, in *Catholicisme VI*, "J. B. de la Salle," 640.
3. Olier, *Divers Écrits* 1:67.
4. La Salle, *Meditations*, trans. Brother Augustine Loes, intro. by Brother Miguel Campos (ed). Winona, Wisconsin: St. Mary's College Press, 1975; 74.

Notes——Chapter 9

1. Bremond, *A Literary History of Religious Thought in France*.
2. Grignion de Montfort, *True Devotion to Mary*.
3. Olier, *Divers Ecrits* 1:67.
4. Huré, *Love of Eternal Wisdom*, chapter 6. In *God Alone*, 67.
5. Daniel-Rops, 288.
6. Grignion de Montfort, *Treatise on True Devotion to the Blessed Virgin*, 1:1.
7. Grignion de Montfort, *God Alone*, 326.
8. Grignion de Montfort, *True Devotion to Mary*, 1:2.
9. André Frossard. *Be Not Afraid*. Trans., J. R. Foster. New York: St. Martin's Press, 1984; 126.
10. A Papasogli. *L'homme venu du vent*. Montreal: Bellarmine, 1984; 333.

Notes——Chapter 10

1. P. Chaunce, *L'Église, Culture et société*. Paris: 1984, 401.
2. Noèmi Hepp, "Femme (Condition de la)," in *Dictionnaire du Grand Siècle*. Paris: Fayard, 1990.
3. *Lettres chrétiennes et spirituelles*, Rouen, 1645; 181.
4. *Lettres inédites*; Paris: Annie Bernes, 1962; 181.
5. *L'honneste femme*, 1632.
6. Bremond, *A Literary History of Religious Thought in France* 2:27.
7. Bremond, Literary History 2:193–94.
8. The text of this letter can be found in Thompson, *Bérulle and the French School*, 192.
9. P. Cochois, *Bérulle et l'École française*. Paris, 1963.

Notes——Chapter 11

1. The Society of Saint-Sulpice has recently published a brochure entitled, "*Pratiques pédagogiques et tradition spirituelle.*" Paris: 6, rue du Regard, 1985.
2. Sauvage, in the Introduction to the *Meditations*.
3. Letter of 5 October 1604. Ed. d'Annecy, t. XII, 306.
4. Y. Congar, "L'esprit des Pères d'après Moehler" (The Spirit of the Fathers According to Moehler) in *Esquisses du mystère de l'Église*. Paris: Cerf. "Unam Sanctam" 8, éd. 1941, Appendix, 130.
5. Lucien-Marie and Jacques-Marie Petit. *Actualité de Jean de la Croix*. Paris: Desclée de Brouwer, 1970; 111, 113.
6. *Bérulle and the French School*, 47.
7. *Lettres* 1:561–63.
8. Amiot, 22–26.
9. Auvray & Jouffrey, eds., *Lettres de Père Charles de Condren*. Paris, 1943; 350–53.
10. *Mémoires* 2:314.
11. Cited by Deville, 166.
12. In *Bérulle et l'École française*, P. Cochois explains a number of words. The publishers of the critical edition of the *Treatise on Holy Orders* have also furnished a detailed glossary.
13. J. C. Guy, "Saint-Benoît 400–1980," in *Études*, 352/3. March 1980, 365–78; here, 373.

Selected Bibliography

Aumann, Jordan. *Christian Spirituality in the Catholic Tradition*. San Francisco: Ignatius, 1985.

Battersby, William J. *De la Salle, Saint and Spiritual Writer*. London/New York: Longmans, Green, 1950.

Bérulle and the French School: Selected Writings. Ed., William M. Thompson; trans. Lowell M. Glendor, S.S. Classics of Western Spirituality. New York/Mahwah:Paulist Press, 1989.

Bremond, Henri. *A Literary History of Religious Thought in France From the Wars of Religion Down to Our Own Times*. 3 Vol. Trans., K.L. Montgomery. London: SPCK, 1928–36.

Bulletin de Saint-Sulpice, e.g., 4 (1978), 5 (1979), 6 (1980).

Condren, Charles de. *The Eternal Sacrifice*. Trans., H. J. Monteith. London: Thomas Baker, 1906.

Daniel-Rops, H. *History of the Church of Christ 6: The Church in the Seventeenth Century*. Trans., J.J. Buckingham. London: J.M. Dent & Sons/New York: E.P. Dutton & Co., 1963.

Eudes, Saint John. *Letters and Shorter Works*. Trans., Ruth Hauser. New York: Kenedy, 1948.

——. *The Admirable Heart of Mary*. Trans. Charles di Targiani and Ruth Hauser. New York: Kenedy, 1948.

——. *The Life and Kingdom of Jesus in Christian Souls: A Treatise on Christian Perfection for Use by Clergy or Laity*. Trans. A Trappist of Gethsemani. New York: Kenedy, 1946.

Glendon, Lowell M. *An Annotated and Descriptive Chronology of the Important Events in the Life of Jean-Jacques Olier* (1608–1657). Baltimore: Society of St. Sulpice, 1987.

Herambourg, C.J.M., Peter. *Saint John Eudes: A Spiritual Portrait*. Trans., Ruth Hauser, M.A. Westminster, MD., 1960.

Huvelin Abbé. *Some Spiritual Guides of the Seventeenth Century.* Intro. and trans., Joseph Leonard. New York: Benziger, 1927.

Kauffman, Christopher J. *Tradition and Transformation in Catholic Culture: The Priests of Saint Sulpice in the United States from 1791 to the Present.* Macmillan, 1988.

La Salle, St. John Baptist de. *John Baptist de la Salle: The Letters.* Trans., Colman Malloy. Romeoville, IL: Christian Brothers Conference, 1988.

———. *Meditations for the Time of Retreat,* Trans., Augustine Loes, Romeoville, IL: Christian Brothers Conference, 1975.

Light From Light: An Anthology of Christian Mysticism, eds. Louis Dupré and John A. Wiseman, O.S.B. No. 18, *Marie of the Incarnation.* New York/Mahwah: Paulist, 1988.

Marie of the Incarnation, Selected Writings, ed., Irene Mahoney, O.S.U. New York/Mahwah: Paulist Press, 1989.

Milcent, Paul. *Saint John Eudes: Presentation and Texts.* Glasgow: John S. Burns, 1963.

Minton, Anne M. "Pierre de Bérulle: The Search for Unity." *The Spirituality of Western Christendom 2: The Roots of the Modern Christian Tradition;* ed., E. Roxanne Elder. Kalamazoo, MI: Cistercian Publications, 1984; 105–23.

Montfort, St. Louis-Marie (Grignion) de. *God Alone: The Collected Writings of St. Louise Mary de Montfort.* Bayshore, NY: Montfort Publications, 1987.

———. *True Devotion To Mary.* Trans., Frederick Faber. Rockford, IL: Tan Books and Publishers, 1985.

———. *The Love of Eternal Wisdom.* Trans., ann., A. Somers. Bayshore, NY: Montfort Publications, 1960.

Muto, Susan Annette. *Pathways of Spiritual Living.* Petersham, MA: St. Bede's Publications, 1984.

Pourrat, Pierre. *Christian Spirituality 3: Later Developments: Pt.1: From the Renaissance to Jansenism.* Trans., W.H. Mitchell. Westminster, MD: Newman, 1953.

———. *Father Olier: Founder of Saint-Sulpice.* Trans., W. S. Reilly. Baltimore: Voice Publishing Company, 1932.

Rapley, Elizabeth. *The Devotes, Women and Church in Seventeenth-Century France.* McGill: Queen's University Press, 1990. This work contains an extensive bibliography and a helpful index.

Sauvage, Michael and Miguel Campos. *St. John Baptist de La Salle: Announcing the Gospel to the Poor: The Spiritual Experience and Spiritual Teaching of St. John Baptist de La*

Salle. Trans., Matthew J. O'Connell. Romeoville, IL: Christian Brothers Conference, 1981.

Thompson, Edward Healy. *The Life of Jean-Jacques Olier: Founder of the Seminary of St. Sulpice.* London: Burns and Oates, 1885.

Thompson, William M. "A Study of Bérulle's Christic Spirituality." *In Jesus, Lord and Savior: A Theopathic Christology and Soteriology.* New York: Paulist, 1980; 226–49.

——. "The Christic Universe of Pierre de Bérulle and the French School." *American Benedictine Review* 29 (1978): 320–47.

Vasey, Vincent R. "Mary in the Doctrine of Bérulle on the Mysteries of Christ." *Marian Studies* 36 (1985): 60–80.

Woodgate, M.V. *Charles de Condren.* Westminster, MD. (No date).

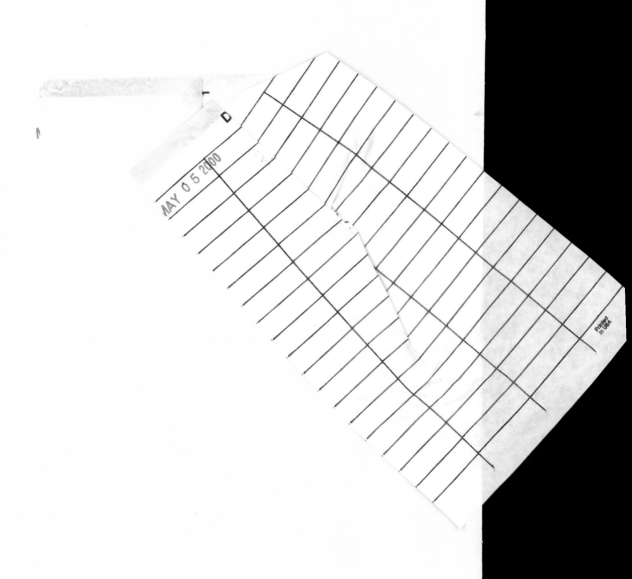